IMAGES
of America

AROUND LAKE OKEECHOBEE

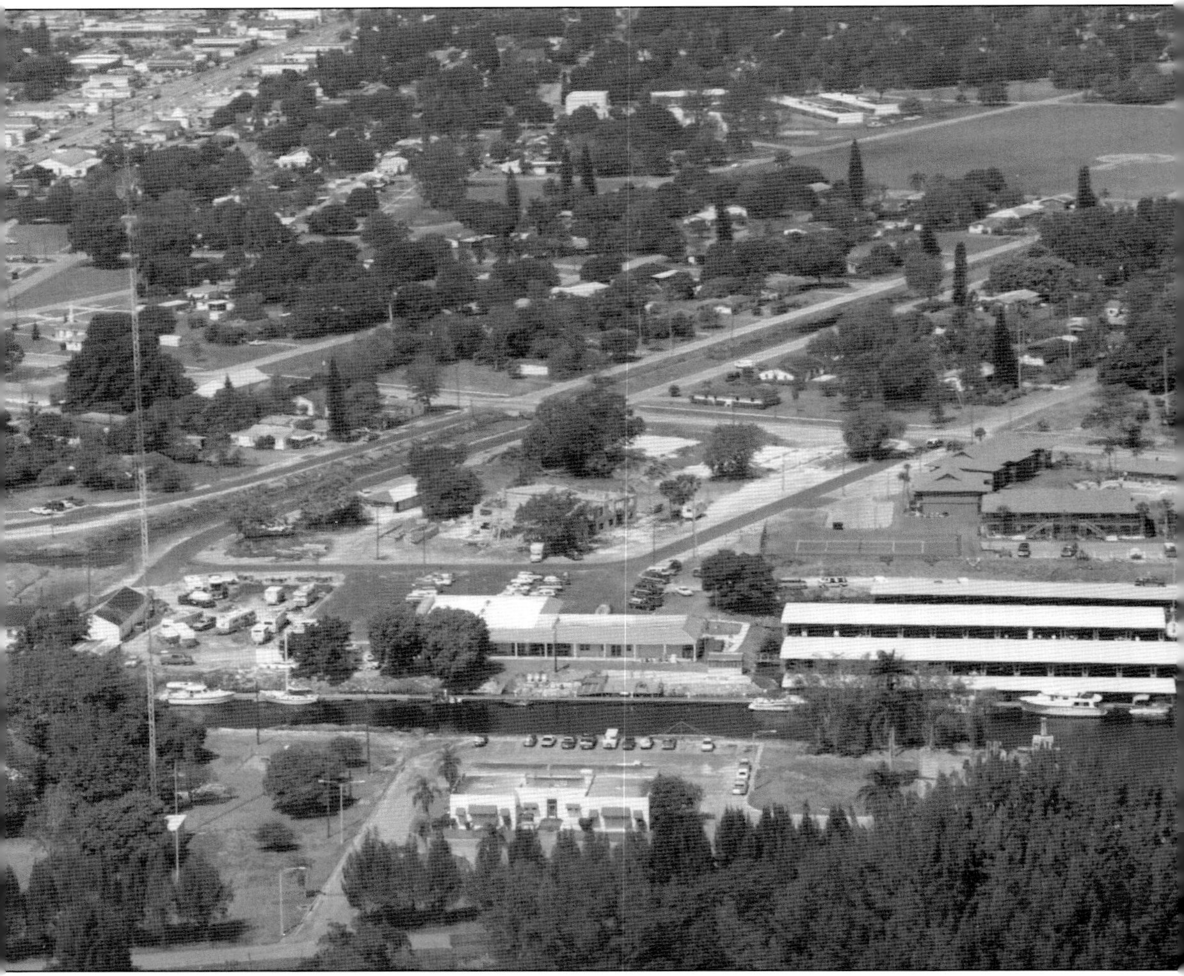

Roland Martin's Marina and Resort, operated by Mary Ann Martin, is shown in this aerial view taken in the mid-1980s. The current owners purchased the property in 1983 from Marvin Vance. Hurricane Wilma destroyed the covered floating docks in 2005. The former Clewiston Marina is nationally known due to Roland Martin's television fishing show and bass sportfishing competitions. There are now condominiums, a restaurant, and a tiki bar on the property. (Courtesy of Mary Ann Martin.)

On the Cover: When this photograph was taken in the 1950s, Brighton Seminole children attended Okeechobee schools. Today there is the Pemayetv Emahakv Charter School, "Our Way School," on the Brighton Reservation, which fosters pride in academic achievement while developing students' abilities in the Creek language and Seminole culture. (Courtesy of the Florida Memory Project.)

IMAGES
of America

AROUND LAKE OKEECHOBEE

Barbara D. Oeffner and Amie Dunning

ARCADIA
PUBLISHING

ISBN 978-0-7385-8564-2

Published by Arcadia Publishing
Charleston, South Carolina

Printed in the United States of America

Library of Congress Control Number: 2009939161

For all general information contact Arcadia Publishing at:
Telephone 843-853-2070
Fax 843-853-0044
E-mail sales@arcadiapublishing.com
For customer service and orders:
Toll-Free 1-888-313-2665

Visit us on the Internet at www.arcadiapublishing.com

To my husband, Thom, for moving with me from Cape Cod to tropical Florida. To Amie Dunning for all her work coauthoring this book.

To Grace Renkens and Carol Lubetkin for their love. To Brendan and Anna and my two grandchildren, Marya and Nina. To Patty, Fran, Heidi, Matt, Paul, Tony, Julia, and Colin.

To God for all the blessings in our lives.

Contents

ACKNOWLEDGMENTS

Thank you to Lindsay Harris, our amazing editor at Arcadia Publishing, who kept her faith in this book throughout the editorial process. Photographs in this book appear courtesy of Mary Ann Martin, the Lawrence E. Will Museum (LEWM), the Clewiston Museum (CM), and the Florida Memory Project at the Florida State Library and Archives (FMP).

Thank you to Thom Oeffner, Phyllis Lilley (Belle Glade branch manager), Missi Luikart, Kimberly Bower, Betty Williamson (president of the Okeechobee Historical Society), Butch Wilson (Clewiston Museum director), Mary Lou Bishop, Walter Vaughn, Mary Ann Martin, Jim Wells, and N. Adam Watson (photographic archivist at the State Archives of Florida). We owe you all a debt of gratitude.

Thank you to the historians and photographers who valued these stories enough to preserve them in books, in albums, in folders, and on discs.

We hope you will enjoy viewing these glimpses of Lake Okeechobee pioneers as much as we did compiling them. The saying that a photograph is worth a thousand words applies to these fantastic snapshots of life around Lake Okeechobee.

INTRODUCTION

The Lake Okeechobee region has been home to many brave and inventive pioneers throughout its colorful history. The towns around the lake were filled with saints and scallywags, aboriginals and Spaniards, as well as moonshiners and sheriffs. Most of the frontiersmen were rugged men and women who were resilient and resourceful.

Visitors to Florida often don't know what beautiful landscapes lie between the east and west coasts. The cattlemen and fishermen prefer it that way. Although Lake Okeechobee sportfishing draws competitors from all over the country to vie for bass fishing prizes, many outsiders are unaware of the gloriously natural Everglades.

The settlers came and farmed the fertile "black gold" soil. It took a certain kind of person to live in this hostile environment. The swamps and cypress hammocks were filled with panthers, otters, bears, bobcats, and rattlesnakes, while the waters brimmed with alligators, poisonous water moccasins, and all kinds of fish.

These photographs introduce some of the Lake Okeechobee characters who stand out as leaders and fighters. The photographs capture the harshness of life, subject as they were to hurricanes, bandits, outlaws, and floods. Life near the Caloosahatchee and Kissimmee Rivers was a constant battle to survive. Working as boatmen, cattlemen, fishermen, and farmers, the settlers carved out a living for themselves despite the hardships. Mail was delivered by boats, and goods were transported by horseback and wagon.

Some 2,000 years ago, the Calusa Indians controlled trade routes throughout this region. Their mounds attest to the fishing and shelling they did along the waterways from Lake Okeechobee and Lake Hicpochee to the west coast on Pine Island and Fort Myers. On Fisheating Creek, they camped and raised corn and other crops. Then the Seminoles and Miccosukees came down from Georgia to settle the region in family groups or clans.

Marian Newhall Horwitz brought high society to Moore Haven from her home in fashionable Philadelphia. She married John J. O'Brien and had big plans for the place. She dreamed of bringing the railroad here much like Henry Flagler brought the trains to Palm Beach. She was elected the one of the first woman mayors in America in 1917, before women gained the right to vote. Her dreams were realized when in 1918 the "Hinky Dink" came from Palmdale to Moore Haven.

One of Florida's toughest pioneers was Dr. Anna Darrow. Nicknamed the "petticoat doctor," she rode on horseback around the lake with her medicines, curing the sick and distraught. She delivered babies to women who couldn't get any medical care in places that no one else would go. Her husband, Roy, tended the office, since his health was frail. She became a heroine for the work she did for all the wild men and women living in the place where American Indians, African Americans, Florida Crackers, cowboys, and catfishermen roamed.

Gangs of bandits were also caught prowling around the lake in the early days of Florida history. Leland Rice, of the notorious Rice gang, got half his jaw shot off one night and had to call for Dr. Anna to patch him up and send him off to a hospital. The ferocious Ashley gang robbed banks in "Bonnie and Clyde" style. Dr. Anna became acquainted with the gang when the mother of John Ashley obtained a tonic for him while he was locked up in a Stuart jail. Dr. Anna was used again when she was led blindfolded 10 miles into the woods to their secret hideout to treat another gang member. Meanwhile, Laura Upthegrove, the only female member of the Ashley gang, was cooking moonshine out in the sawgrass.

John Nolen was an educated city planner. He platted out the streets of Clewiston and made a very attractive plan for development. He also designed Venice, on Florida's west coast. He laid out circular streets, designed a recreation unit, and left room for parks and green space. The Wantanabes, a Japanese immigrant family, ran the Clewiston Inn before it burned down and was rebuilt on its present site on Royal Palm Avenue in Clewiston. They left to go back to Japan. The magnificent million-dollar mural in the present Everglades Lounge was painted in 1926.

After canals were built to try to control what Marjorie Stoneham Douglas called "the River of Grass," the Everglades experienced two catastrophic hurricanes, one in 1926 and another in 1928. Photographs from these hurricanes are included in this collection. The shallow lake broke through the muck levees that had been built around it and flooded the surrounding communities. Pres. Herbert Hoover visited the area in 1928 and provided government funds to construct around the lake what has been called the "Herbert Hoover Dike" in his honor.

Inventors and entrepreneurs Henry Ford, Thomas Edison, and Henry Firestone summered in this area and built cars, tires, and lights for the residents to enjoy. Roads, bridges, and railroads brought commerce and allowed local farmers and cattlemen to sell their products to markets on both coasts.

During World War II, Clewiston built Riddle Airfield to train the Royal Air Force flying troops. Arcadia, Florida, also had a training camp for air force personnel. Current resident Walter Vaughn, whose father, Henry, built the library during his tenure as president of U.S. Sugar in 1967, remembered playing in the school band for the Royal Air Force troops.

Agriculture took a leap forward with the discovery of sugarcane as a cash crop. Clewiston is still nicknamed "American's Sweetest Town" as headquarters for U.S. Sugar Corporation.

Rowland Martin's Marina attracts sportfishermen, boat enthusiasts, and tourists who want to relax and enjoy the peace and quiet of the lake. Many fishing camps and RV parks around the lake provide scenic spots for campers to inhabit during the warm winter months in Florida.

Culled from various sources, these photographs provide a historic look at an area that is stunning in its natural beauty and rich in stories of survival. Some of the most colorful people that lived around Lake Okeechobee are also featured in this book.

One

Glades Pioneers

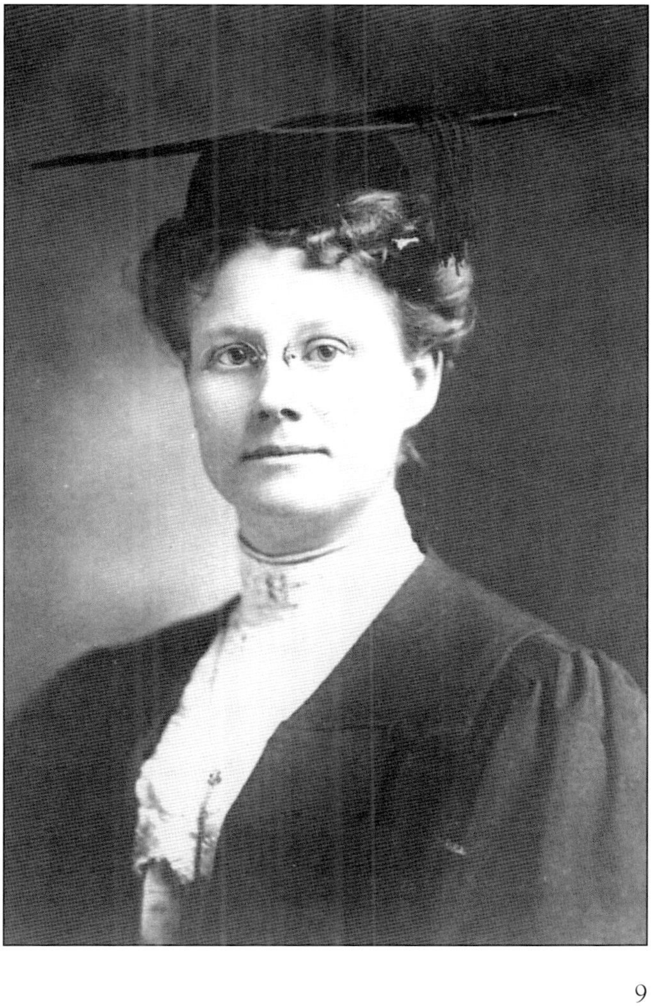

One of Florida's toughest pioneers was Dr. Anna Darrow. Nicknamed the "petticoat doctor," she rode on horseback around the lake with her medicines curing the sick and distraught. She delivered babies to women who couldn't get any medical care in places that no one else could reach. Her husband, Roy, tended the office, since his health was frail. A member of the notorious Rice gang, Leland Rice got half his jaw shot off one night. Pretending to be his mother, Doc Anna held his hand, bandaged up the outlaw, and sent him to a hospital in St. Augustine. She also pumped out the stomach of a new doctor who bragged he was "going to run the petticoat doctor out of town." The doctor had accidentally swallowed poison intended for another purpose. (LEWM.)

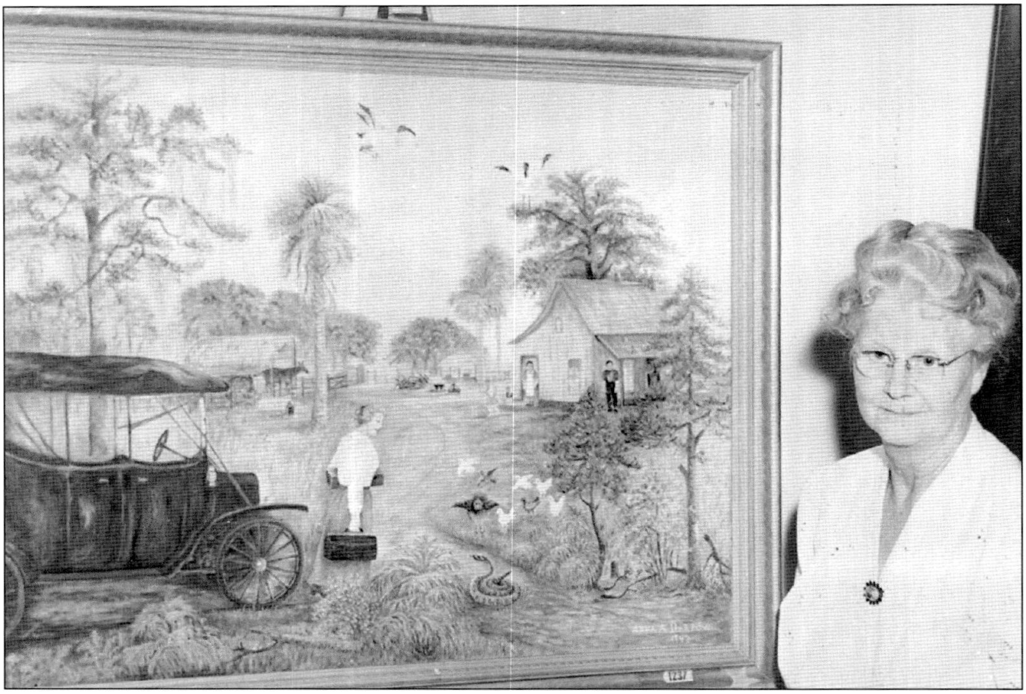

Dr. Anna shows her painting. She won second prize, a bond worth $1,000 in the Medical Art Exhibition sponsored by Mead-Johnson Company during the 1947 American Medical Convention. The year's theme was "Courage and Devotion Beyond the Call of Duty." (LEWM.)

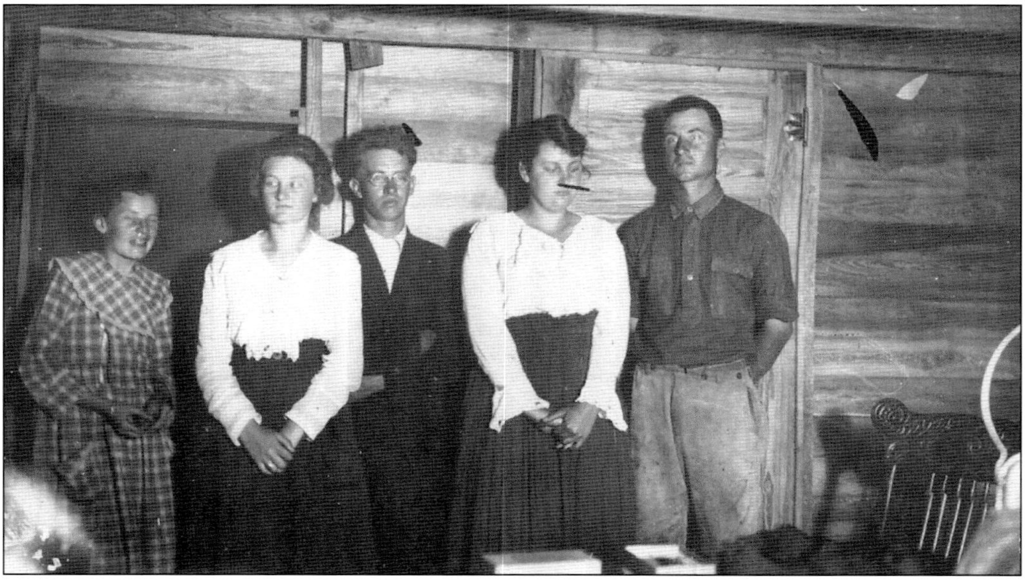

Lawrence E. Will (center) is standing with the Poulter girls (left and in white right) in 1919. Will wrote books about the early days around the lake: *A Cracker History of Okeechobee*, *A Dredgeman of Cape Sable*, *Okeechobee Hurricane and the Hoover Dike*, *A Pioneer Boatman Tales of Okeechobee Boats and Skippers*, *Okeechobee Catfishing*, and *Swamp to Sugar Bowl*. In these true accounts, he relates his boating experiences in the pioneer days of Lake Okeechobee settlement. (LEWM.)

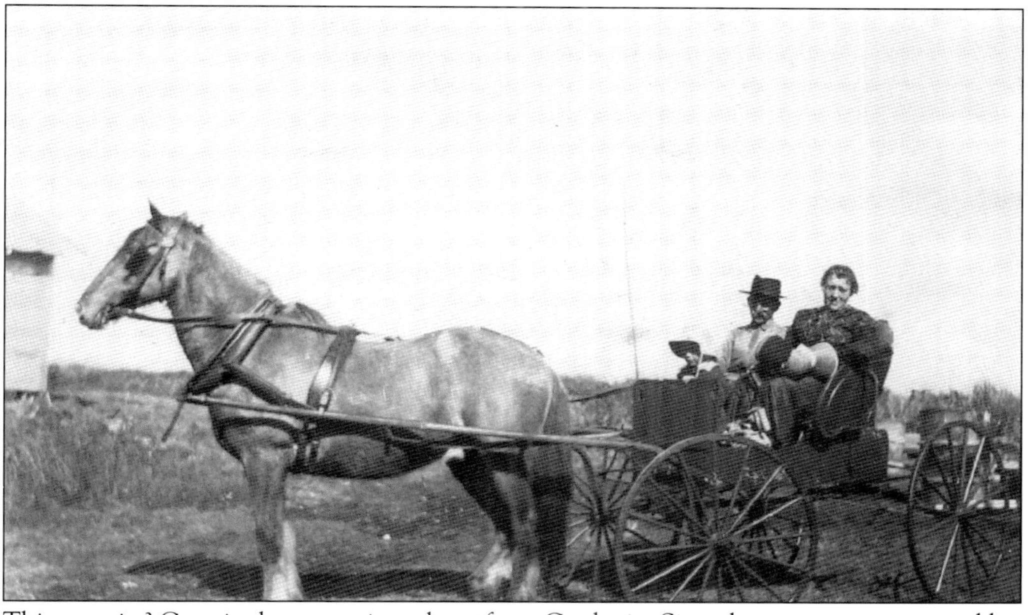

This man is ? Cunningham, a guitar player from Gardenia. Since he was expecting a sudden stroke, he dug his own grave in a canal bank, but he lived to return to England. With Mrs. Little and her granddaughter, he drove 8 miles on Bolles Road from Gardenia to Okeelanta on the Miami Canal. (LEWM.)

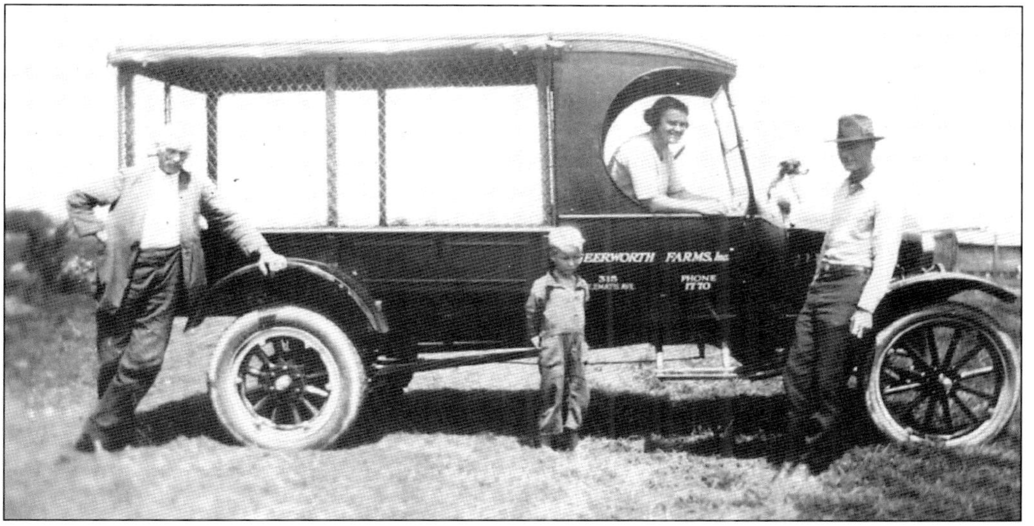

Black Gold is a festival celebrated every year in Belle Glade. A high school or college girl is selected from several candidates to be Miss Black Gold. The event is held at the Dolly Hand Cultural Center auditorium and is judged professionally. The women dress up in evening gowns and give the audience information about their goals. They are asked a question and are judged on their responses. The term "black gold" refers to the rich soil of the farmland, where sugarcane, corn, beans, and other crops are harvested every year. In this photograph, Mr. and Mrs. John C. Heck, Dave Hetherington, and a Bishop boy are shown at Geerworth in the spring of 1925. (LEWM.)

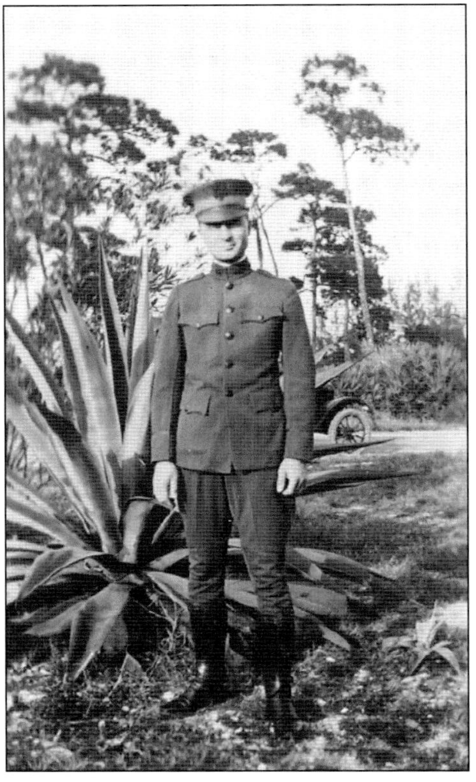

The Lawrence E. Will Museum in Belle Glade was founded in 1976 in honor of the United States bicentennial. Dr. Orseingo, director of the Glades Historical society, was director for many years. He received his doctorate in agronomy and soil science from Cornell University in 1948. In World War II, he served his country in an army armored field artillery unit. In 1933, he received his undergradute degree in agronomy and statistics from Cornell University. In 1955, he joined the Instituto Interamericano de Ciencias Agricolas, in Turrialba, Costa Rica. He later joined the staff of the University of Florida Everglades Experiment Station (EREG) in 1957. He worked diligently for the betterment of Glades farmers until 1975. At the research center, he held several positions, including horticulturist and professor of plant physiology. Upon his retirement in 1975, he was named professor emeritus. "He helped more farmers in more ways to be successful than anybody you have ever known. He was a friend of the whole industry," said Joe Marlin Hilliard, owner of Hilliard Brothers of Florida in Clewiston. "He was a heck of a scientist." In 1976, he became the director of agricultural research for the Florida Sugar Cane League in Clewiston. (LEWM.)

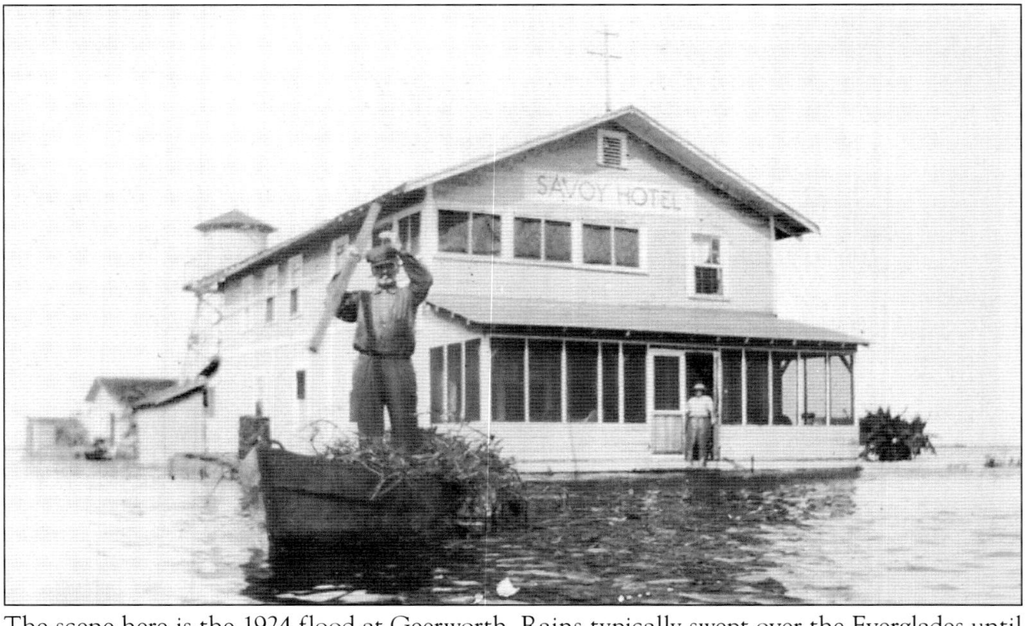

The scene here is the 1924 flood at Geerworth. Rains typically swept over the Everglades until canals and levees were built to contain the waters. Hurricanes still hit Florida during the wet season between June 1 and November 1. (LEWM.)

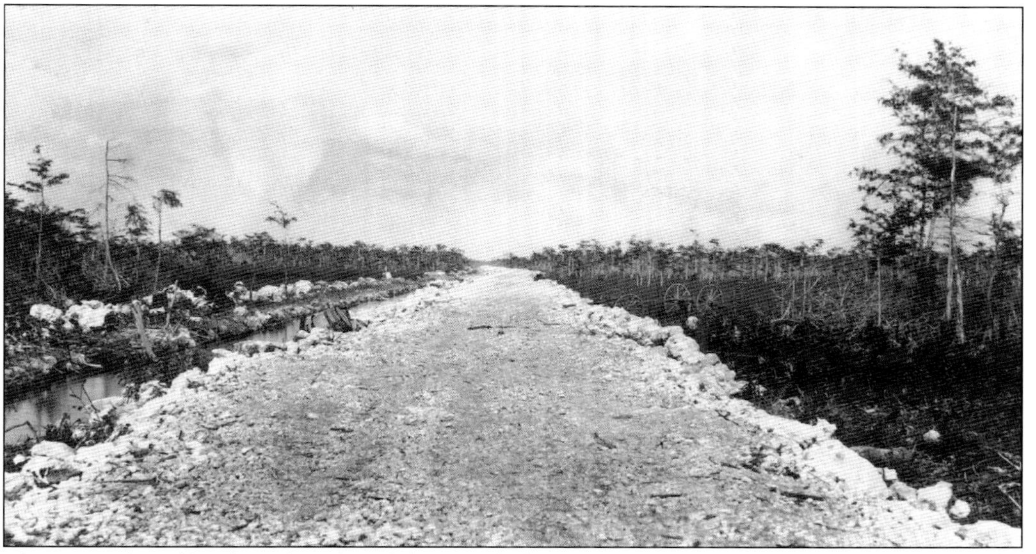

This typical road leads to the edge of the Everglades. In 1839, U.S. soldiers started boating up the Caloosahatchee River and along Fisheating Creek on the north side of the lake. This comprised the first community, called Fort Center, erected on the banks of Fisheating Creek on the site of a former Calusa Indian village. It was one in a series of army installments from Fort Myers to Fort Jupiter that crossed the state. Observation Island was another camp at the southwest end of Lake Okeechobee. (LEWM.)

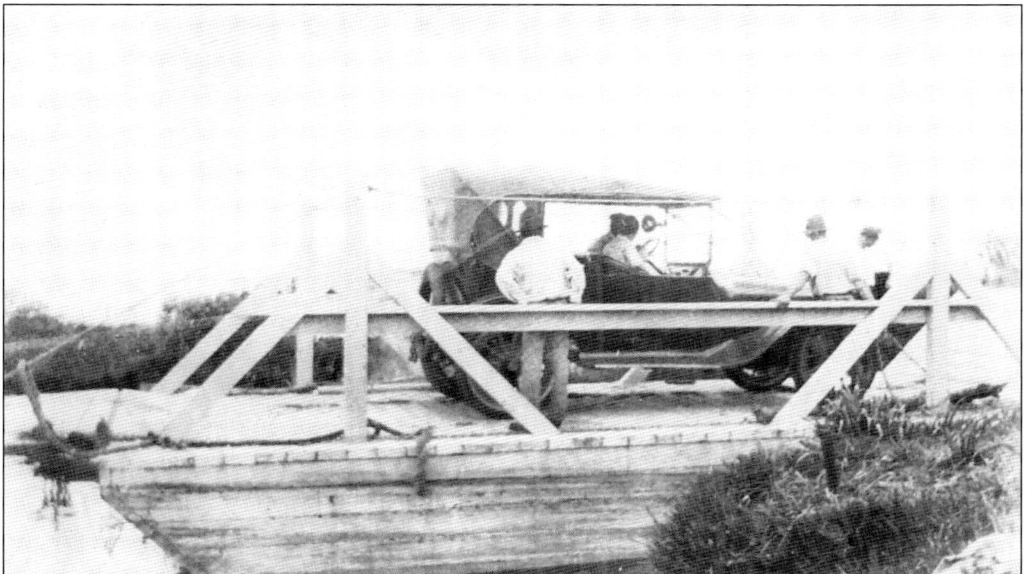

Here was the first automobile to drive to Okeelanta from anywhere farther than South Bay or Gardenia (8 miles). The Model T "Tin Lizzie" was an automobile that was produced by Ford Motor Company from 1908 to 1927. Ford dealer G. C. Barco drove from West Palm Beach to Okeelanta in May 1921. The road was graded but not surfaced. The three main canals were crossed on barges similar to the one shown here crossing the North New River Canal at Okeelanta. This was before bridges were built. (LEWM.)

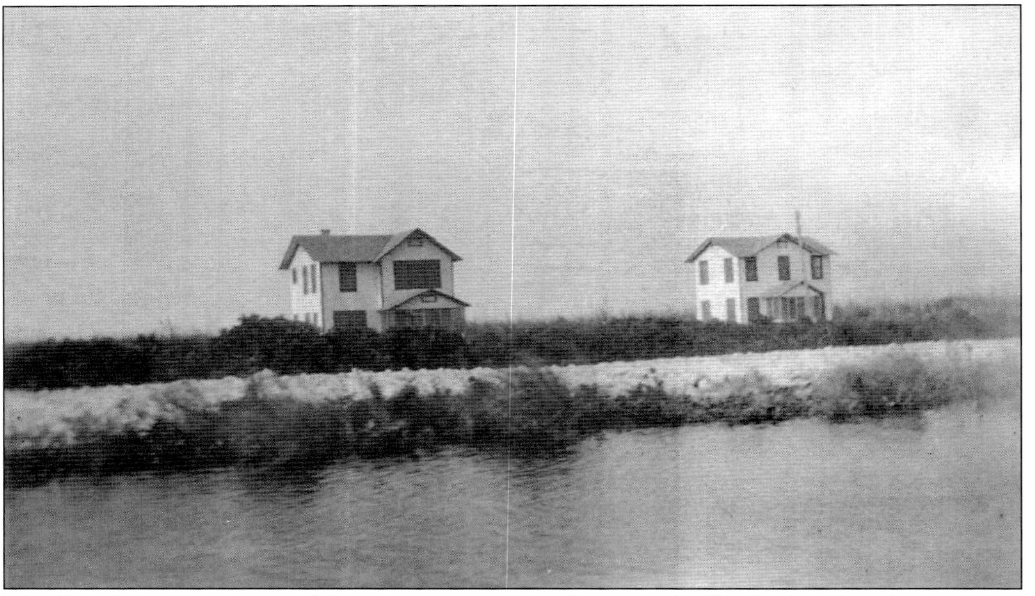

The Everglades Experimental Station is situated 3 miles east of Belle Glade. This photograph is from November 1923. In back, the station has a concrete marker that shows how much the muck has sunk down. The Sugar Cane Growers Cooperative, an organization of 22 independent cane farmers, uses this facility to improve their varieties of sugarcane. Scientists, entomologists, and geneticists from all over the world come to do research here. The University of Florida runs it today. The librarian is Kathy Krawchuck. (LEWM.)

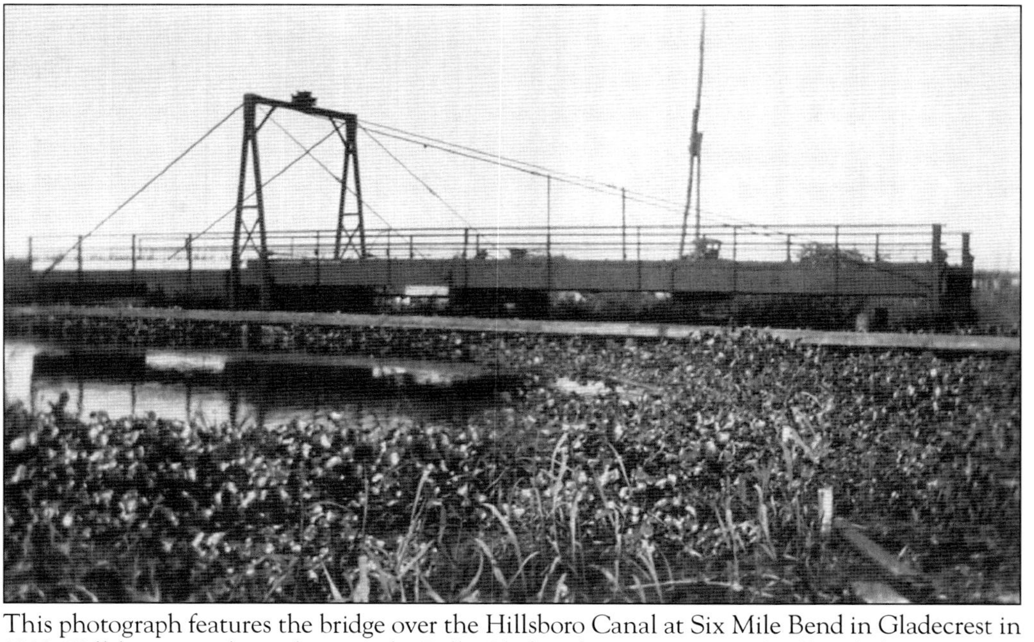

This photograph features the bridge over the Hillsboro Canal at Six Mile Bend in Gladecrest in 1923. Hillsboro was the early name for Belle Glade. The town motto of Belle Glade is "Her soil is her fortune." (LEWM.)

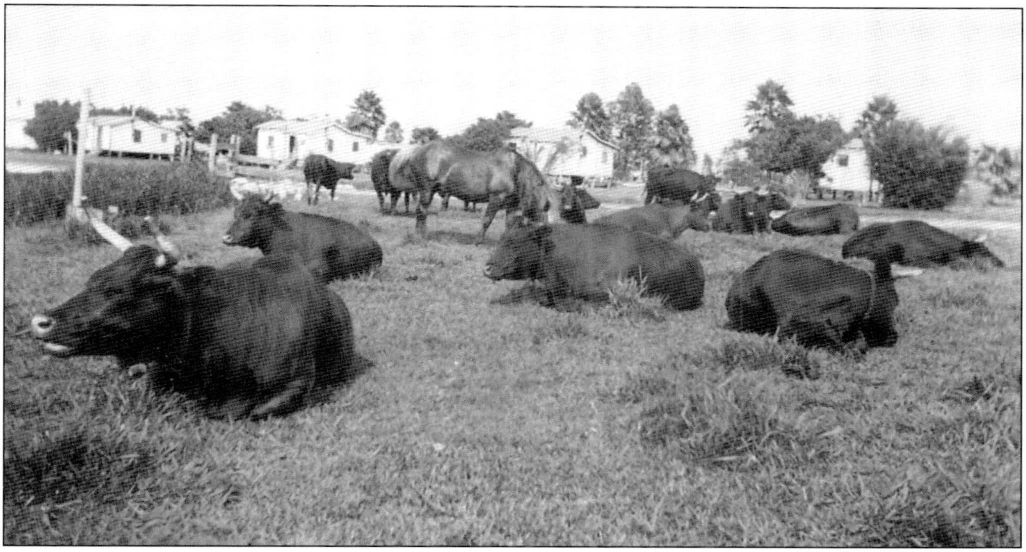

This view of a herd of Devon cattle was taken on September 6, 1936. Cattlemen settled the Florida frontiers and had to be independent and resourceful. When there was a storm or heavy rains, water would get deep enough that yearlings would have to swim to get from one high spot to another. Canals were dug to drain the land. There used to be a livestock market in Belle Glade, and the land all along Route 80 abounded in cattle ranches. In Glades County, the large pioneer cattle ranchers are the Bronsons, the Pepples, and Lykes Brothers. (LEWM.)

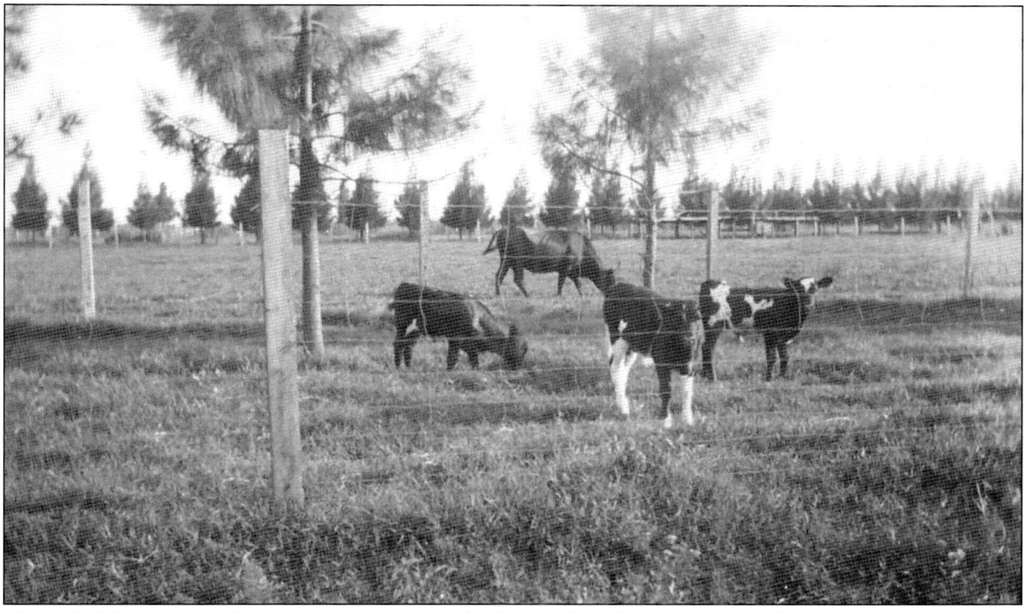

These half-breeds are Devons and range cattle. Since the 1500s, range cattle derived from Spanish imports roamed free throughout Florida. They were herded to Port Rassa and sold to boatmen from Cuba. The Hilliard brothers of Hendry County were some of the early Florida ranchers. When cowmen were weaning heifers, mosquitoes could suffocate them by blocking their nostrils. Cowboys covered themselves in tar to protect their skin from mosquito bites. They also wore bee hats with material to protect their faces and necks. (LEWM.)

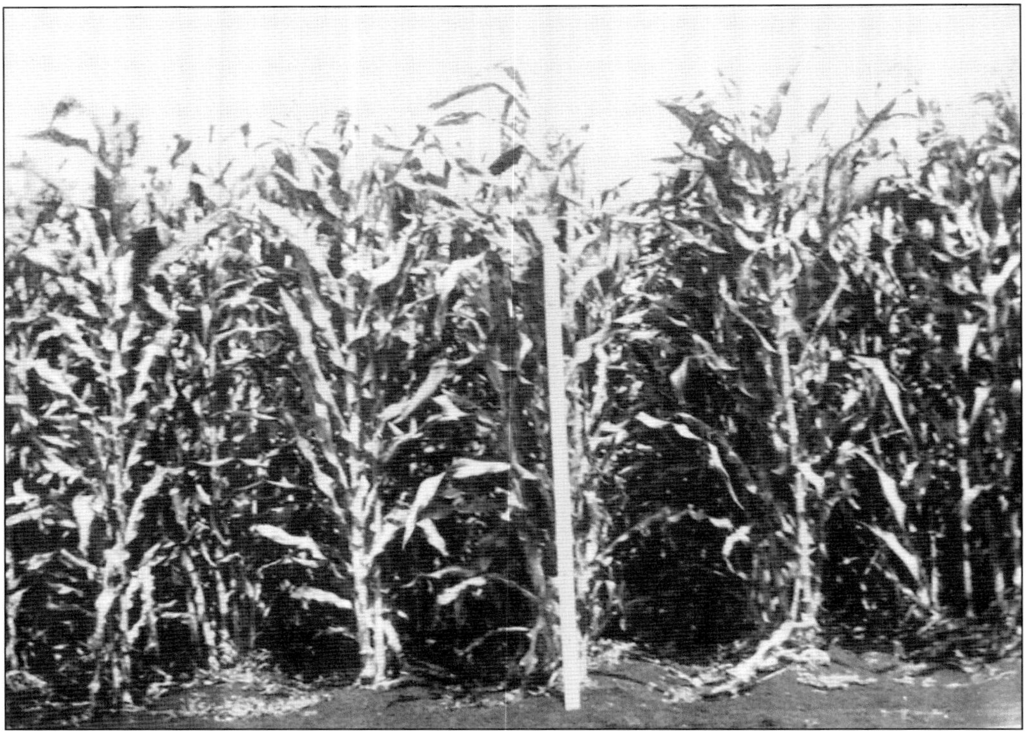

This variety of corn, called tuxpan, was all-around good, sweet corn. This shows a seven-foot stake at the Everglades Experimental Station in 1936. (LEWM.)

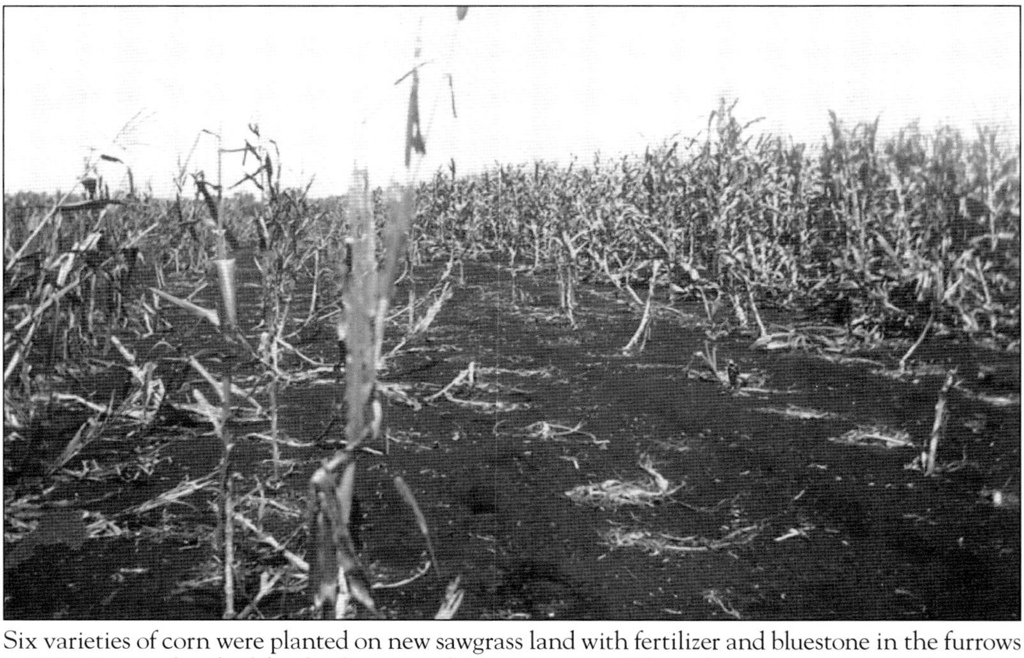

Six varieties of corn were planted on new sawgrass land with fertilizer and bluestone in the furrows in 1930. It was ploughed for the first time the previous year. The only variety to grow and produce was Nassau (right), with a yield of 12 bushels to the acre. (LEWM.)

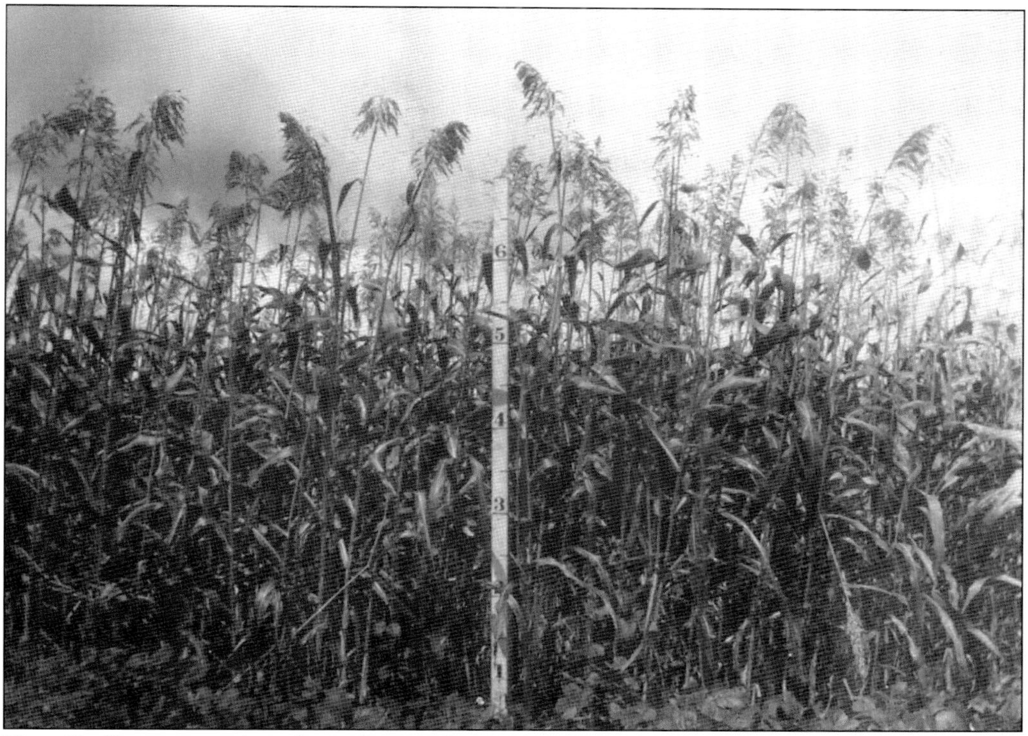

This Shallu variety of sorghum does well in summer. Recent experiments include wheat and maidencane to produce ethanol for biofuel. (LEWM.)

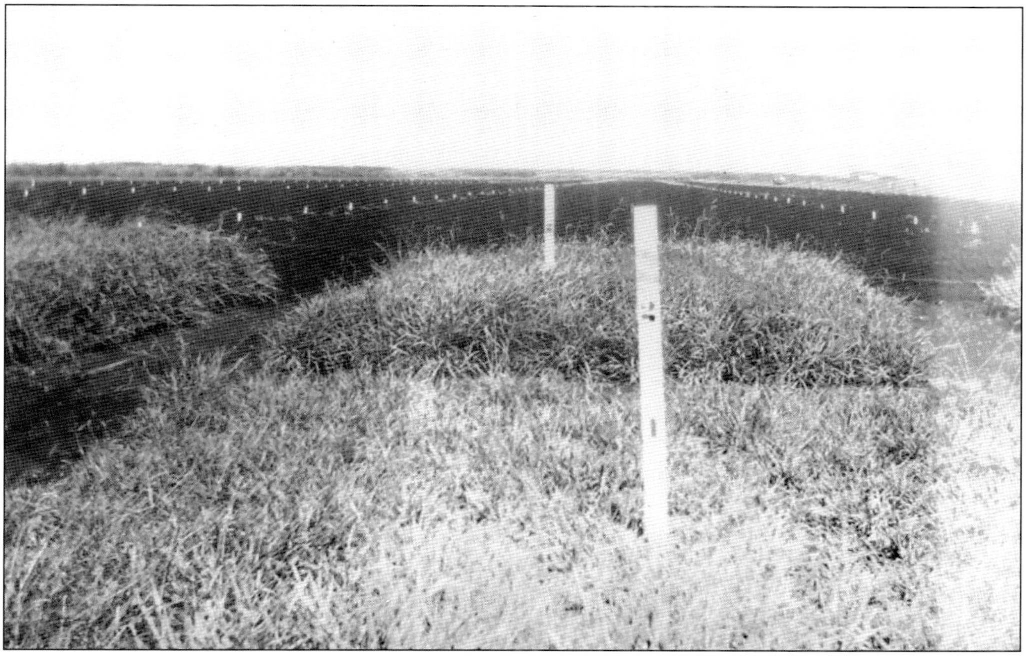

The difference in growth here is due wholly to the back plot being fertilized. Geneticists have continued to research plant varieties to generate the best possible strains. (LEWM.)

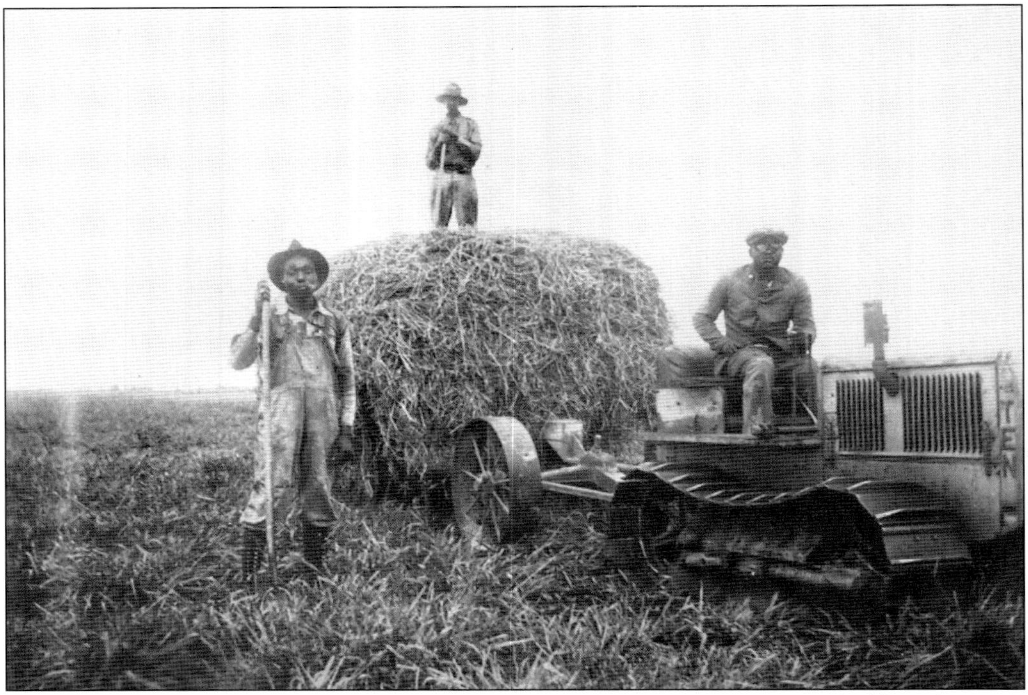

This brand of hay is called Dallas grass. Raising cattle has always been a profitable industry in Florida. The Spanish brought them in the 1500s, when Florida was under their flag. Florida has been under five flags throughout its history. Many varieties of cattle thrive in the heat and humidity of the tropical climate. The number of beef cows raised here today is second only to Texas. (LEWM.)

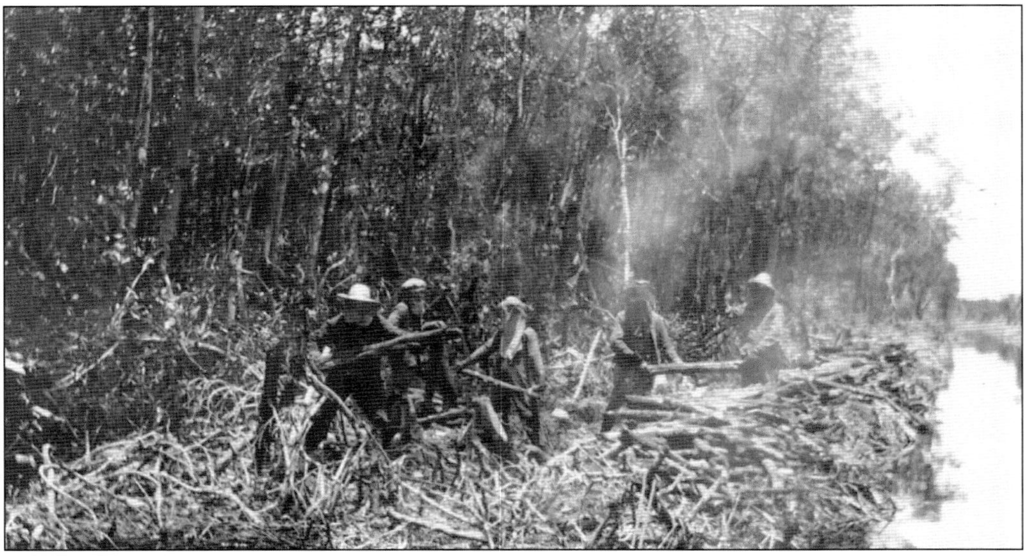

Pictured here is a dredge crew loading firewood from a canal bank near Bear Lake. The dense growth of red mangrove trees, which were cut in clearing the right-of-way, was stacked in cords. Here it is being piled on the "roll" along the canal to get it out of the water. Wood crews waded in the water. They wore veils, gloves, and used smudge smoke as protection from mosquitoes. (LEWM.)

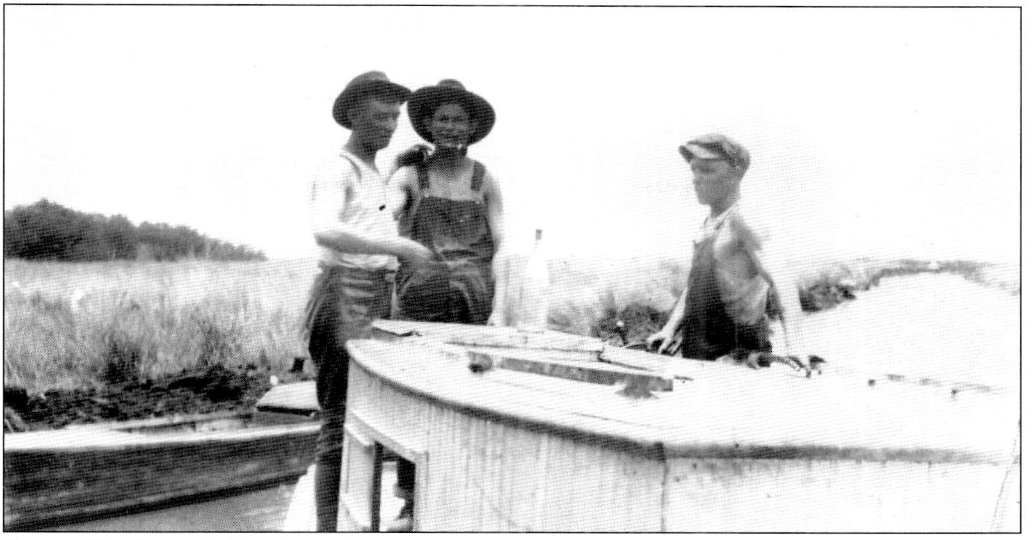

A trio of backwoods Crackers takes time out from their busy schedule. These men are, from left to right, Thad Padgett, Jim Porter (fireman), and Blondy Pritehard (launchman). Florida Crackers drove cattle hundreds of miles over Florida's old "Cracker Trail" to markets in Tampa and Punta Rassa before the lands were fenced off. During calving season, cowboys rode into bunches of cattle, selected a cow or calf, and roped it for branding and inoculations. (LEWM.)

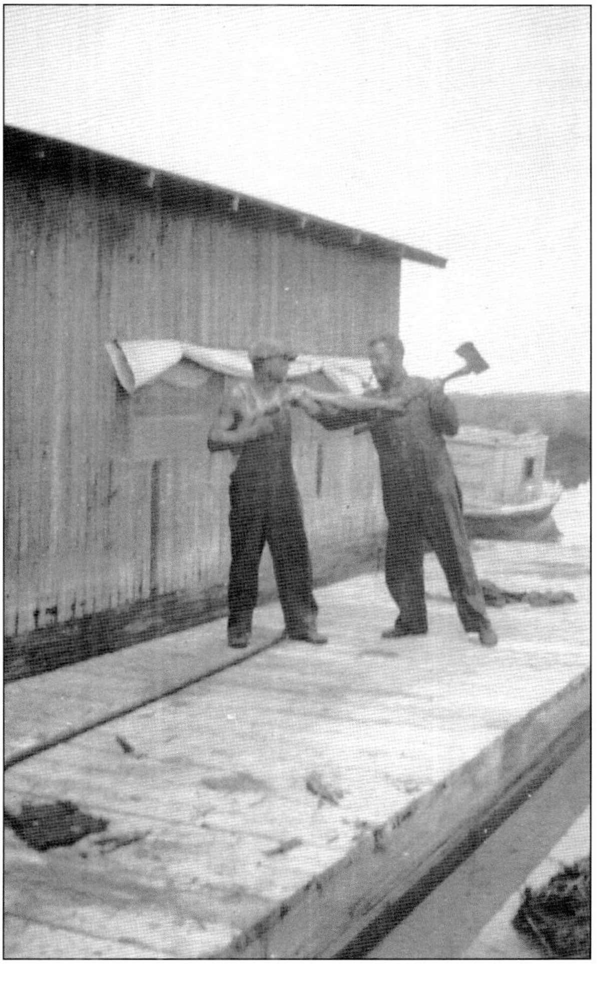

Blondy Pritehard (left) and Gus Roberts (right) duel on the water barge. These boats were used to transport goods and equipment throughout the Everglades. (LEWM.)

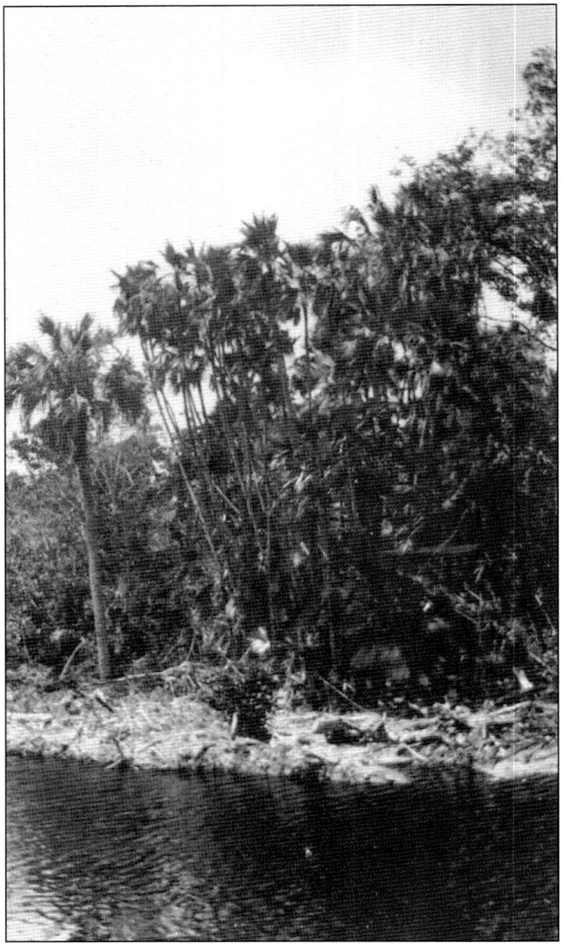

American Indian tribes left behind remnants of shells, fish bones, and other materials in mounds like these around this area. Notice the silver palms at west end of mound. This photograph shows a heavy growth of large trees, including wild royal palms. This shows dense undergrowth and a clump of paurotis palms near the mound. The stable Belle Glade Indian culture, as evidenced from fossils recovered from the Pleistocene Epoch, occupied the Fort Center area for more than 2,000 years. It is believed that these fossils were washed up on high ground by the waters and were used by American Indians. Fossil hunters Mark Renz and Virginia Douglas from Moore Haven have made impressive discoveries over the past decades, including a giant tortoise, a woolly mammoth, spears, and many shells and skeletal remains. (LEWM.)

This machinery is pulling ahead in the "soup doodle" terrain. Take note of the raised spud with a large foot beyond the dipper handle. During rainy season, it was difficult to navigate through the mucky soil. (LEWM.)

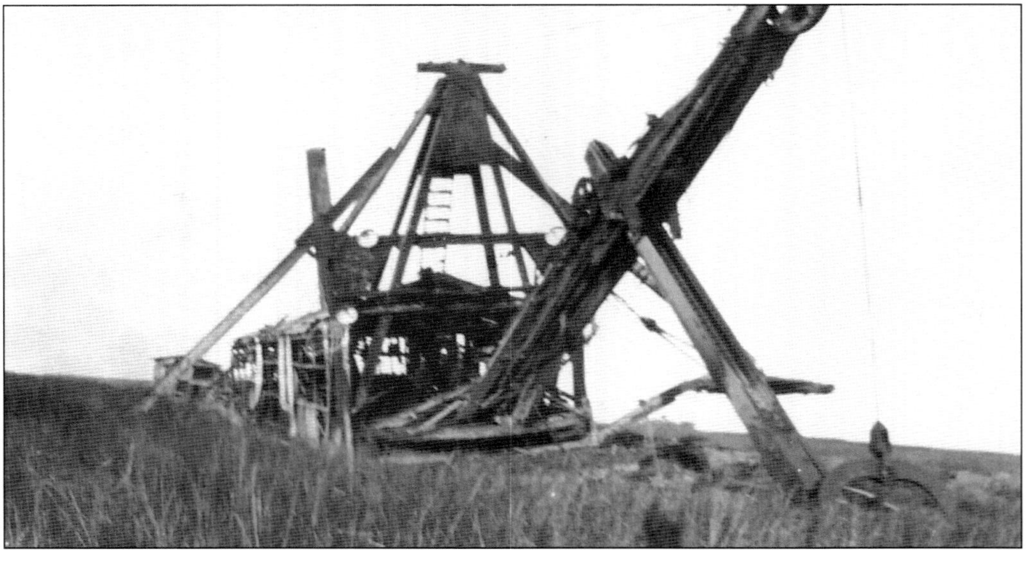

Farming always involved plowing, which is seen taking place at Okeelanta around 1936–1937. A bagasse plant is now located here to power the sugar plant. When Bror Dahlberg started cane production in the Glades, he envisioned using the raw bagasse to produce Celotex wallboard. In 1929, sugar was produced. The first sugarcane season lasted 35 days, grinding 12,969 tons of cane, which resulted in 745 tons of raw sugar. These were such astonishing figures that the use of bagasse for wallboard was forgotten. The bagasse was used to fuel the boilers. (LEWM.)

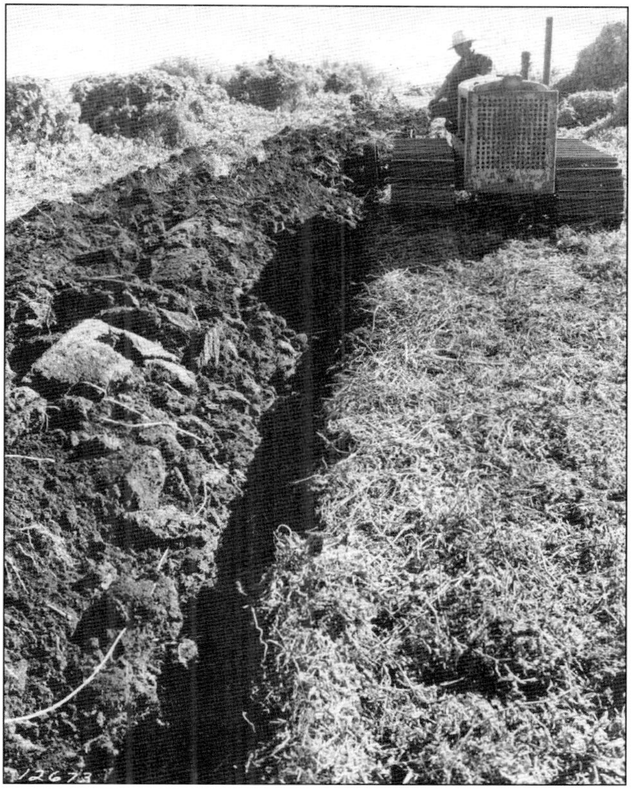

This area is filled with scenes like this of sugarcane fields with men on tractors. Sugarcane is planted with short stalks of seed cane. Green shoots emerge from the stalks and grow into ripe sugarcane. (LEWM.)

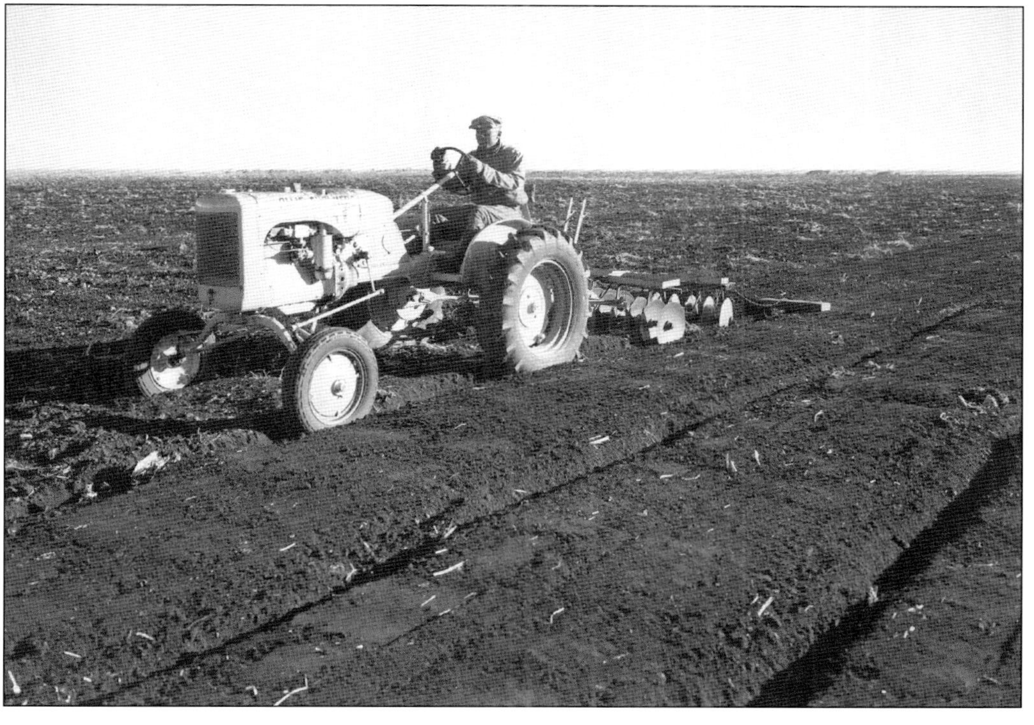

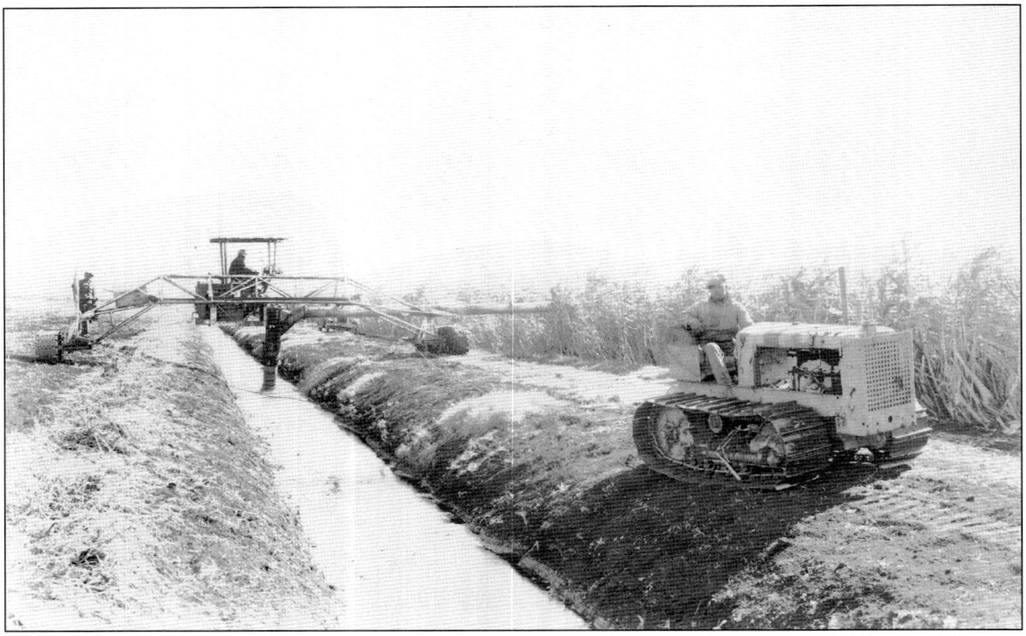

U.S. Sugar Corporation used these portable irrigation pumps on its many cane fields. Work begins at the end of the summer and continues until spring, when the harvest is complete. (LEWM.)

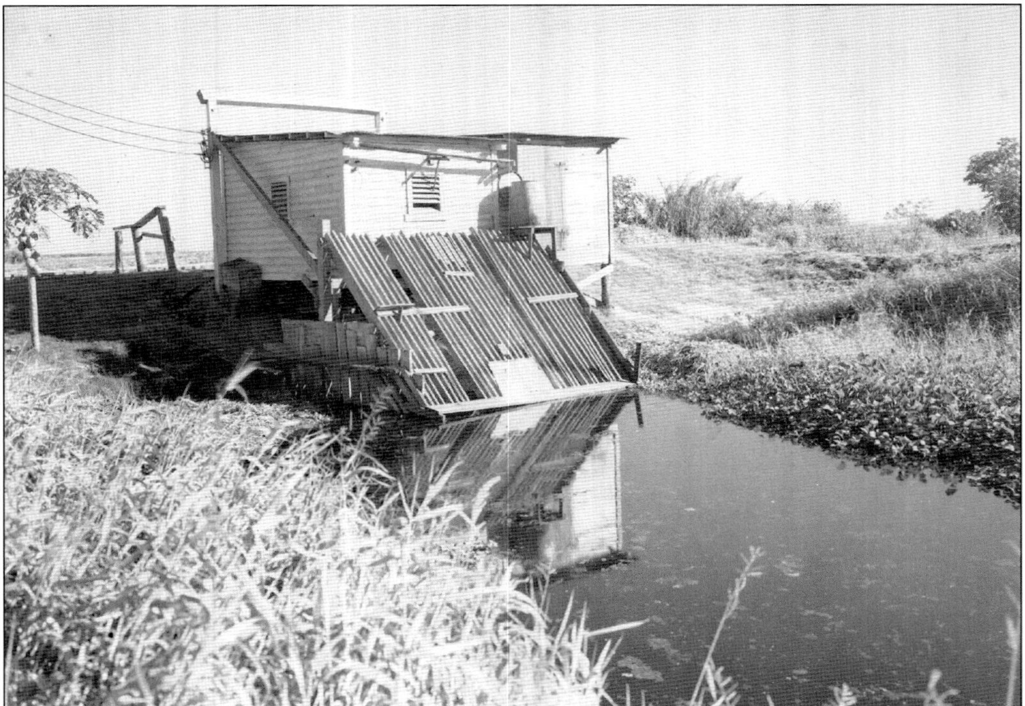

Here is the South Florida Conservancy District Pump House in South Bay before being rebuilt in 1948. South Bay was named for the southern arm of Lake Okeechobee at the corner where it is situated. (LEWM.)

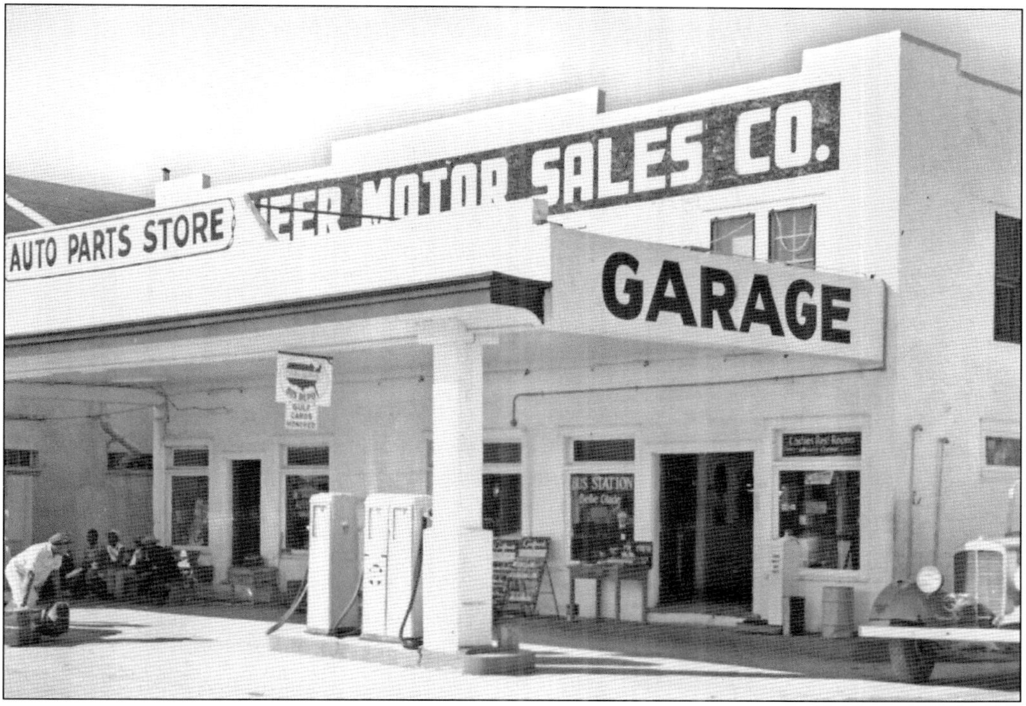

This October 1950 photograph shows a Belle Glade garage. Shops have built up on Main Street along with commercial buildings over the years. (LEWM.)

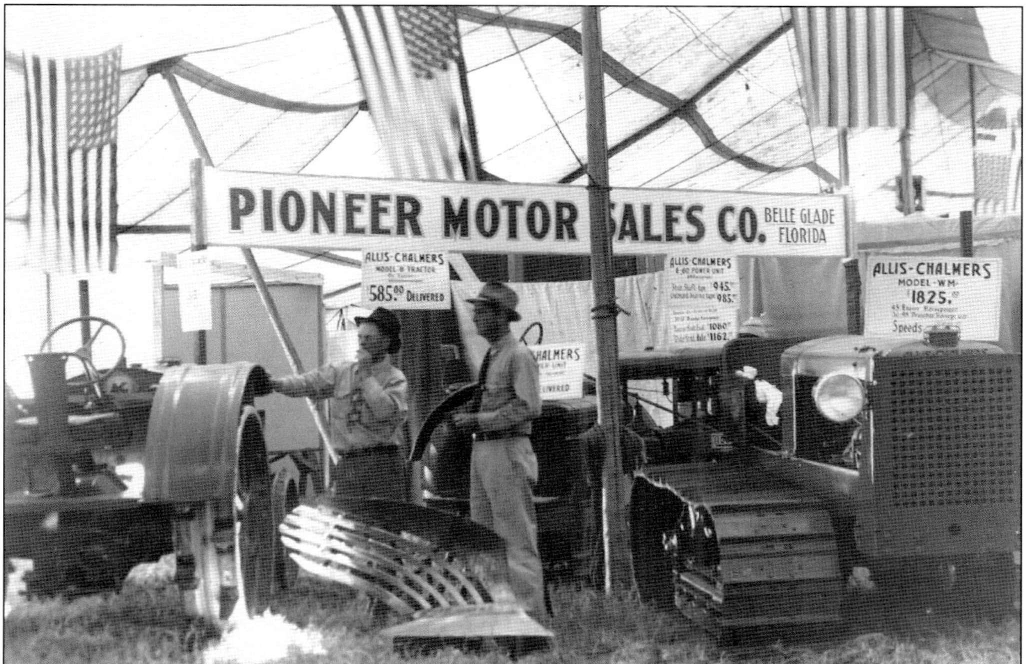

Fairs are popular for local social events as well as for displaying prize livestock. Here Jay Sample attends the Legion Fair. (LEWM.)

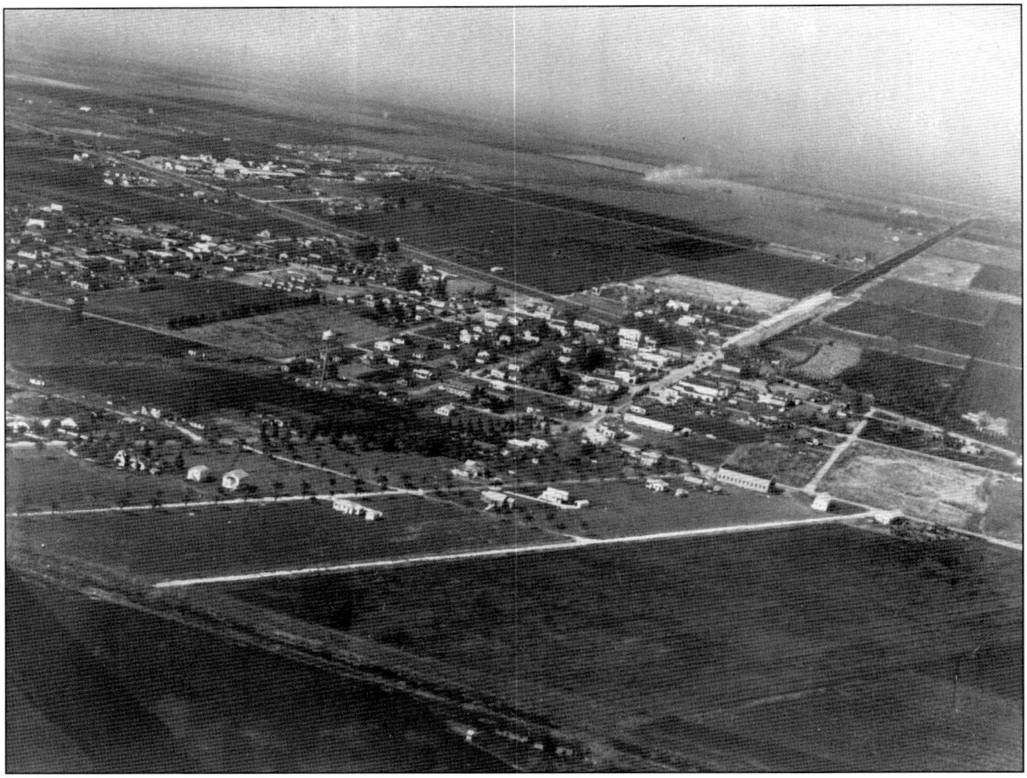

Belle Glade looked like this around 1940, looking north from the Hillsboro Canal to Lake Okeechobee. The area has grown and benefited from the Palm Beach Community College and the Dolly Hand Cultural Arts Center in the west end of town. (LEWM.)

Here is a view of Belle Glade's Main Street, looking north from Avenue B. Belle Glade RV Park used to occupy a location along the lake, but Hurricane Wilma destroyed it in 2005. (LEWM.)

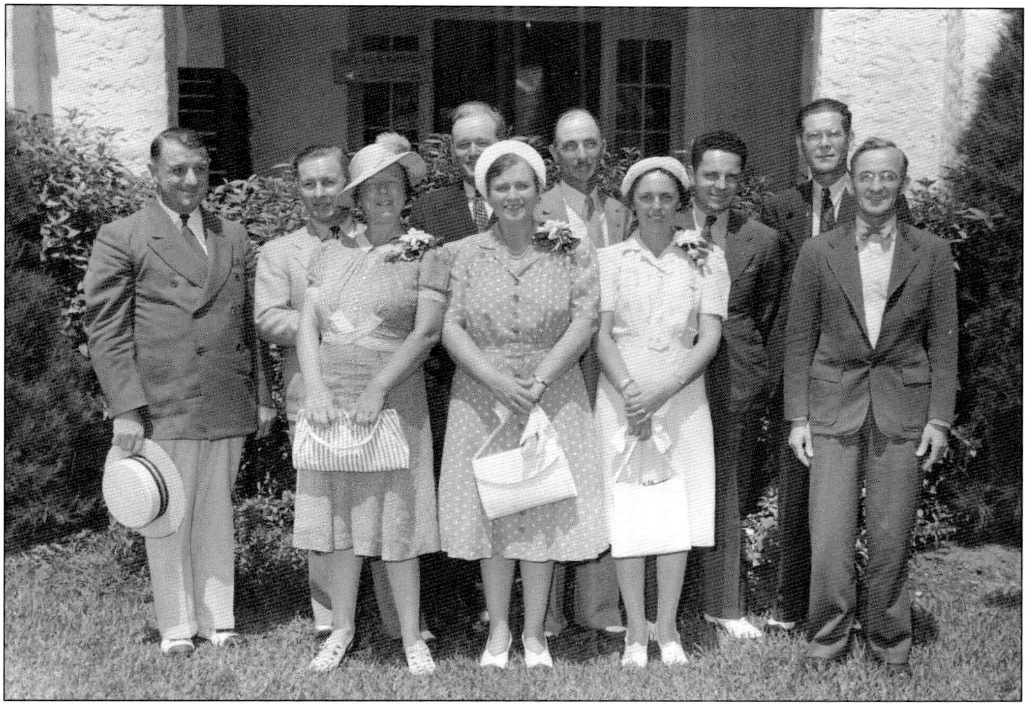

These members of Belle Glade civic organizations are attending a pioneers meeting at the Hollywood Rotary Club. Included here are A. E. "Slick" Kirchman, Mrs. Braddock, Rosco L. Braddock, Mrs. M. E. Granger, Lawrence E. Will, Eleanor Hearn Currier, Thurmond W. Knight, and Rev. J. O. Jameson. Two members are unidentified. (LEWM.)

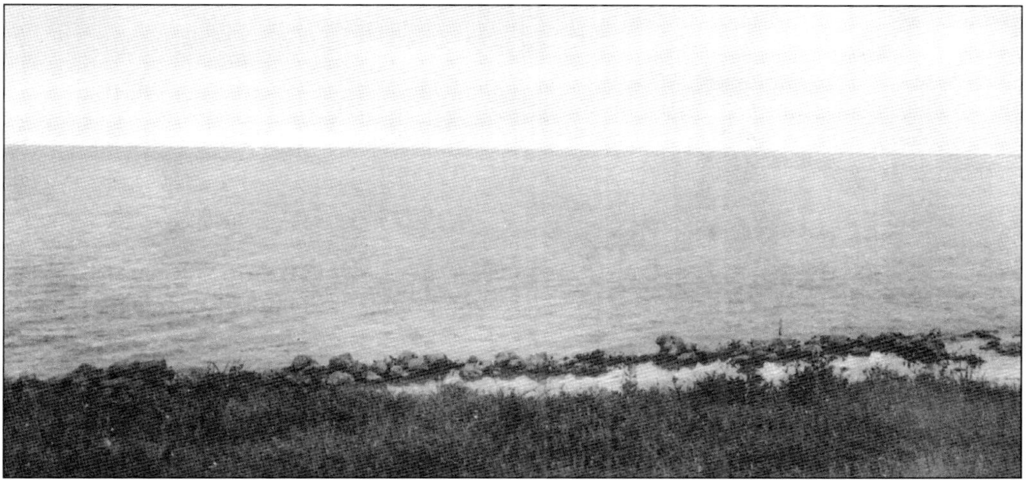

Lake Okeechobee is the second largest freshwater lake wholly within the United States. The lake is very shallow and varies in depth from 18 feet after the summer rains to 9 feet in the dry winter season. Winter festivals occur yearly in the surrounding towns. Lakeport, on the north side, hosts the Sour Orange Festival in February each year. Quilting contests are held and handmade quilts are on display and for sale. There are dancing performances and musical concerts. Children sift through haystacks for prizes buried inside. Vegetables and craft items from local vendors are displayed on tables. Entertainment from clowns includes face painting and balloon animals. (LEWM.)

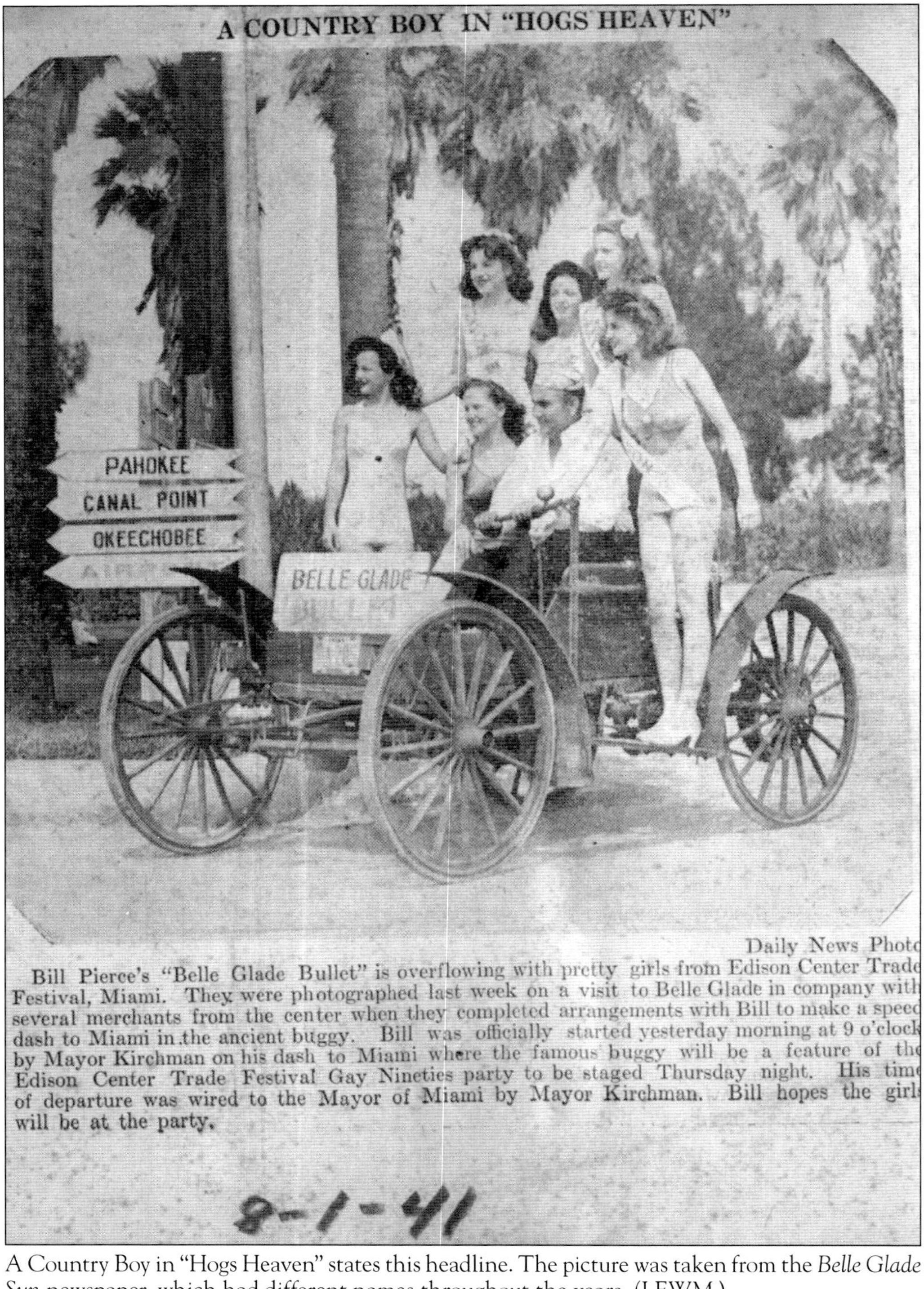

A COUNTRY BOY IN "HOGS HEAVEN"

Daily News Photo

Bill Pierce's "Belle Glade Bullet" is overflowing with pretty girls from Edison Center Trade Festival, Miami. They were photographed last week on a visit to Belle Glade in company with several merchants from the center when they completed arrangements with Bill to make a speed dash to Miami in the ancient buggy. Bill was officially started yesterday morning at 9 o'clock by Mayor Kirchman on his dash to Miami where the famous buggy will be a feature of the Edison Center Trade Festival Gay Nineties party to be staged Thursday night. His time of departure was wired to the Mayor of Miami by Mayor Kirchman. Bill hopes the girls will be at the party.

8-1-41

A Country Boy in "Hogs Heaven" states this headline. The picture was taken from the *Belle Glade Sun* newspaper, which had different names throughout the years. (LEWM.)

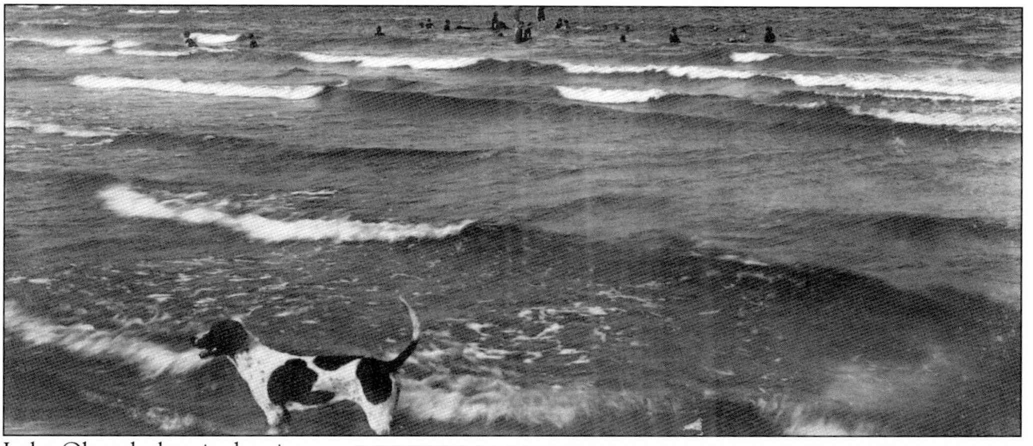

Lake Okeechobee is the site of the "Big O" hike every year. The hike is usually scheduled for November, and members of the Florida Trail Association hike 110 miles around the lake in 9 days. Campers stay in tents, motels, or at RV campgrounds along the route. In 1993, this lake trail was dedicated as part of the Florida National Scenic Trail system, where hikers and bikers share the paved pathway. From this elevated trail visitors and locals can view the breathtaking scenery. (LEWM.)

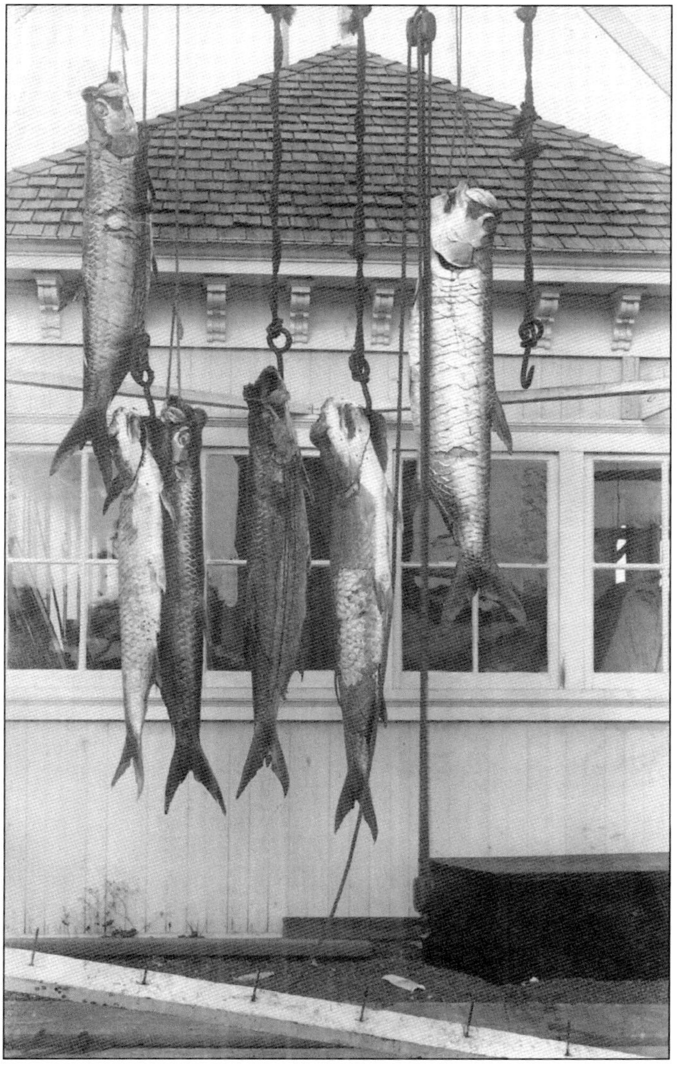

Fishermen try for big catches from the lake such as bass, bluegill, crappie, catfish, and other prizes. They compete in tournaments throughout the year using bass boats to maneuver around. Before the introduction of nylon, fishermen used natural fibers to construct their nets. The Calusa Indians were the first to use special tools, much as fishermen did in the 1920s, to mend their nets. (LEWM.)

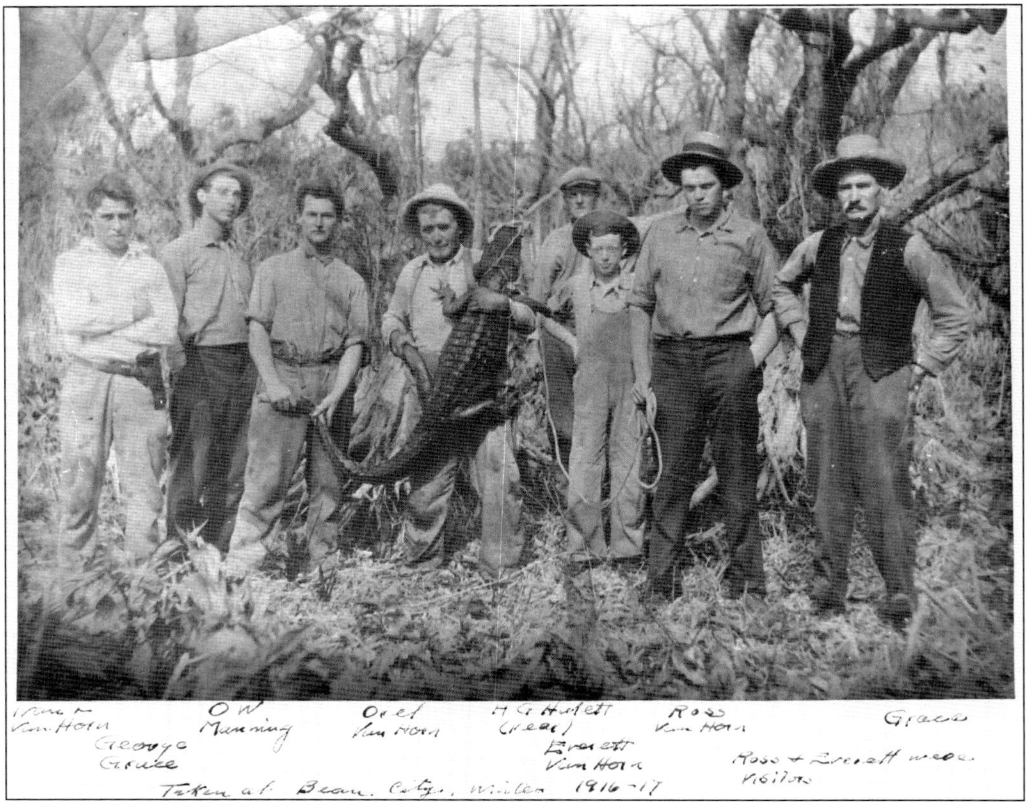

A classic pose shows these men holding an alligator. Alligator wrestling has been a tourist attraction in Florida for a long time. It is said that there are 10,000 alligators in Lake Okeechobee today. (LEWM.)

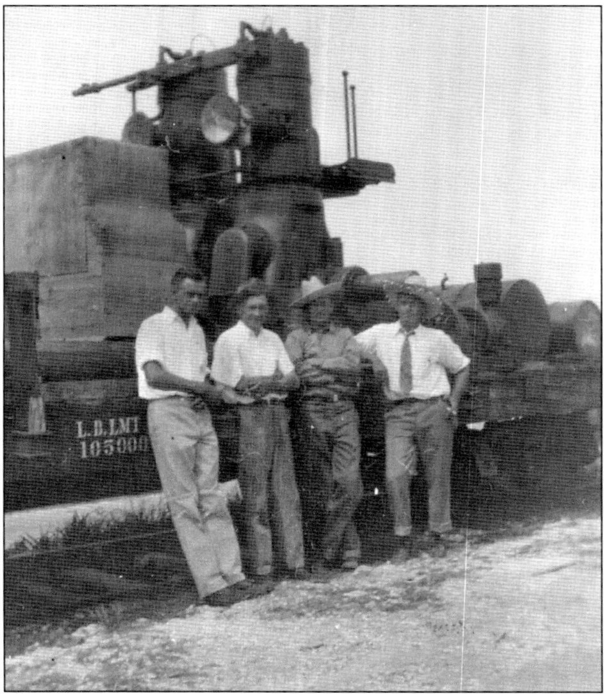

A diesel engine approaches a railroad crossing at Sebastian and continues to the site of the power plant at Belle Glade in this December 1928 photograph. (LEWM.)

The Ashley gang was the "Bonnie and Clyde" of the lake. They terrorized bank employees by riding up and holding them up for their cash. While Laura Upthegrove (left), the only female member of the notorious Ashley gang, was distilling moonshine out in the sawgrass, her boyfriend, John Ashley (right), and his brother were in Pahokee robbing banks. The local sheriff was determined to catch them and eventually did. (LEWM.)

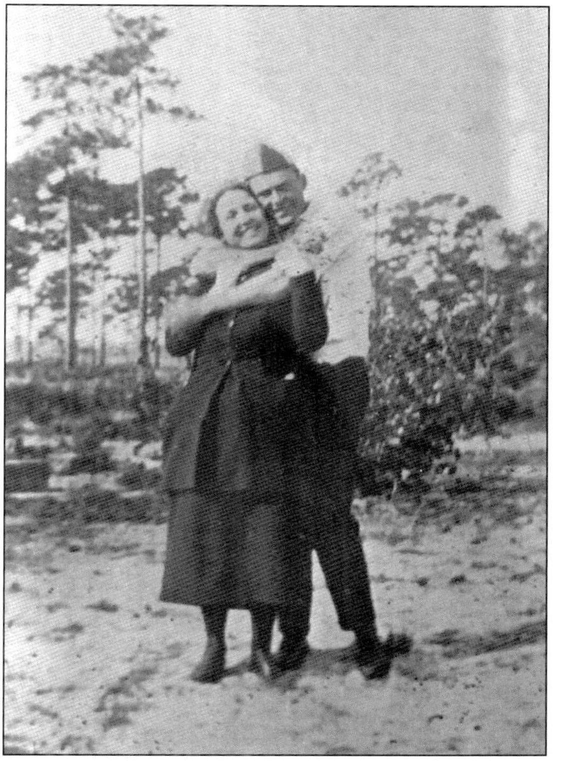

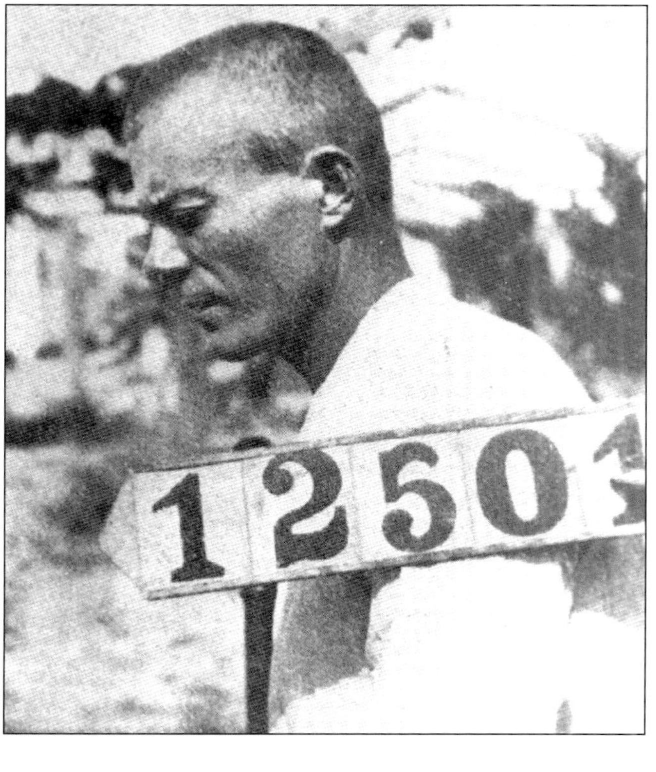

Dr. Anna Darrow became acquainted with the notorious Ashley gang when the mother of John Ashley, a gang member, concerned about her son's health, obtained a tonic for him while was in a Stuart jail. Dr. Anna's services were utilized once again when she was led blindfolded 10 miles into the woods to their hideout to treat another gang member. (LEWM.)

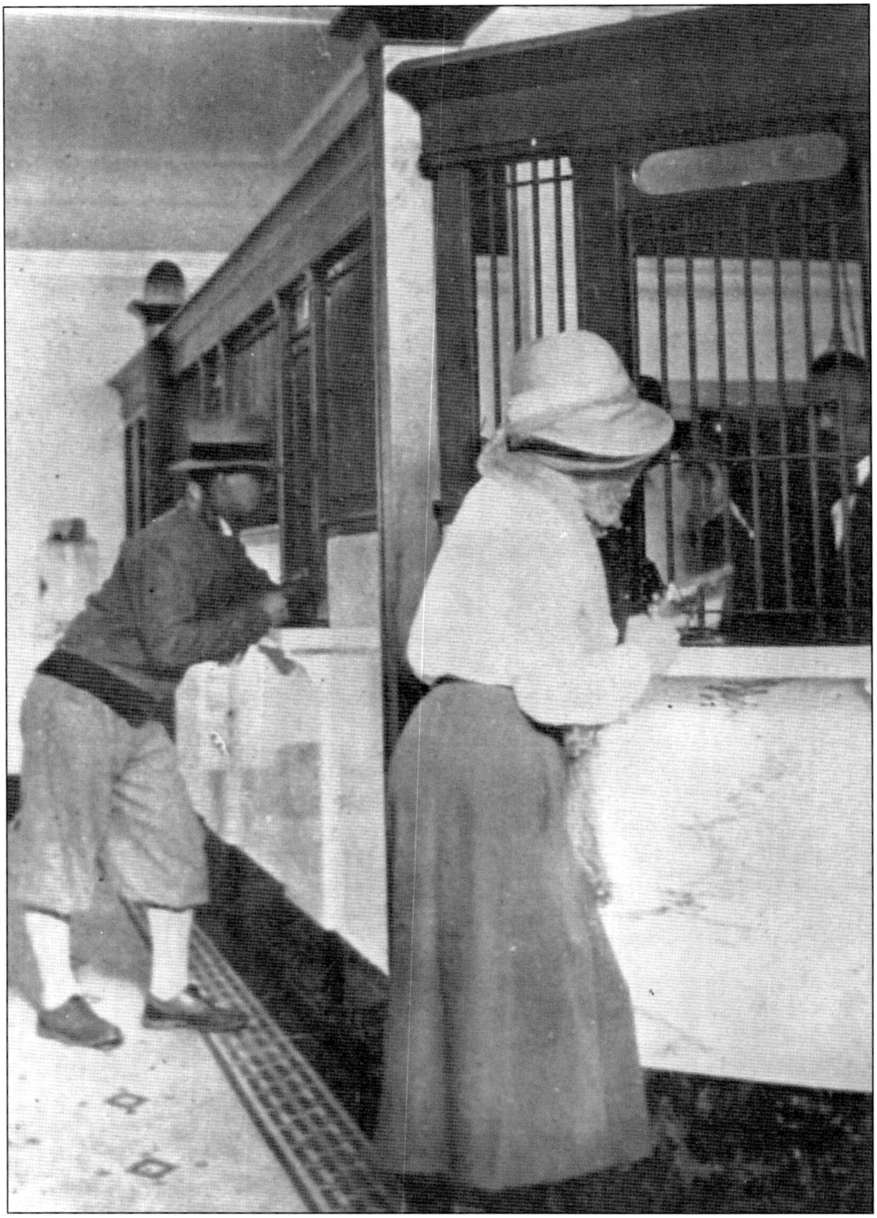

This is a staged reproduction of a bank robbery by John Ashley and Laura Upthegrove at the bank in Stuart. Laura Upthegrove, called the "Queen of the Everglades," was described as an "Amazon of a woman" who packed a .38 caliber revolver strapped to her hip. Ashley was captured 12 miles southwest of Stuart. Before the trial began, Ashley pleaded guilty and was sentenced to 17.5 years in Raiford State Prison. On March 13, 1918, he was sent to a road camp, but he escaped three months later. Most of the gang was apprehended at Plant City. In 1924, Sheriff John Merritt apprehended the gang at the Sebastian Bridge. After being warned not to make a move, John Ashley disobeyed. The deputies fired, killing the entire gang. The sheriff took John Ashley's glass eye and made a key chain out of it. Laura Upthegrove said she would get it back and she did. (LEWM.)

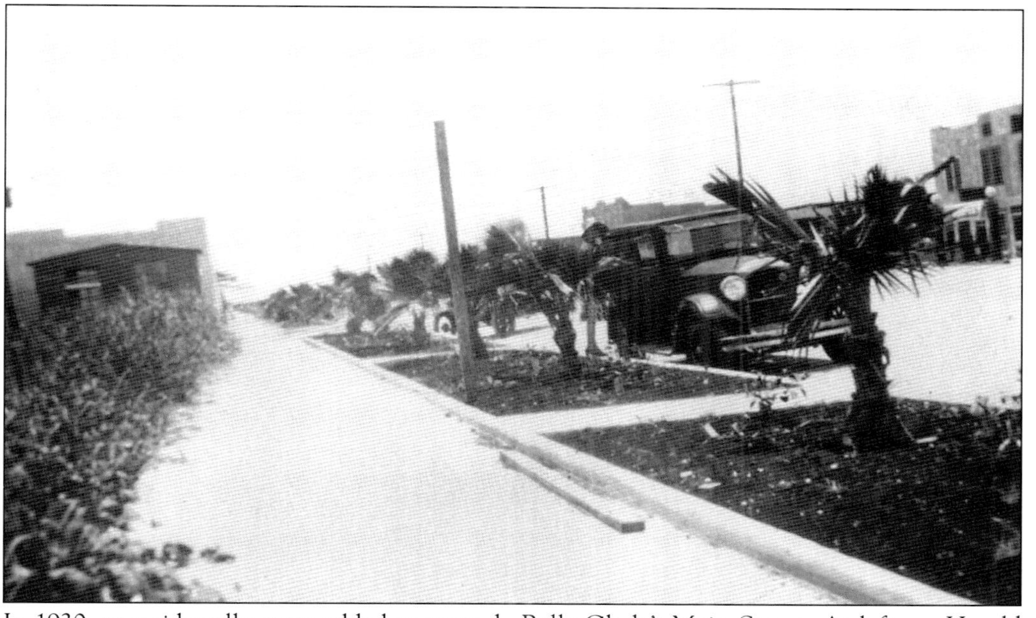

In 1930, new sidewalks were added to upgrade Belle Glade's Main Street At left are Harold Riedel's battery shop and Glades Chevrolet. At right are the Pioneer Service Station and Borce Grocery. (LEWM.)

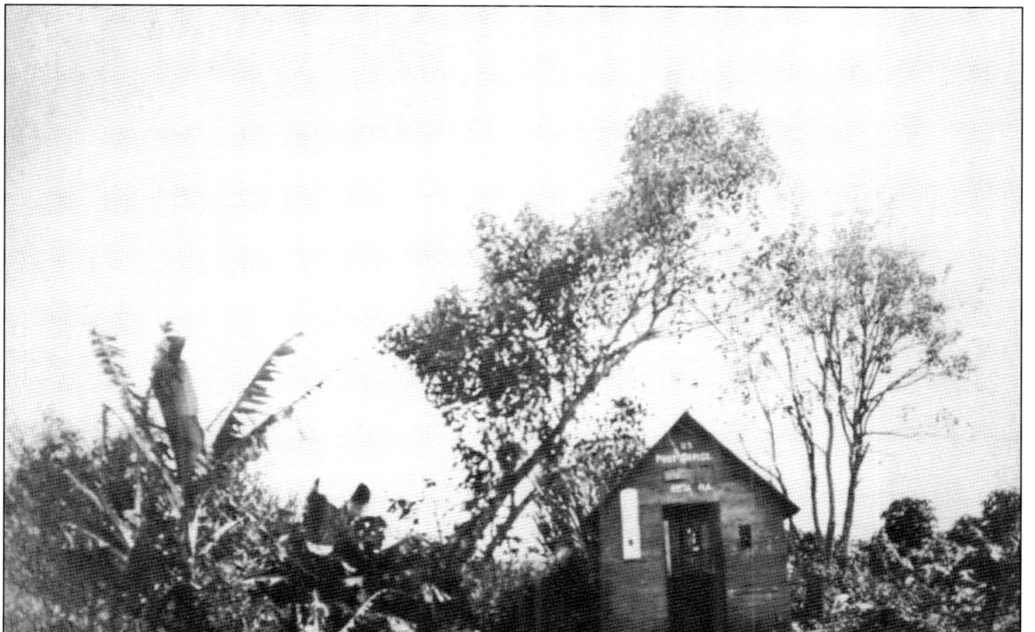

This building is the first U.S. post office at Ritta near Bolles Hotel. J. R. Leatherman, a preacher from Virginia who had a reputation for drinking, got a school but wanted a post office too. To get one, the town required a name. The name Chosen was selected in 1921 as a good, biblical name, because theirs was "a Chosen Place." (LEWM.)

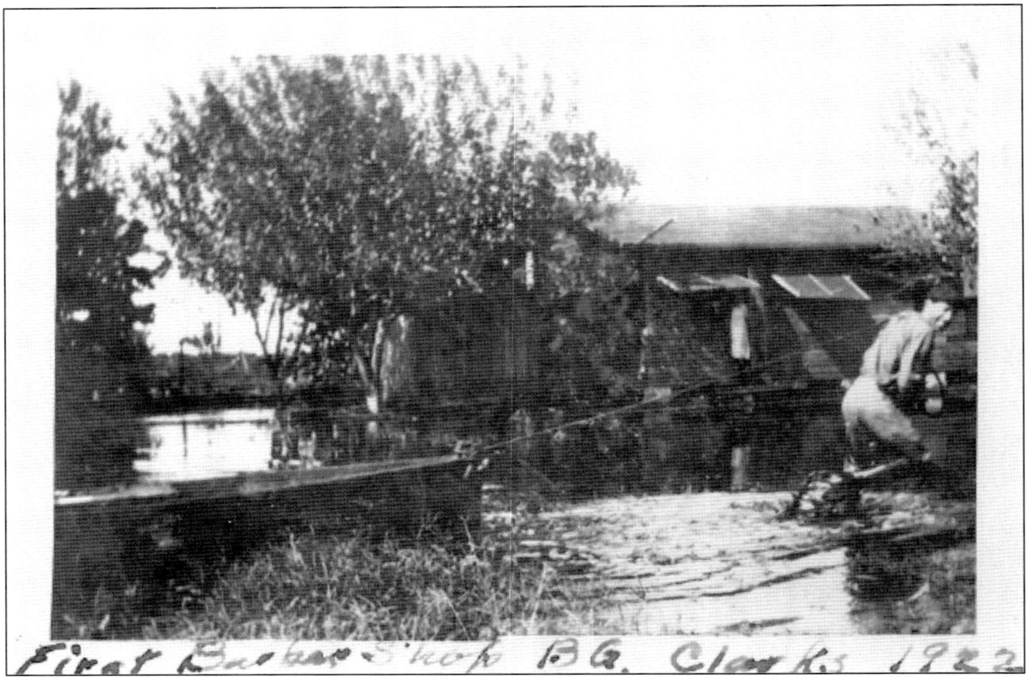

Clark's was the first barbershop in Belle Glade in 1922. Here are Clark's home and his barbershop. (LEWM.)

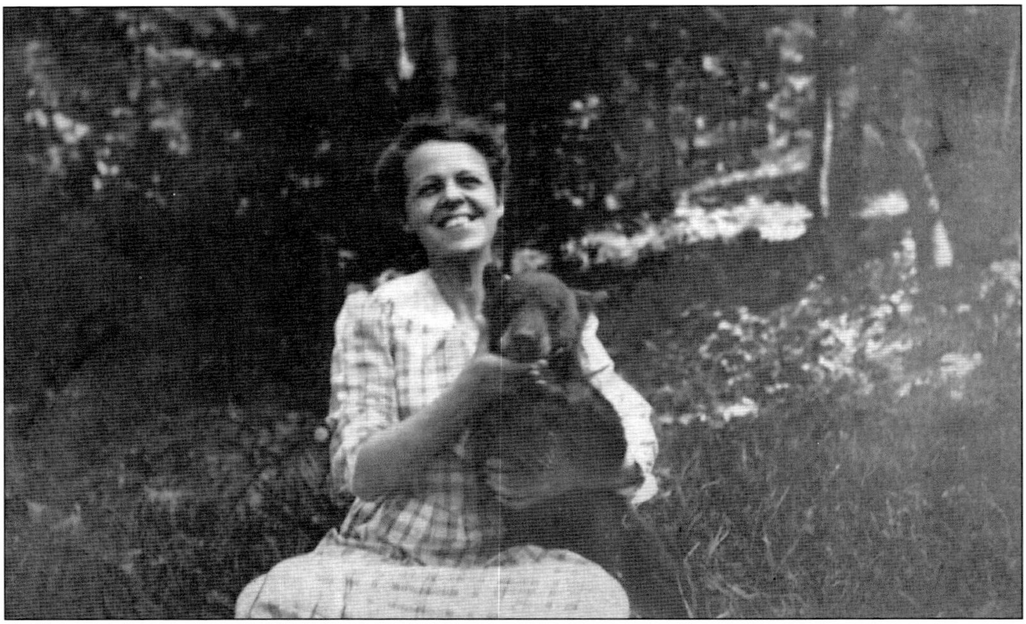

Alberta Von Stroup poses with a Florida black bear cub in 1912 or 1914. Black bears still wander around the Everglades and live near Fisheating Creek in Lakeport. Black bears have also been photographed and captured on the Big Cypress Seminole Indian Reservation. They have been sighted searching for bananas in Moore Haven by the authors and also in many towns around the lake to this day. (LEWM.)

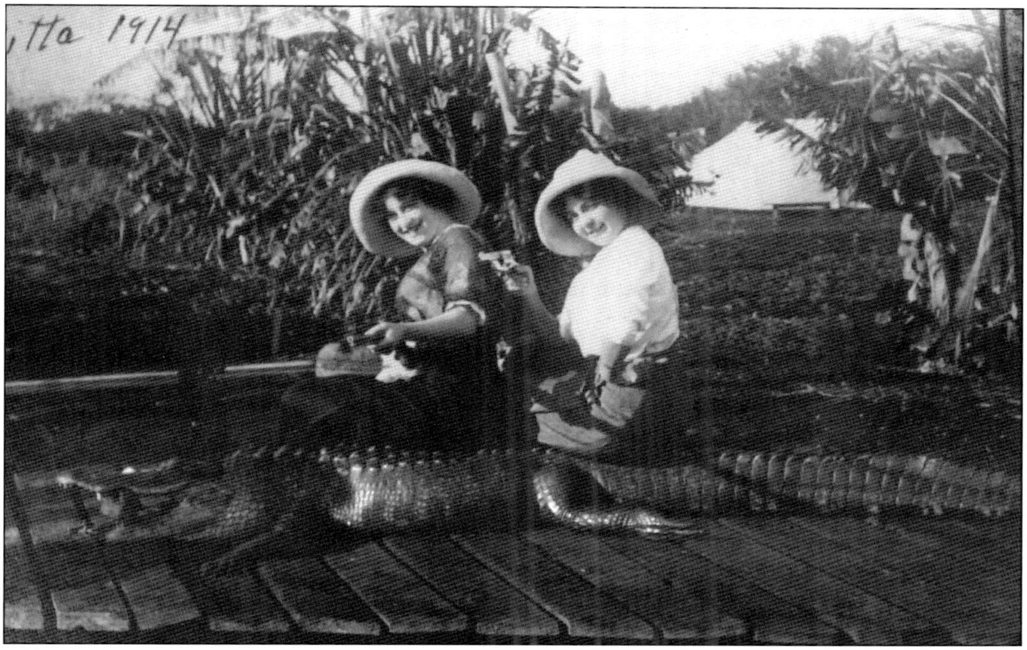

Alberta Von Stoup and her friend go on a gator ride at Ritta in 1914. Hats like these were very fashionable and generated a market in plumes around the beginning of the 20th century. (LEWM.)

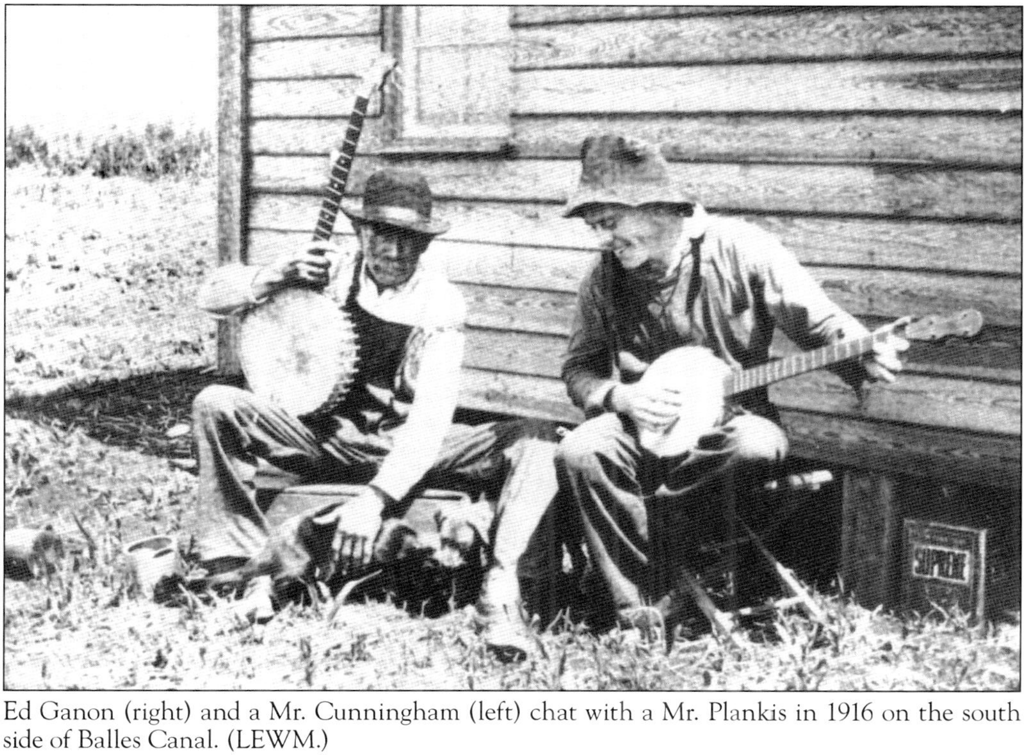

Ed Ganon (right) and a Mr. Cunningham (left) chat with a Mr. Plankis in 1916 on the south side of Balles Canal. (LEWM.)

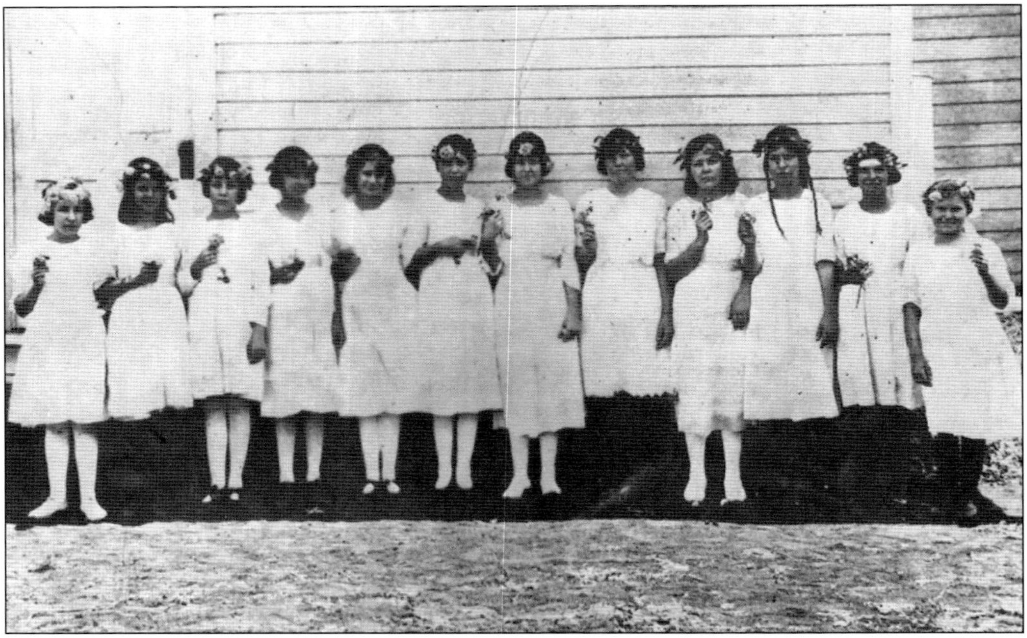

The staff of South Bay School is seen in this 1920 photograph. From left to right are Catherine Clark (LaByer), Edith Fisher, Wanda Marvin, Thelma Fitzhugh, Margaret Gist, Opal Hartline, Zelma Lockmiller (Betzmer), Alice Thigpen, Margaret Clark, Bessie Dean, Hazel Fisher, and Laura Hudson. (LEWM.)

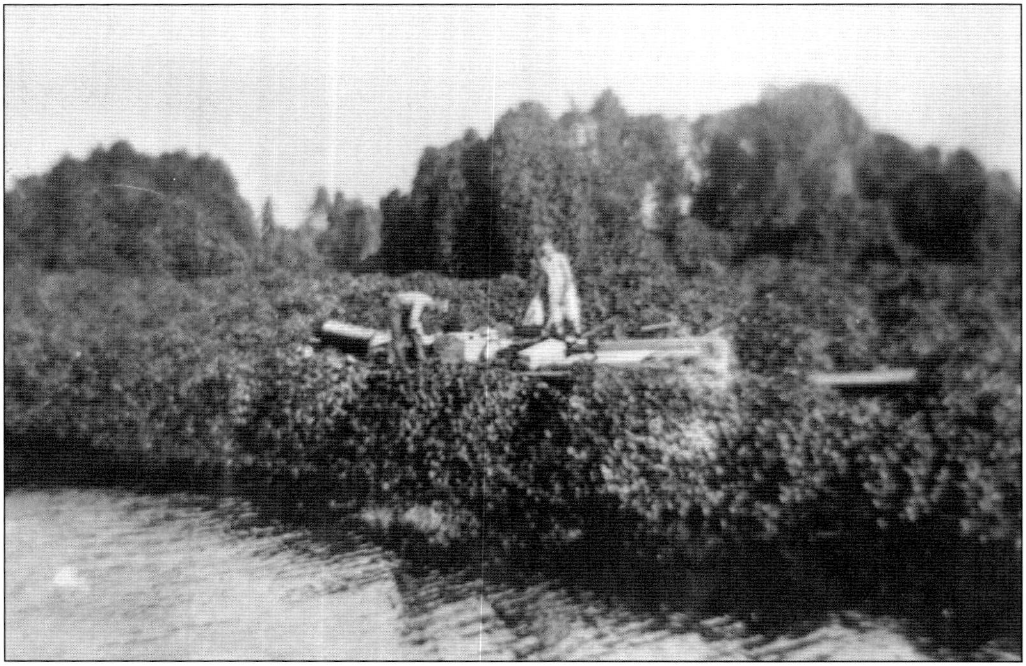

Here is the lumber for the first house in Belle Glade, which was built by Orna Manning and Bert Gaylord in June 1915. The school was located on the north side of the canal a quarter-mile east of Main Street. The trees here are custard apples covered by moon vines. (LEWM.)

From left to right are Clarence Everett, Dr. William J. Buck, unidentified, and Henry T. White. Dr. Buck made calls on patients at the Okeelanta Hotel and once walked across the North New River Canal on a sea of water hyacinths. The only natural enemies of the water hyacinth plant are freezes and salt water. It was brought to Florida from a lady living on the St. Johns River visiting the New Orleans International Cotton Exposition in 1884, who admired its gorgeous lavender blossoms. She brought the water hyacinth back and hoped it would grow in Florida, where it thrived. This plant has clogged Florida's waterways ever since. (LEWM.)

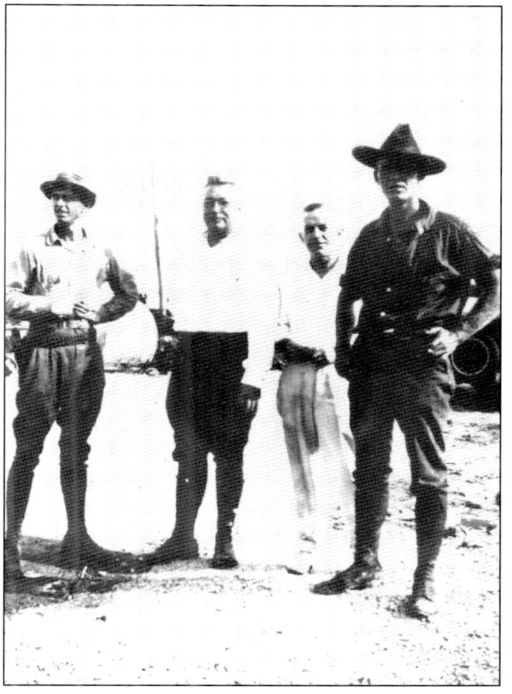

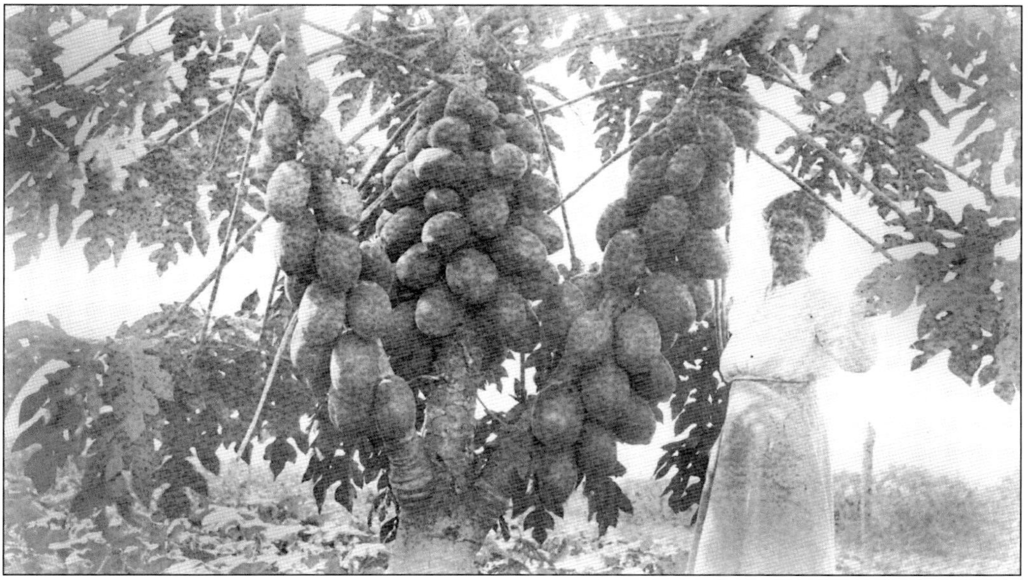

Clara Hart shows off her large papaya tree. Agriculture has always been important to the local economy. Agriculture Day is celebrated in the towns around the lake on March 20 every year. Also in March, Chalo Nitka, or "the Day of the Big Bass" in the Seminole language, takes place. Seminoles participate each year in the festival on the Moore Haven Chalo Nitka fairgrounds. Celebrated on the first weekend of March, it features a parade, rodeo, the Glades County Youth Livestock Show, a carnival, and many other activities to celebrate the paving of Moore Haven's Main Street since 1949. Each year a Chalo Nitka Queen is chosen from Glades County's high school girls at one of the oldest continuous celebrations in Florida. (LEWM.)

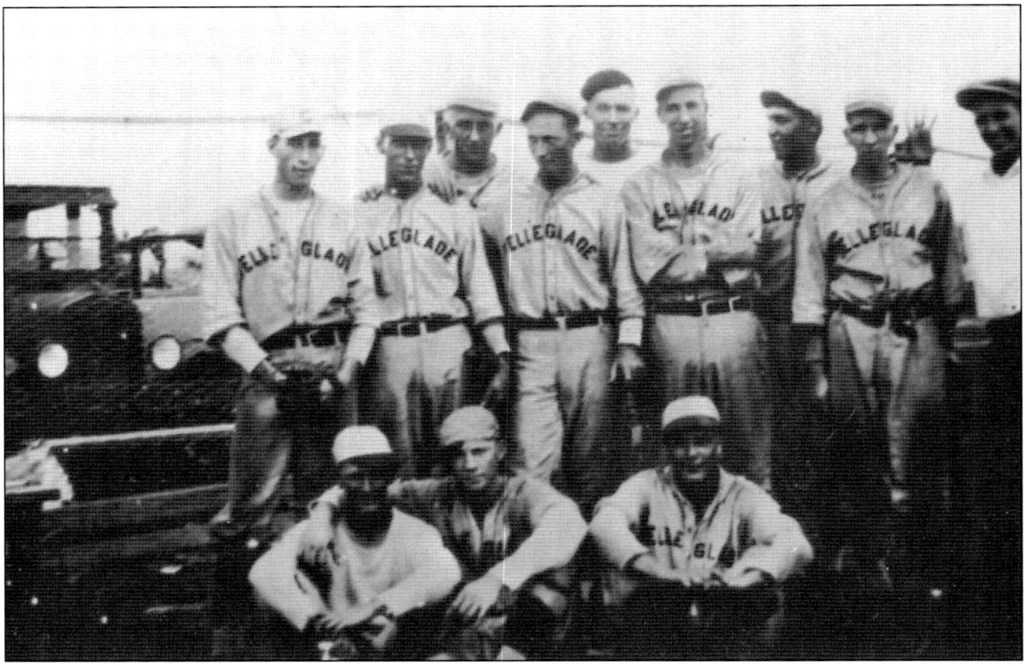

Belle Glade's first baseball team poses for the fans in 1928. Standing from left to right are Woods, Mitchell, Fred Greer, T. W. Lee, four unidentified, and Lou Betzner (far right). (LEWM.)

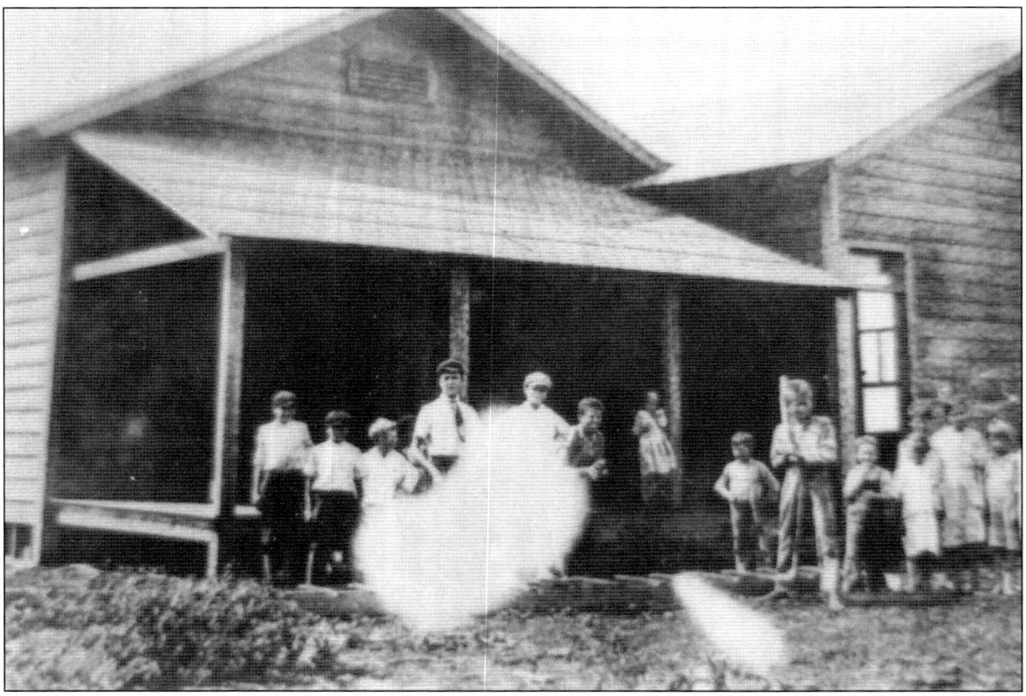

This photograph depicts the first schoolhouse in Belle Glade. In Glades County, a two-room school had opened in 1916 with Mrs. W. J. Young as the teacher. In March 1919, a school was opened for black students, and 35 children enrolled. (LEWM.)

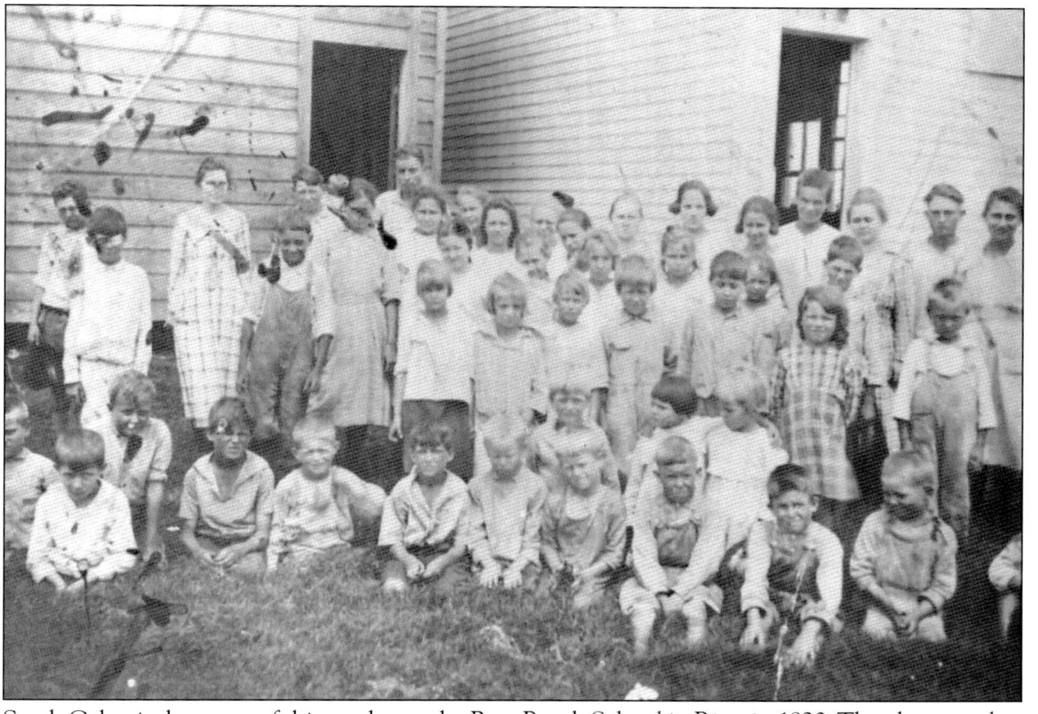

Sarah Calan is the name of this teacher at the Bare Beach School in Ritta in 1920. The photographer was E. K. Plank. (LEWM.)

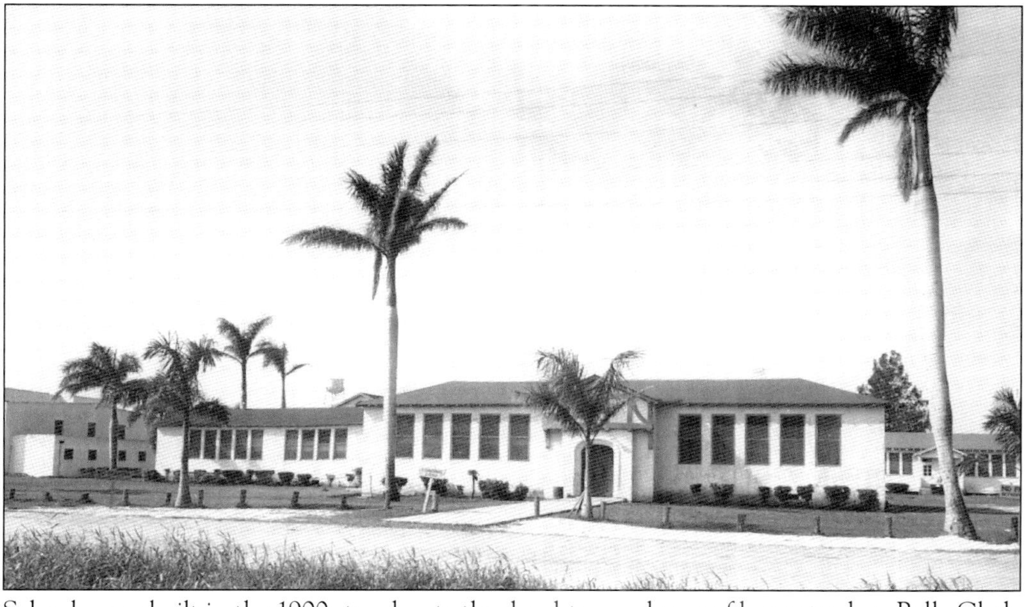

Schools were built in the 1900s to educate the daughters and sons of homesteaders. Belle Glade grammar school and high school (at left) were built to teach what were called the three R's: reading, writing, and arithmetic. (LEWM.)

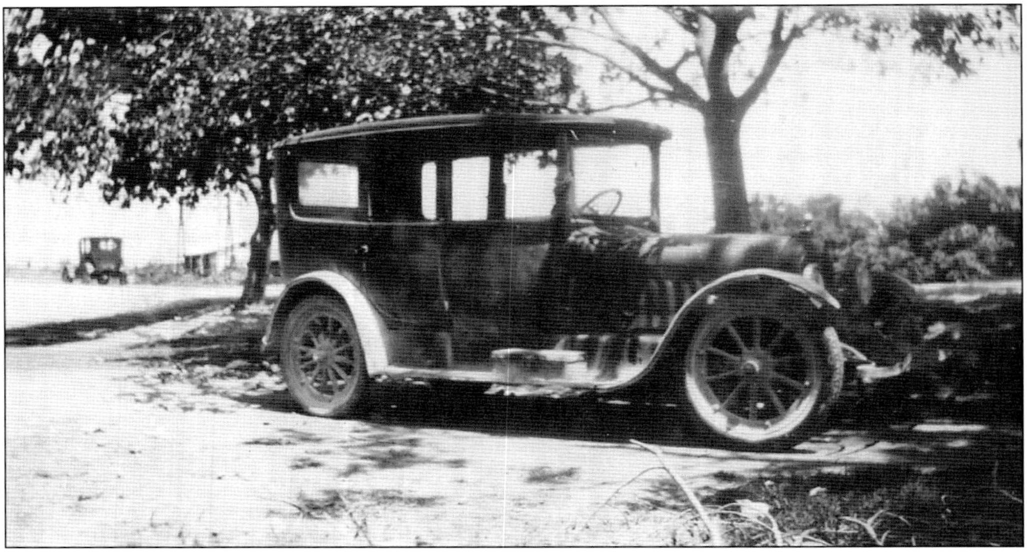

This automobile was Belle Glade's first bus, which was operated by a Captain Benjamin. Before Conners Highway was finished in 1924 from the east coast to the lake, cross-state travel had been mostly by boat. One of the first men to drive a bus from coast to coast, Ed Kettner, was also famous for saying, "I'd walk a mile for a Camel." (LEWM.)

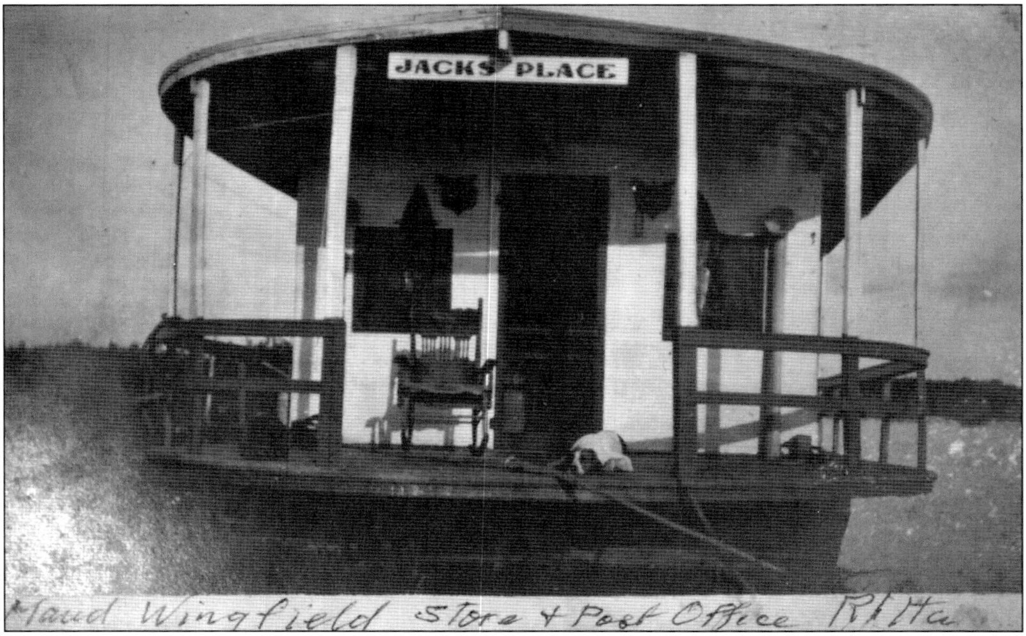

Here is Maude Wingfield's first store and post office at Ritta and Bare Beach. The first store boat was the powered sloop of pioneer storekeeper J. M. Baker, who delivered groceries to Glade Crest down the Hillsboro Canal and to Ritta, where he supplied Maud Wingfield until she got big enough to buy direct. Often early post offices were in women's homes. The first post office in Hendry County was in a town named Tasmania, north of LaBelle. Moore Haven's first postmaster was also a woman, Rhinda Daniels. The post office opened at 8:00 a.m. and was supposed to close at 8:00 p.m. but occasionally was open longer when the mail arrived late. (LEWM.)

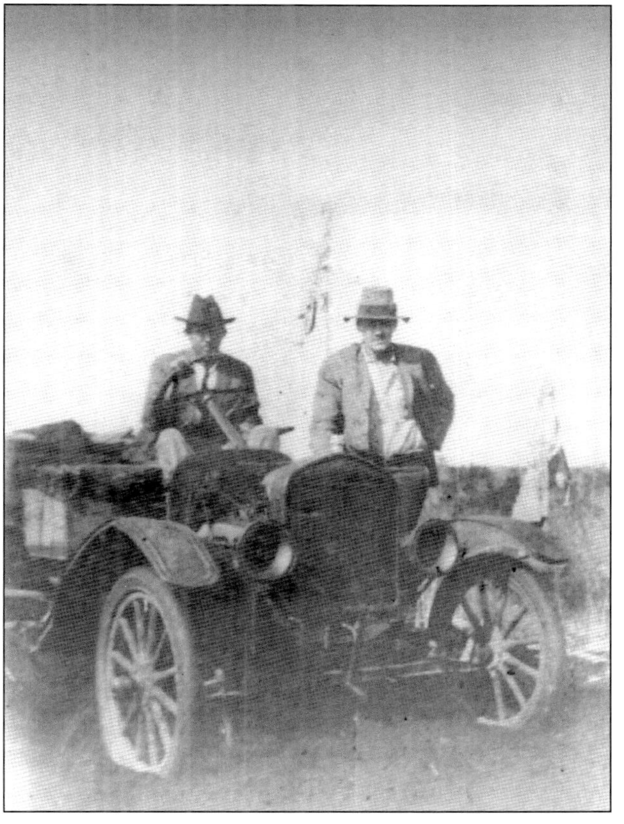

Allen and Walter Greer arrive at 20 Mile Bend. Walter Greer was Belle Glade's first mayor. The first car to drive from Belle Glade to West Palm Beach was a chain-drive Ford truck. This event took place in 1921, before the road was paved or leveled. (LEWM.)

This scene is of an early voting booth under the flag. Only 13 voters were eligible in the Glades. It also depicts Mrs. King's hotel. The ballot contained a proposal for a Ritta bond election to finance the Palm Beach inlet in August 1916. (LEWM.)

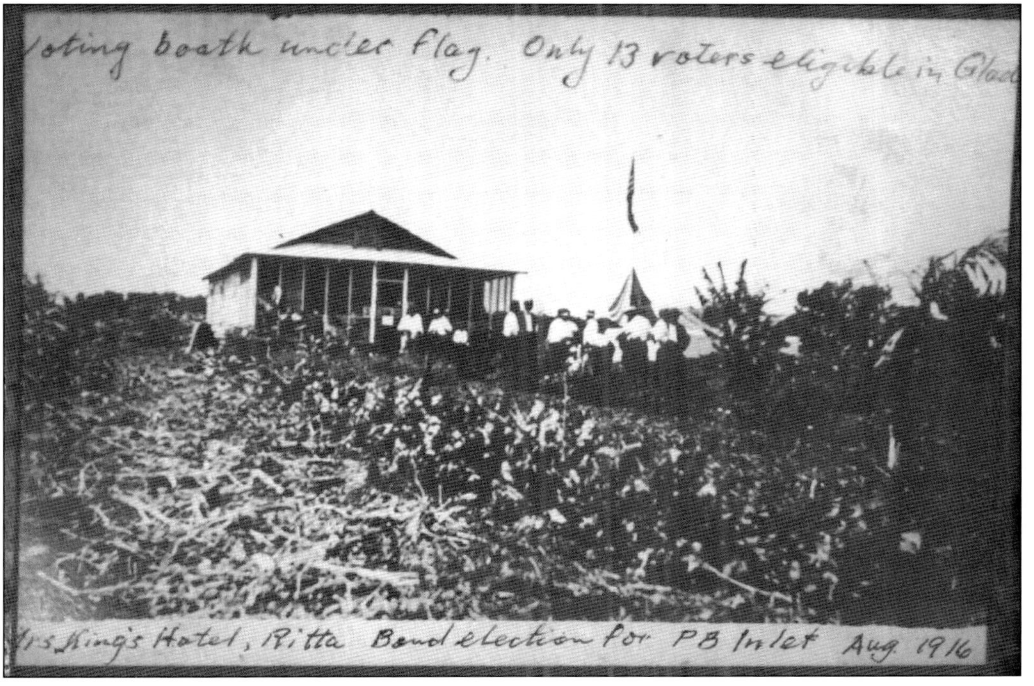

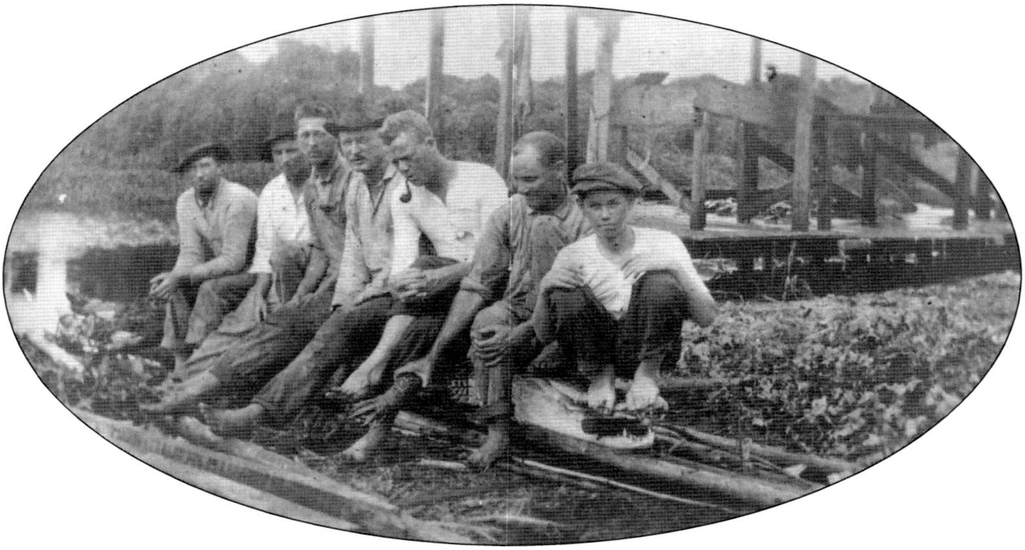

These catfishermen working at Kreamer Island pose on top of an alligator. Catfishing was a huge industry around Lake Okeechobee. There are custard apple trees and moon vines in the background. Young W. A. "Cricket" Cross sits on the alligator's head. (LEWM.)

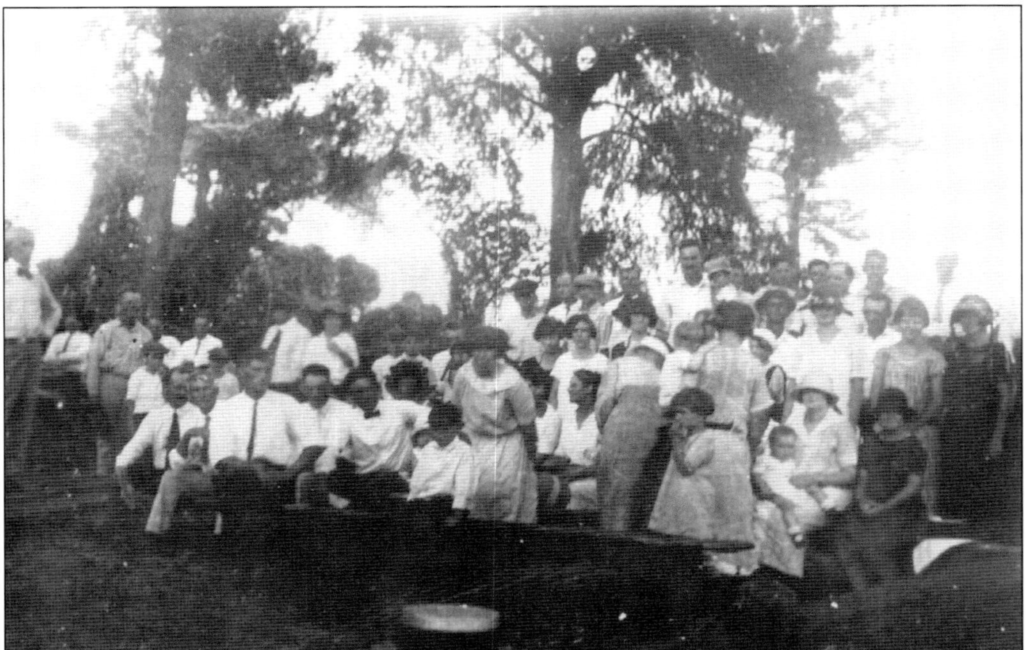

Here was the spot for the first church service at Lake Harbor, which was held under the trees before the church building was constructed. Today the church is known for the home-baked cakes and pies its ladies sell at Thanksgiving to raise money. (LEWM.)

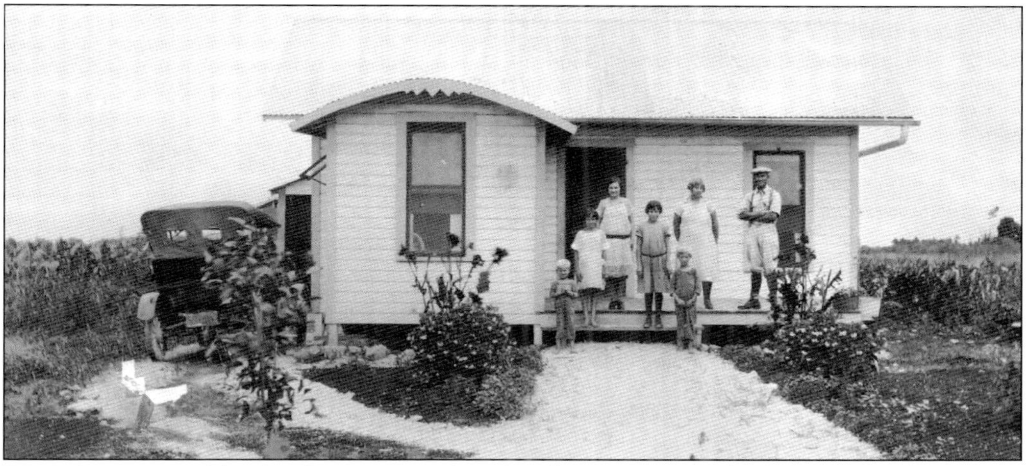

W. H. Savango and his family are pictured at their home is a typical Glades frontier homestead portrait in 1925. The first settlement was called Tantie, after Tantie Huckabee, a redheaded schoolteacher who came to Okeechobee from South Carolina. Early in the 1920s, the Florida East Coast Railway took over the settlement and laid out a model town. It was named Okeechobee, meaning "Big Water," after Lake Okeechobee. (LEWM.)

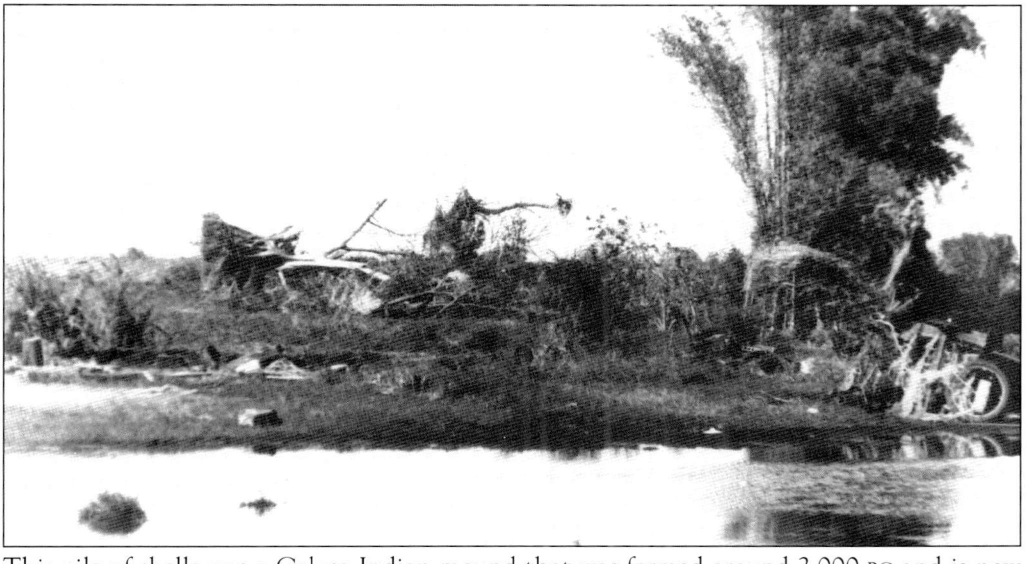

This pile of shells was a Calusa Indian mound that was formed around 2,000 BC and is now surrounded by bamboo. American Indian Day is celebrated on September 25 every year in Florida with festivals at the Hollywood, Big Cypress, Immokalee, Fort Pierce, and Tampa Seminole reservations. It was first observed in 1912; Dr. Arthur C. Parker, a Seneca Indian, asked the Boy Scouts of America to set aside a day for the First Americans. For three years the scouts adopted such a day. In 1915, at the annual congress of the American Indian Association meeting in Lawrence, Kansas, a plan to celebrate American Indian Day on the fourth Friday in September was formally approved. In 1990, Pres. George Bush approved a joint resolution designating November as National American Indian Heritage Month. On American Indian Day, canoe races, horse races, concerts, golf and pool tournaments, cooking contests, clothing contests, storytelling, alligator wrestling, log peeling, archery, fishing, and plenty of traditional American Indian food like fry bread give both tribal members and visitors a fun-packed day. (LEWM.)

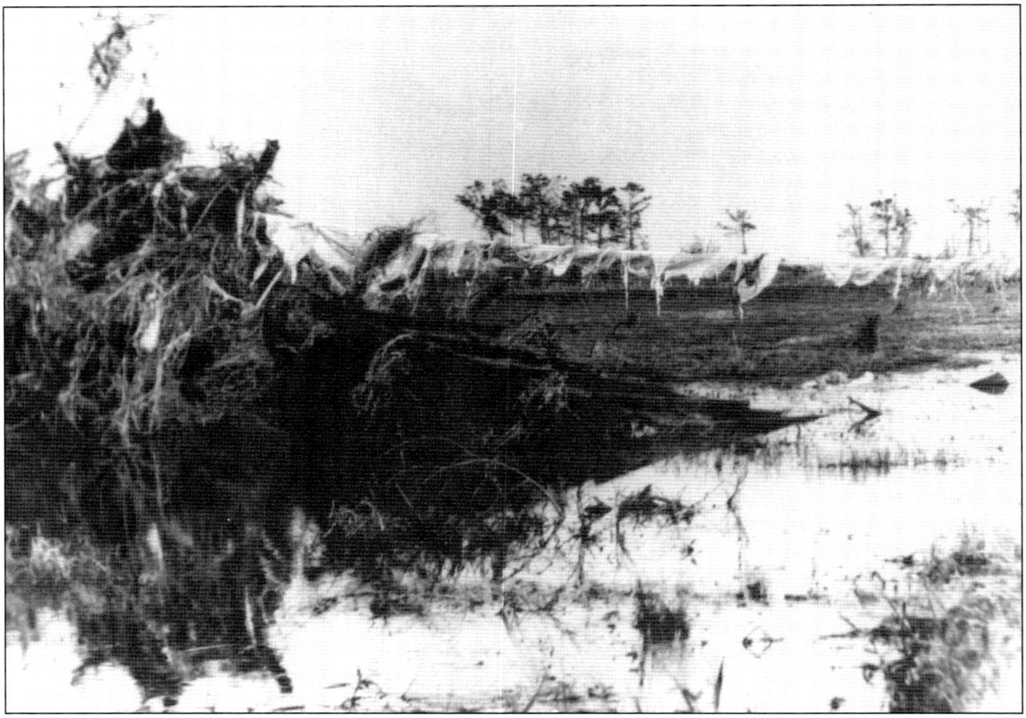

The Chosen Indian mound was excavated, and a timeline by soil depth along with relics, shells, and bones can be seen at the Lawrence E. Will Museum attached to the current Belle Glade Library. These trees were uprooted by the hurricane. (LEWM.)

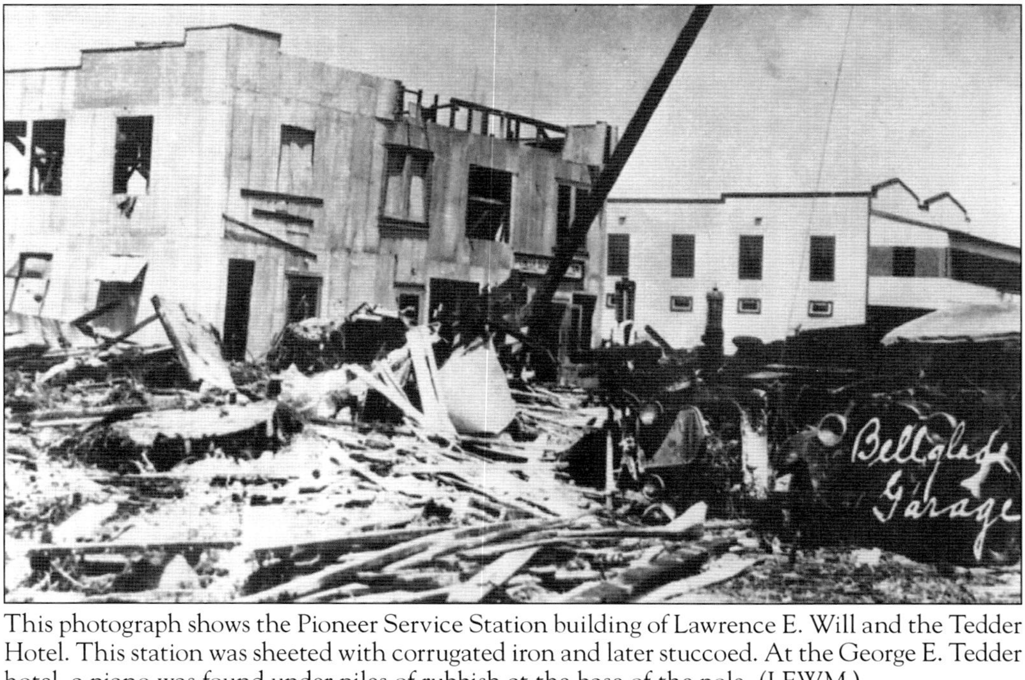

This photograph shows the Pioneer Service Station building of Lawrence E. Will and the Tedder Hotel. This station was sheeted with corrugated iron and later stuccoed. At the George E. Tedder hotel, a piano was found under piles of rubbish at the base of the pole. (LEWM.)

Two

Storm of 1928

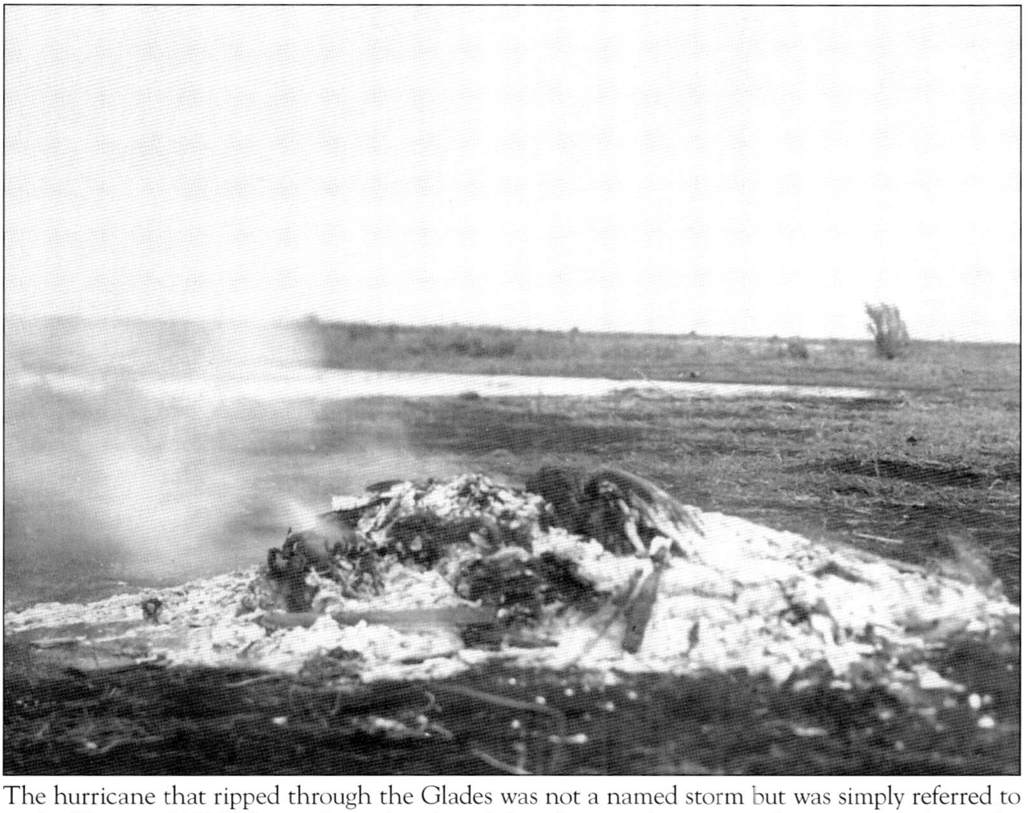

The hurricane that ripped through the Glades was not a named storm but was simply referred to as the "Storm of 1928." It was downplayed, and therefore people were caught unawares when gale-force winds blew water from the lake over the towns of Belle Glade, Pahokee, and Clewiston. This photograph shows corpses that were burned after the destruction brought upon the towns. Other bodies were transported to Woodlawn Cemetery in West Palm Beach for burial. (LEWM.)

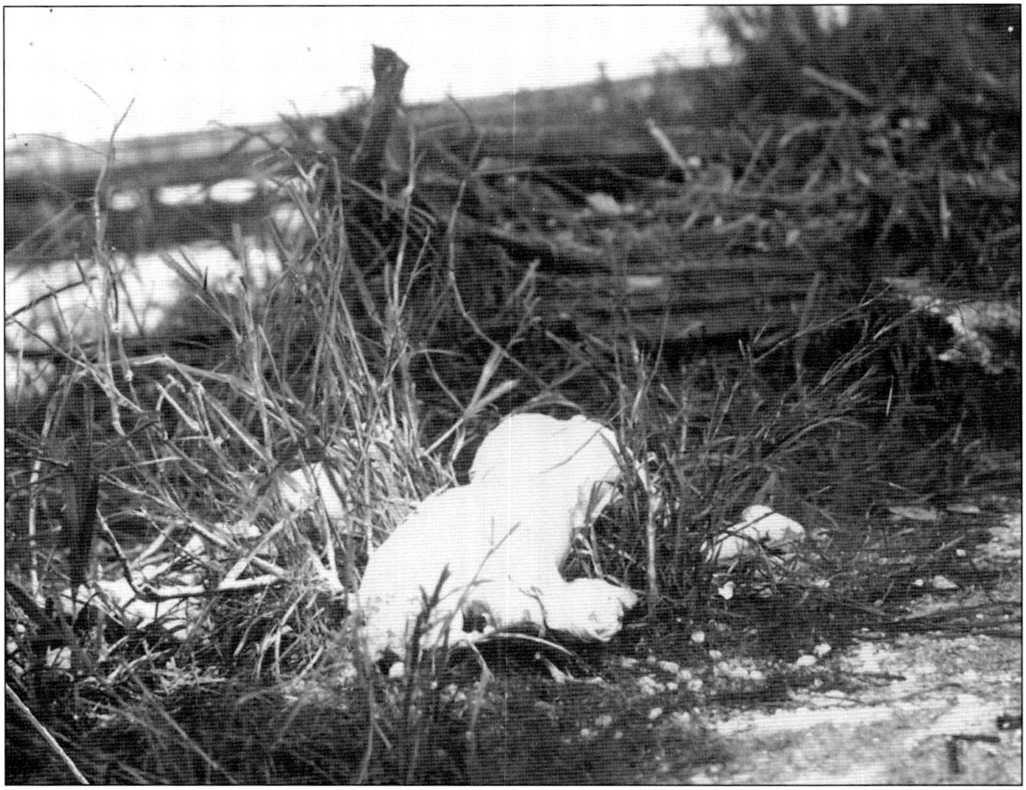

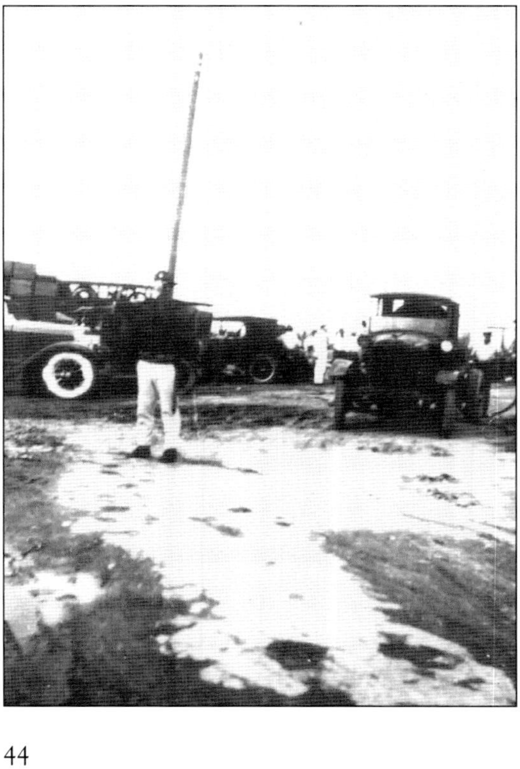

The report of 2,000 dead was not an accurate one, because black residents were not counted in this survey. Recent speculation goes that there were perhaps 3,500 people killed by this hurricane and the flooding caused by Lake Okeechobee's overflow. This death toll made it the second deadliest storm in United States history. (LEWM.)

At the bridge, Belle Glade caskets guard a crude oil tank truck. Snakes were displaced from their waterlogged habitats, and numerous snakebites were reported. (LEWM.)

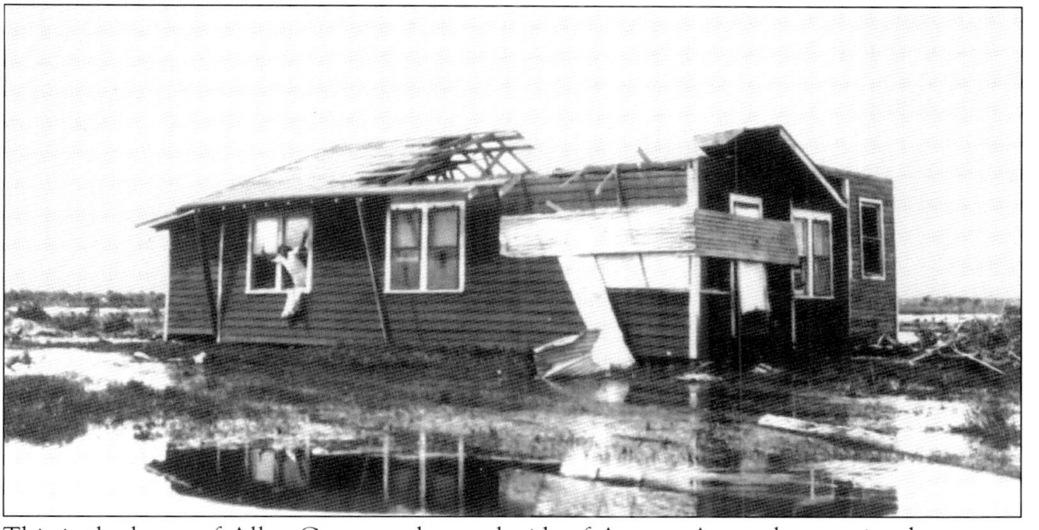

This is the home of Allen Greer on the south side of Avenue A, nearly opposite the present city hall. After the hurricane, 38 dead African Americans were found piled up in front of this house. (LEWM.)

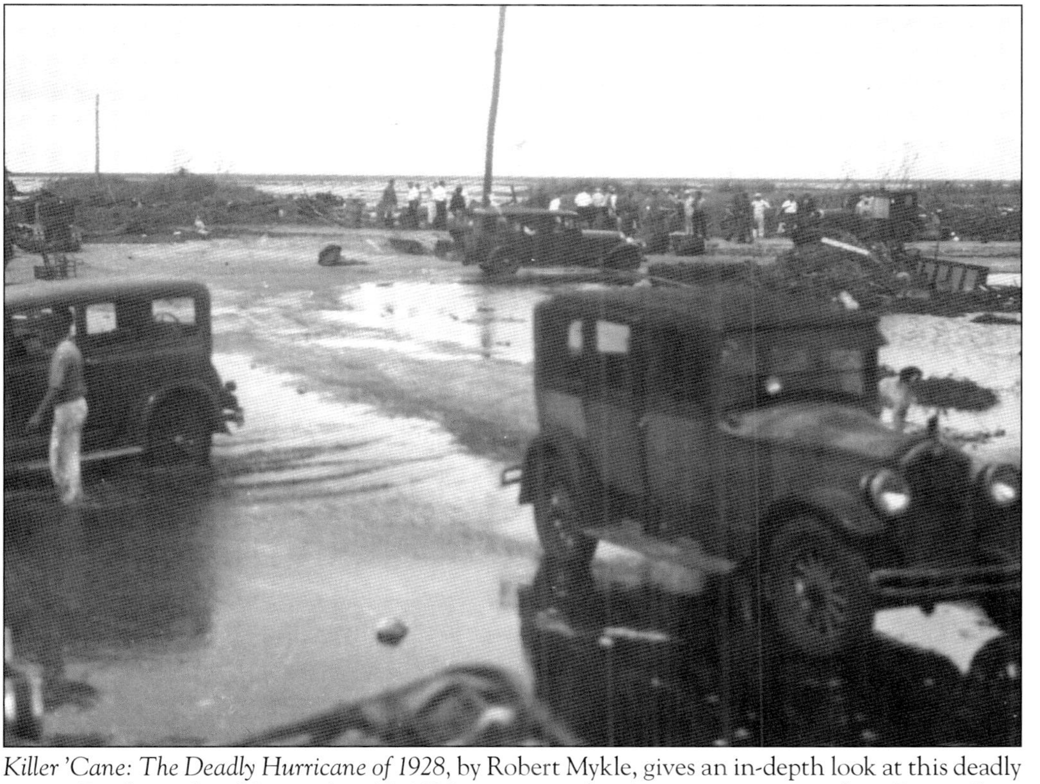

Killer 'Cane: The Deadly Hurricane of 1928, by Robert Mykle, gives an in-depth look at this deadly storm. On the night of September 16, 1928, a category four hurricane swept up from Puerto Rico and slammed into Palm Beach County. Streets like these flooded and caused excessive water damage to surrounding towns. Word of the destruction in the Bahamas was not disseminated, because it was felt that it would adversely affect tourism. (LEWM.)

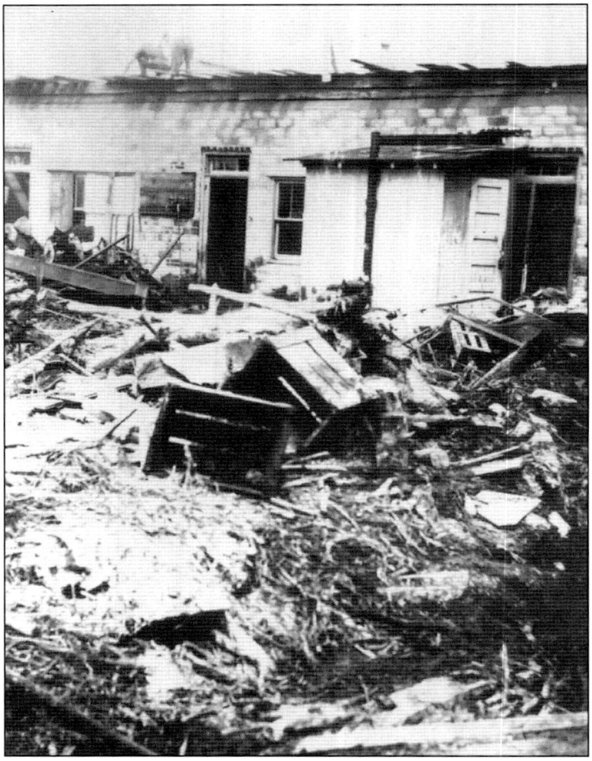

Businesses along Main Street in Belle Glade included Darden's building from the back, Alston Drug, and Pace Furniture stores. (LEWM.)

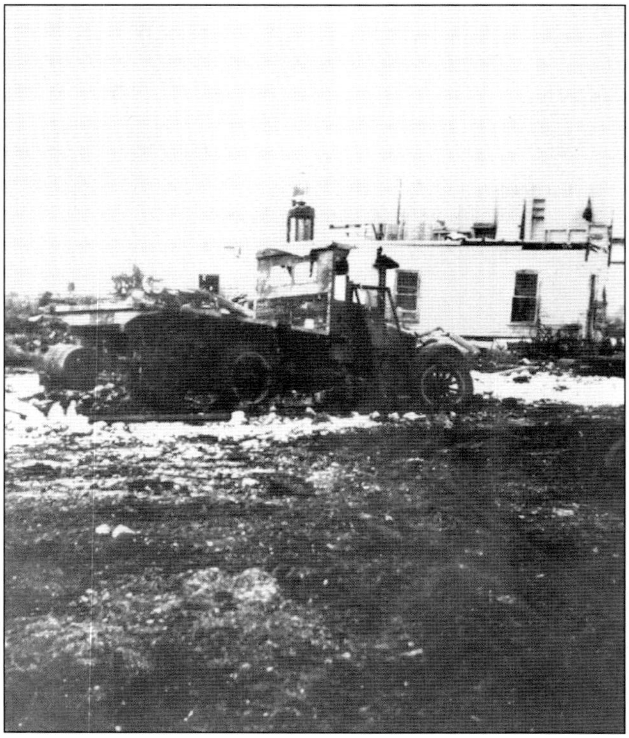

A scene from the aftermath of the horrific storm of 1928 features a flatbed truck waiting for coffins. Stacks of coffins were shipped over to Woodlawn Cemetery in West Palm Beach for burial. A mass grave was also created in Port Myaca Cemetery for the hurricane victims. (LEWM.)

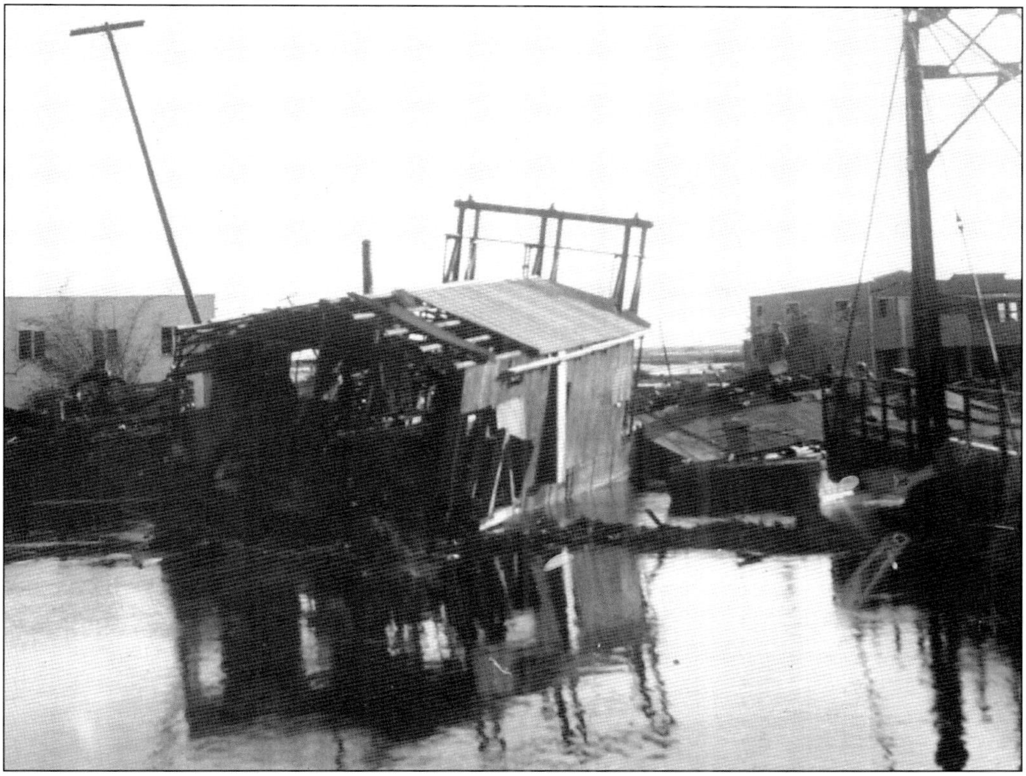

Chosen, a town west of Belle Glade, was the location of the Hooker and West store. This town was also sometimes called Indian Mound due to the location of an early Calusa mound situated here. (LEWM.)

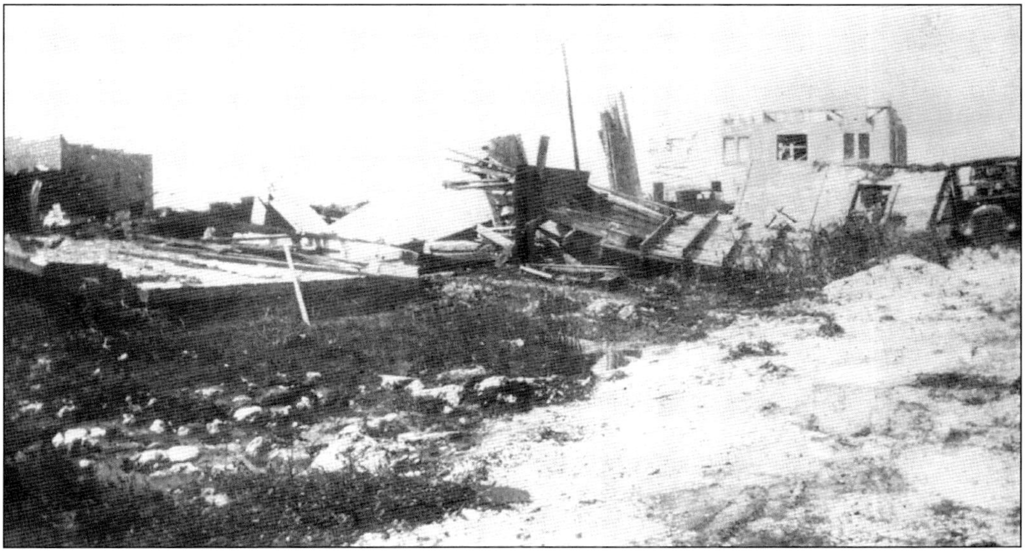

This scene was shot looking west from Rieder's Power Plant on Southeast Avenue B. The building at left was the Boree Building; at right was the Pioneer Building; and at center in the foreground is the floor of Ford garage. (LEWM.)

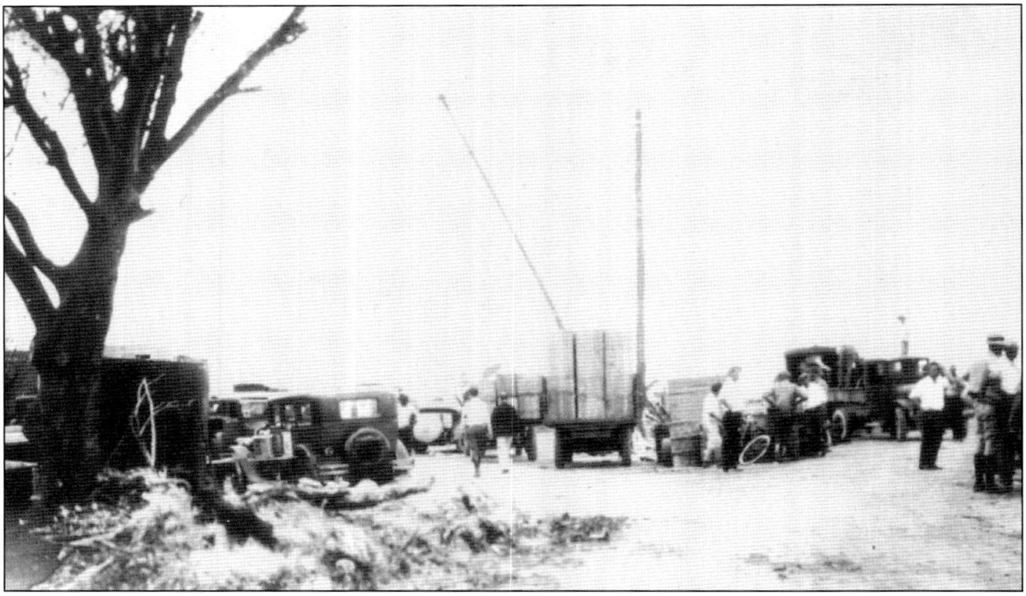

While unused caskets were being returned to West Palm Beach, bodies were now being burned after the devastating 1928 storm. (LEWM.)

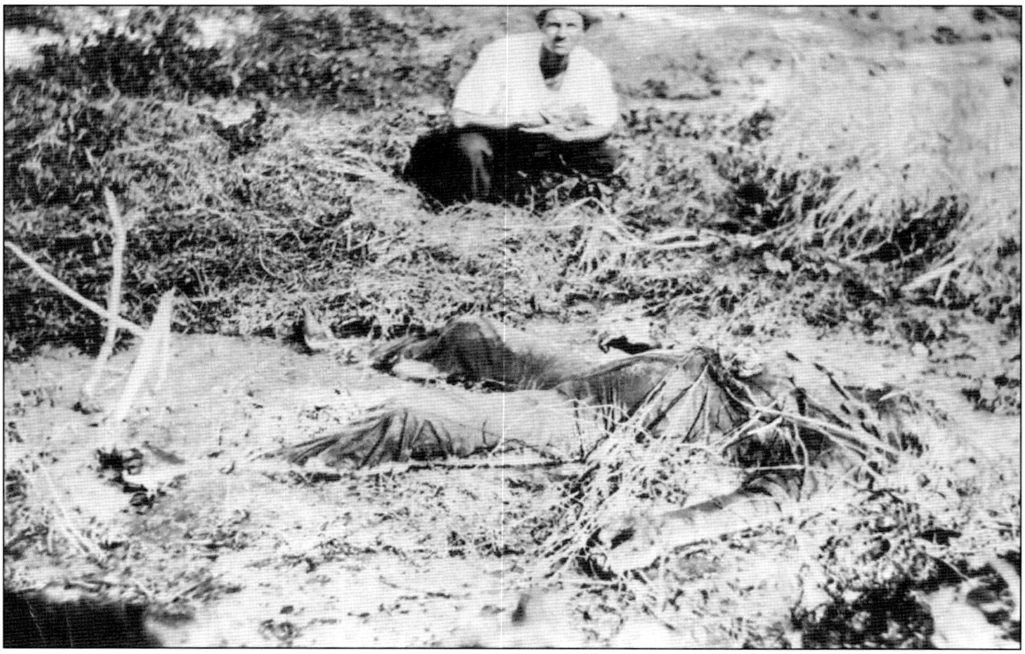

This photograph shows the body of an African American preacher who was identified by his gold teeth. He carried his money in a Bull Durham sack around his neck. The information was supplied by Victor V. Bullock of the U.S. Coast Guard. (LEWM.)

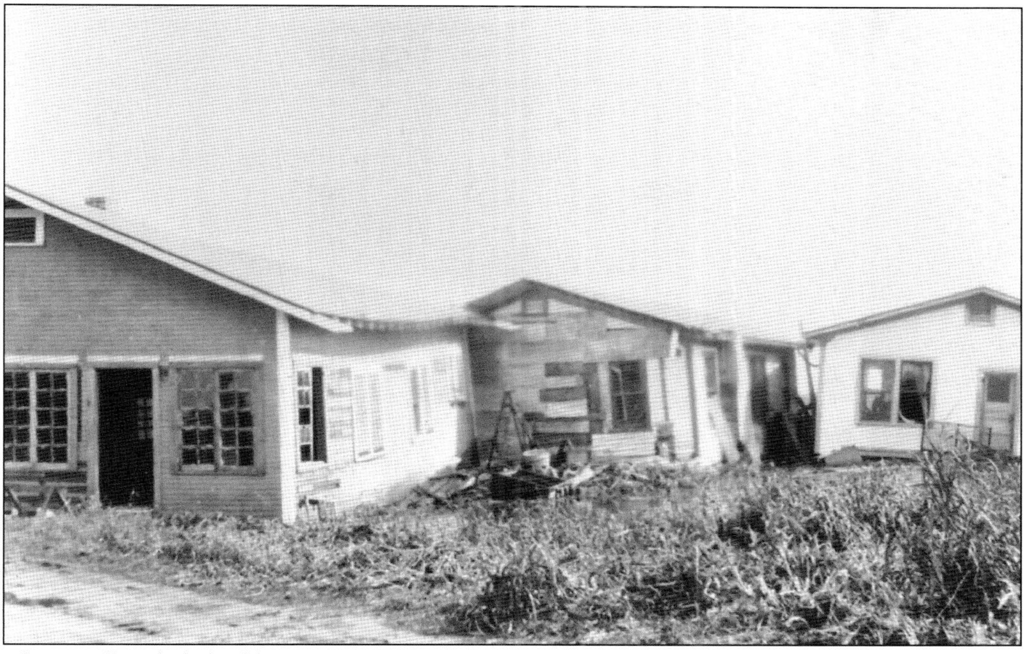

These Belle Glade buildings drifted together in the 1928 storm. Hurricane-force winds whipped through the town and surrounding fields before the people had time to flee. Over 3,500 people were drowned. (LEWM.)

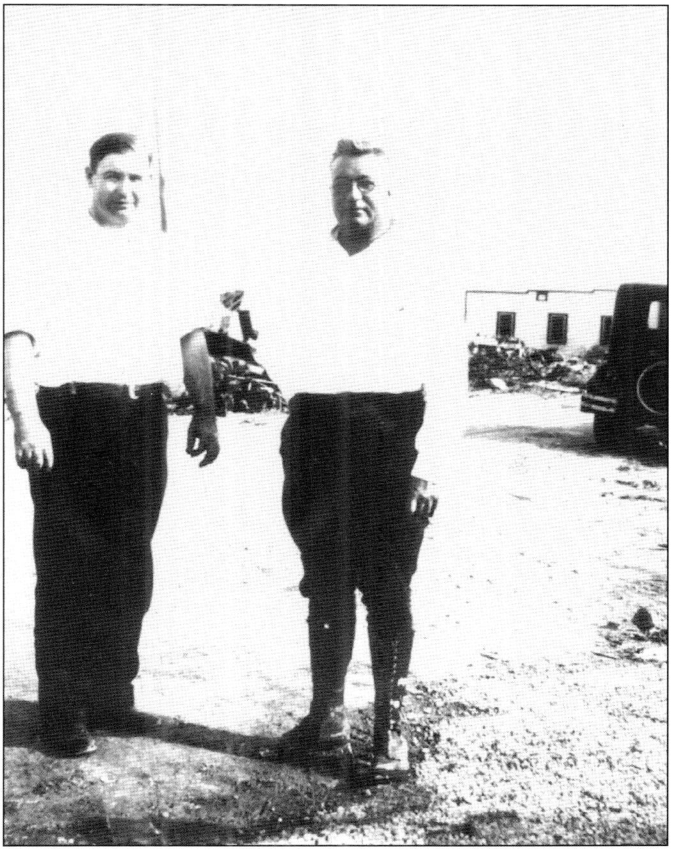

D. Buck (right) and Charlie Grantland, a visiting official, came to Belle Glade to survey the damage after the hurricane. (LEWM.)

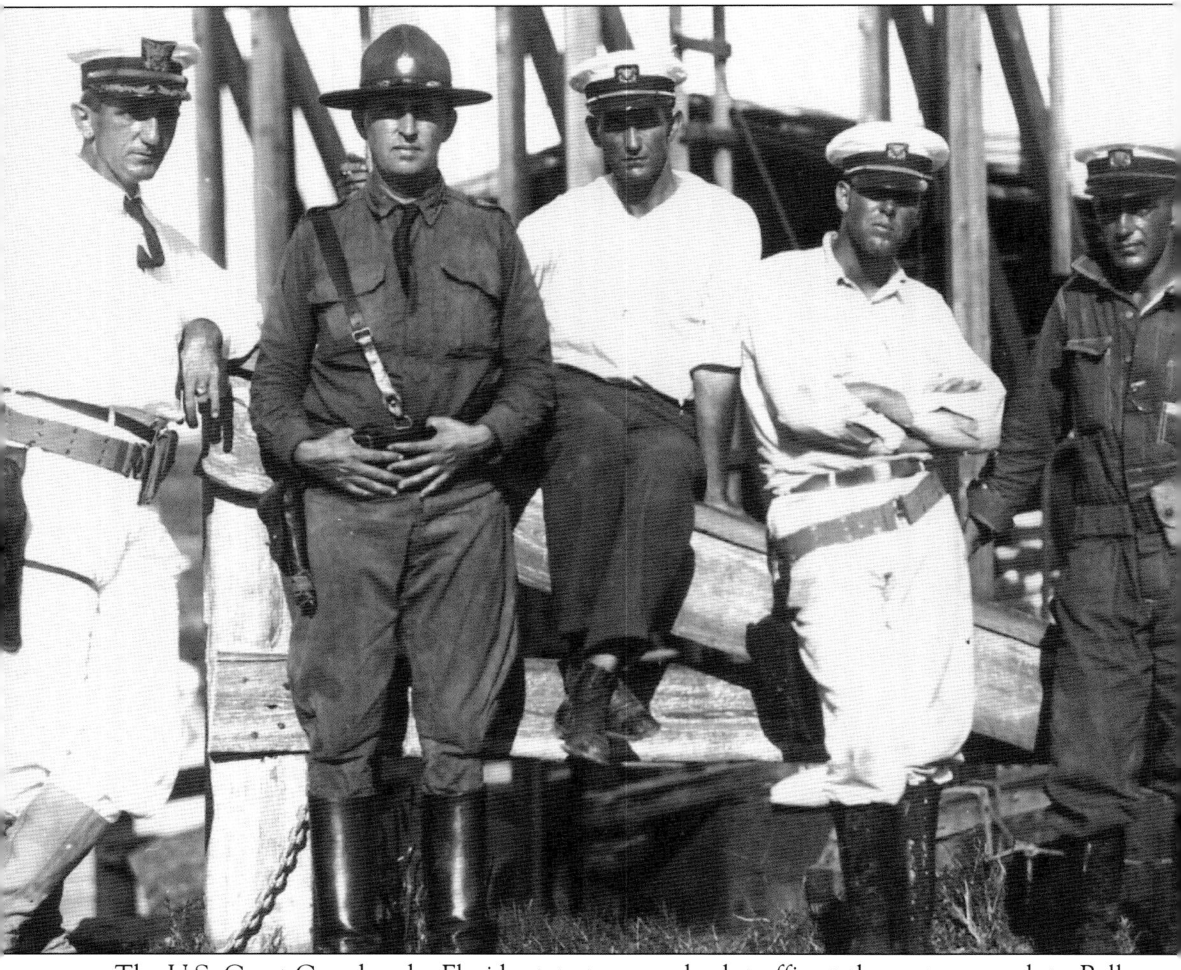

The U.S. Coast Guard and a Florida state trooper check traffic at the east approach to Belle Glade after the 1928 hurricane. (LEWM.)

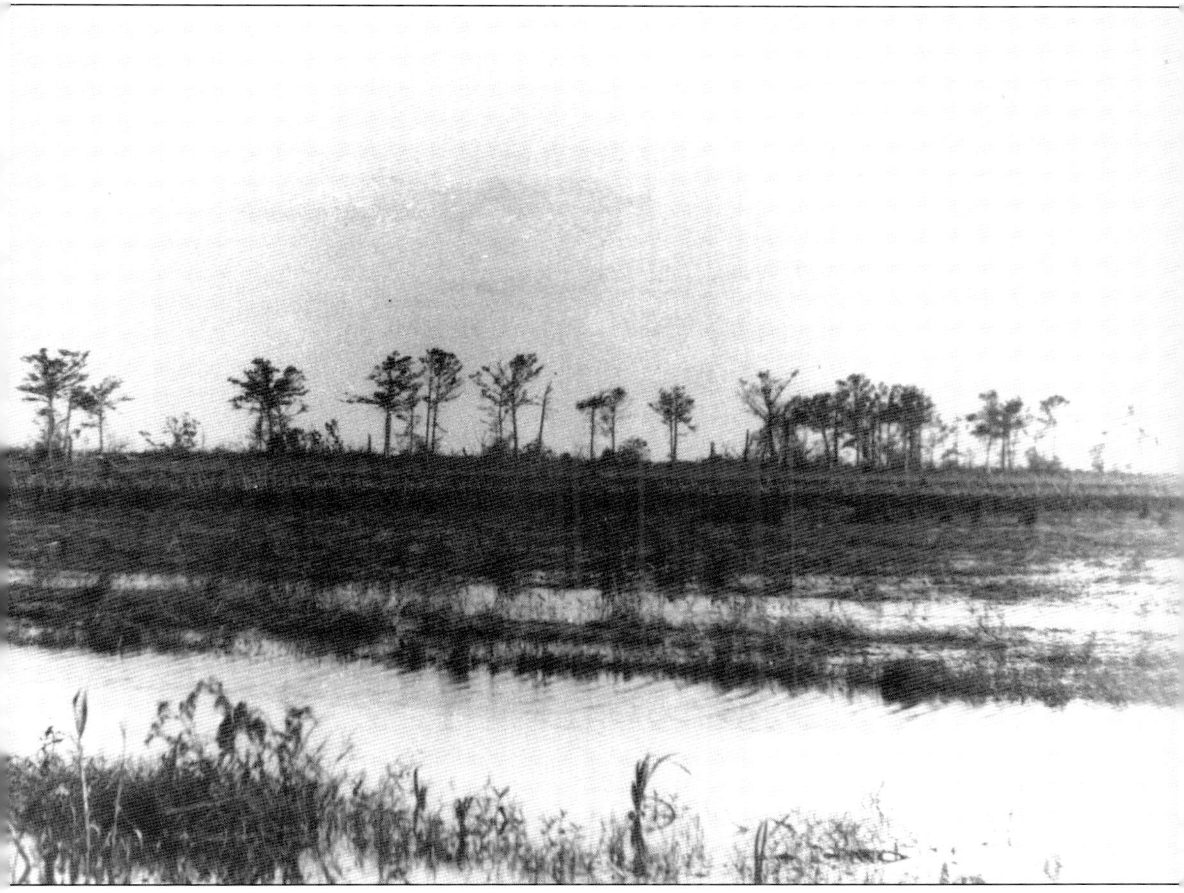

Here there are cypress trees near the Indian mound at Chosen after 1928 storm. The Cypress Knee museum used to exist in Palmdale, run by Tom Gaskins, where American Indian dugout canoes and cypress knees carved into a variety of shapes and famous people were on display. Across the street, a boardwalk was cut through the cypress swamp, and visitors could walk along the wooded trails. The land was owned by Lykes Brothers, and the museum on it was eventually torn down. (LEWM.)

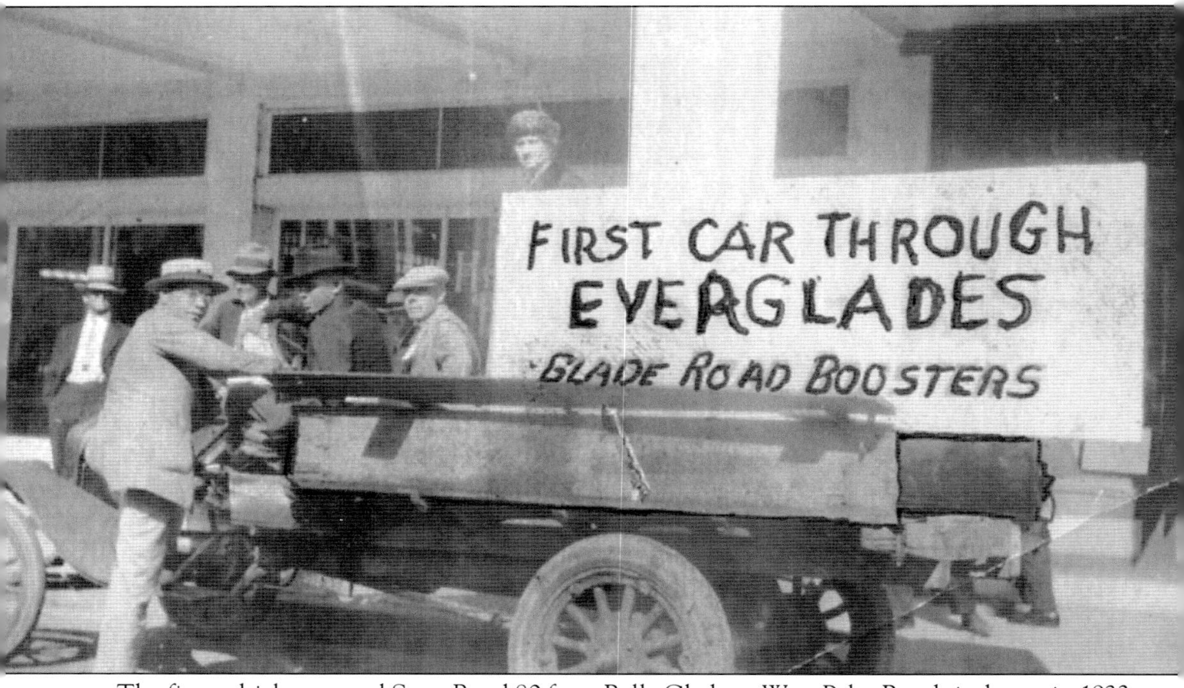

The first vehicle to travel State Road 80 from Belle Glade to West Palm Beach is shown in 1923. Local men include Allen Greer (straw hat), Walter Greer, and Dan O. Patton. Mrs. Walter Greer (Claire) is standing behind the sign. An old Cracker saying is, "Never hire a man who rolls his own cigarettes or wears a straw hat, as he won't do anything but roll cigarettes or chase his straw hat." (LEWM.)

Three

Early Days in Belle Glade

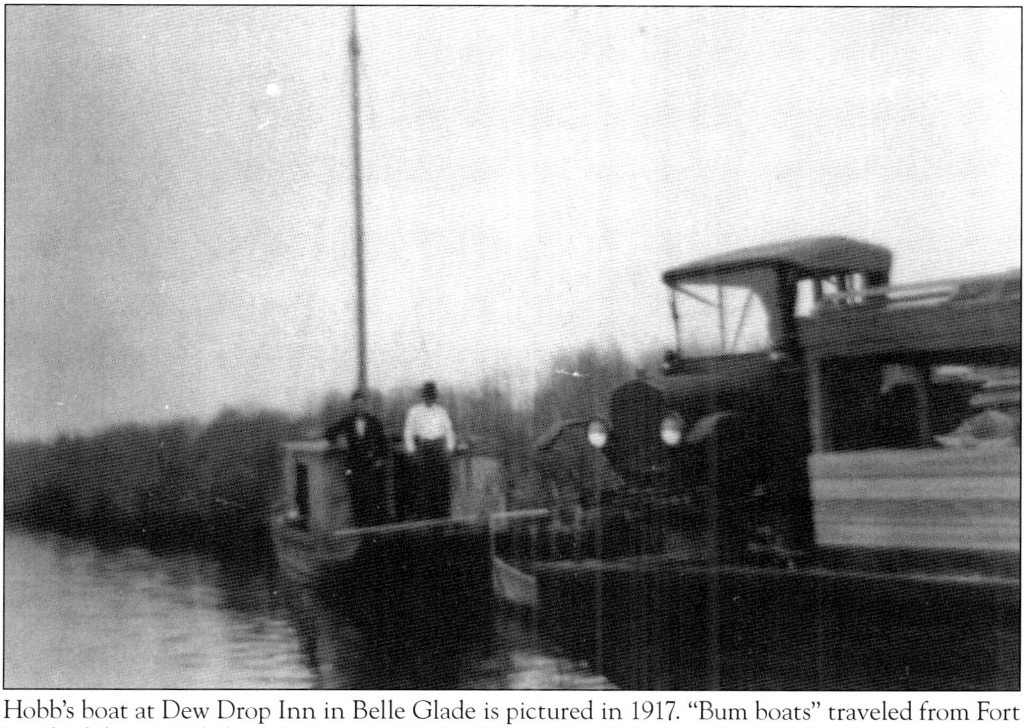

Hobb's boat at Dew Drop Inn in Belle Glade is pictured in 1917. "Bum boats" traveled from Fort Lauderdale around the lake to provide the housewives living in these isolated towns canned goods, cloth, and other items used in the home. The boatmen often had to barter their goods for vegetables or fish. The bum boats gave way later on to country stores as the towns grew and roads were created. (LEWM.)

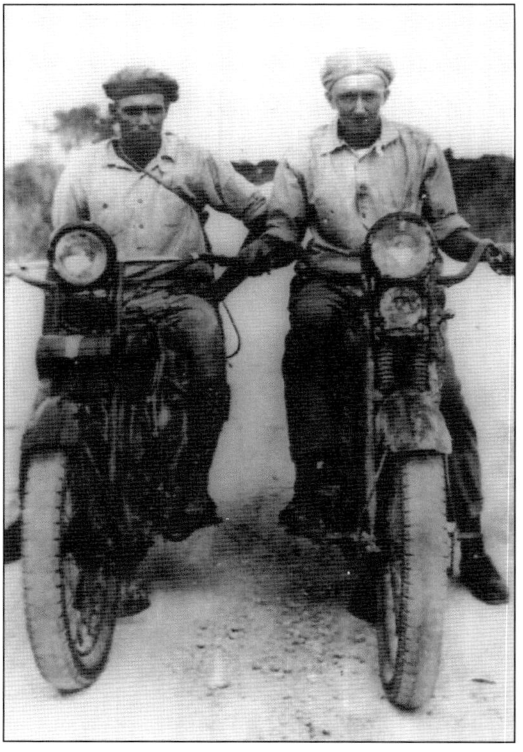

Pictured here are Fritz Stein (left) and Fred Greer, two local townsmen. Hans and Fritz Stein were the lock tender's sons. Lawrence Will tells that when the water hyacinths clogged the lock gate at Chosen, he barely made it through with a passenger boat. A Seminole tried to follow in his dugout canoe but was unable to make it through. Hans and Fritz jumped down to help out, and the three men, standing on the hyacinths, picked up the heavy boat and pushed it along on top of the plants. Water hyacinths divide in only two weeks' time and can multiply to 65,000 plants in eight months. (LEWM.)

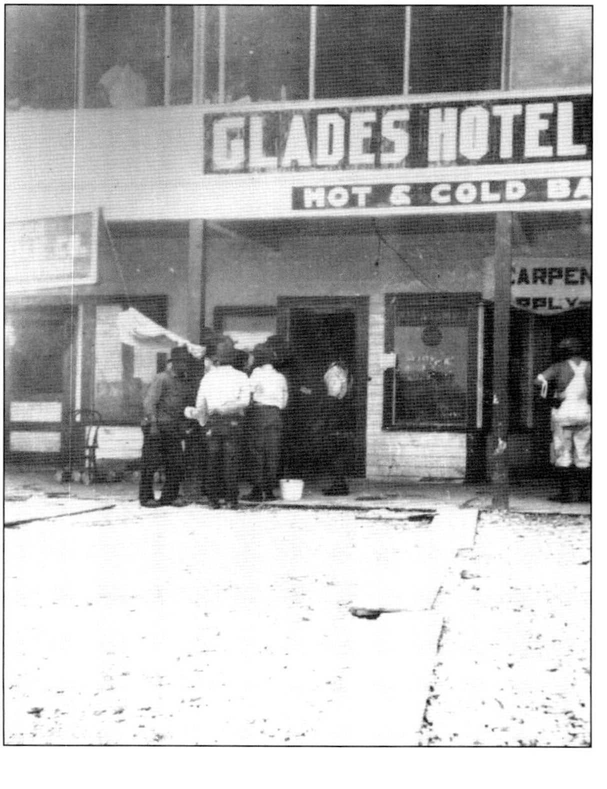

The Glades Hotel was a landmark in the community. F. M. Myer was the proprietor of the Pioneer Hotel in Belle Glade. (LEWM.)

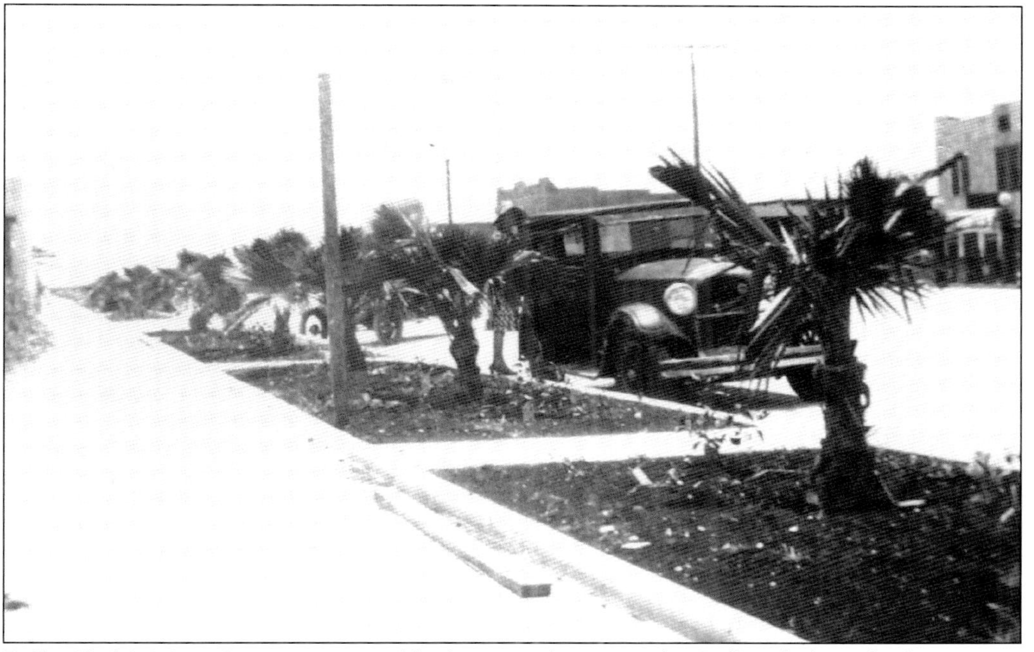

Belle Glade's Main Street is pictured looking southwest. Today Belle Glade is the largest city within the 2,862,000-acre Everglades in the heartland of Florida. (LEWM.)

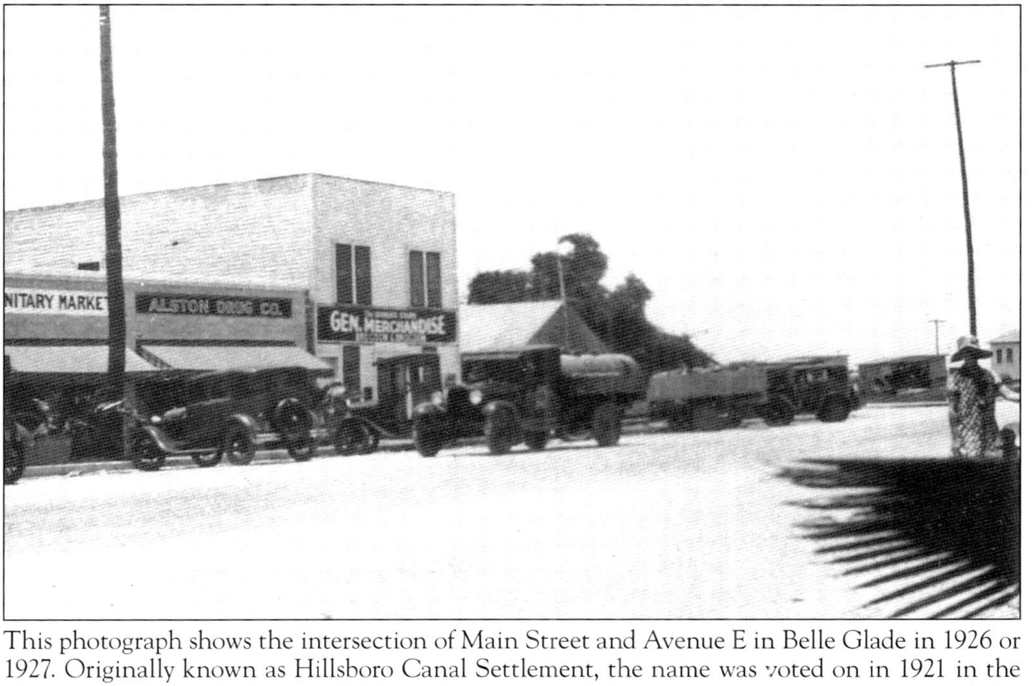

This photograph shows the intersection of Main Street and Avenue E in Belle Glade in 1926 or 1927. Originally known as Hillsboro Canal Settlement, the name was voted on in 1921 in the Pioneer Hotel lobby, where a blackboard was available. A group of tourists making a trip down the canal from West Palm Beach after traveling through the Everglades stated that it was "the belle of the Glades." Elsie Myer, wife of the proprietor, quickly added this entry to the list. Citizens chose the name Belle Glade from the list of candidates. (LEWM.)

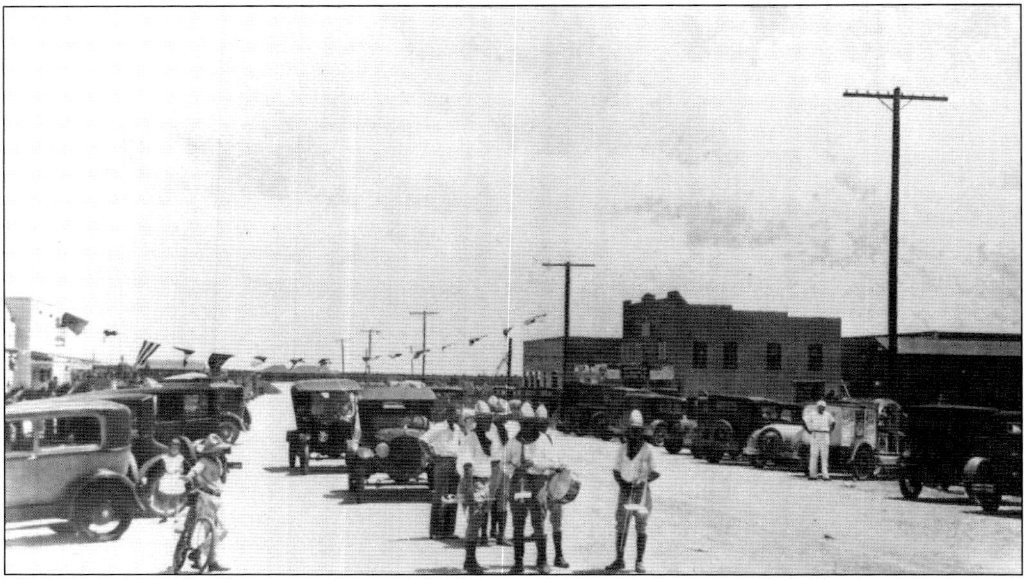

The Brown Farm Band was a local group of musicians that entertained for family weddings and other civic festivities. They would not hire anyone to play unless they were talented. This photograph was taken in Belle Glade on July 4, 1929. The two-story Pioneer building is shown at right. (LEWM.)

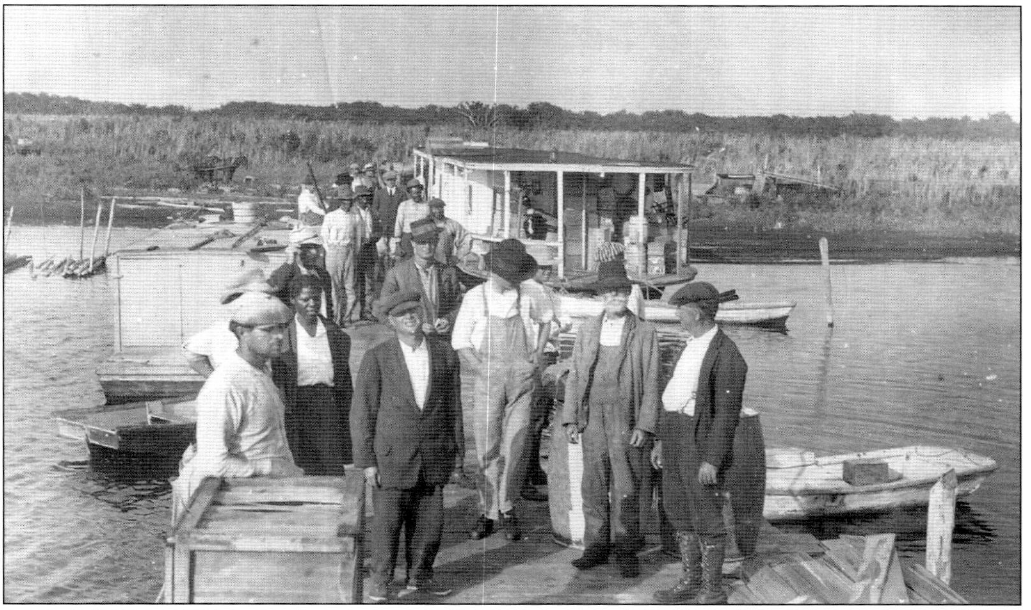

Here is the first dock in Belle Glade with fishermen trying it out. Lawrence Will, recording the word of early settler Sam Grey, relayed that in the spring of 1900 there were five hunters on the lake. Their names were Will Curry, William Strickland, Charley Chandler, Bill Leitner, Sam Luckey, and Sam Grey. Curry and Strickland had been in the area the longest, having arrived by boat from Fort Myers in 1897 accompanied by Curry's wife, Lula, and brother, Luke. Will credited Curry and Strickland with having caught the first catfish shipped from Lake Okeechobee, which were picked up by Capt. Ben Hall in his steamer *Naomi II* in 1900. (LEWM.)

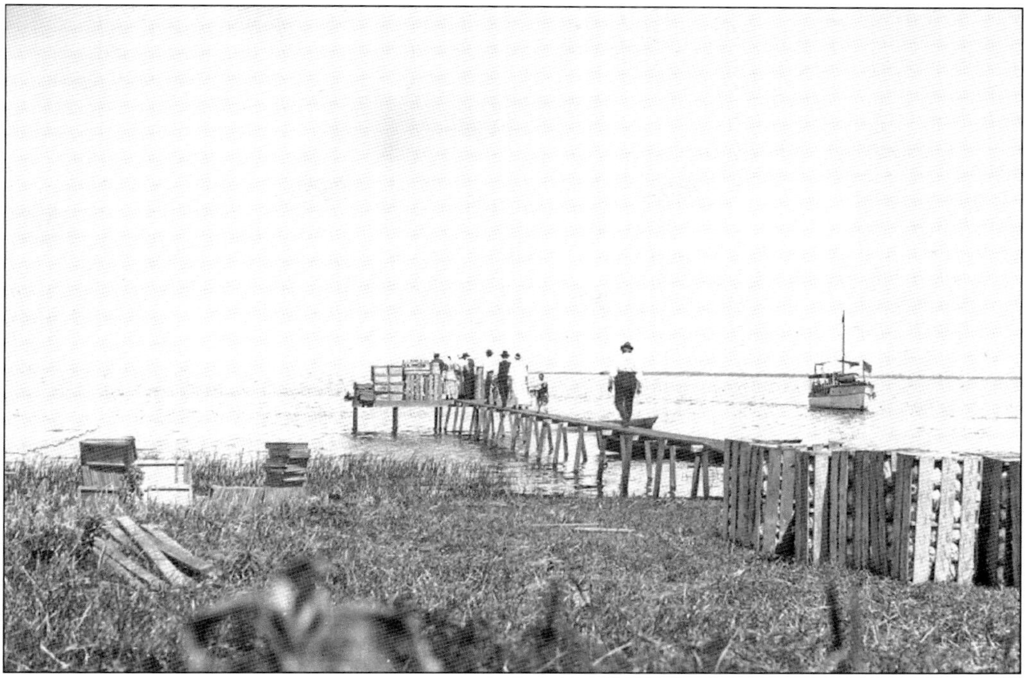

This dock with men and a boat is representative of many around the lake. After his success in bringing the first steamboat up the Caloosahatchee River in 1900, Captain Hall changed his occupation and became the first commercial fisherman on Lake Okeechobee. He would supply trotlines to men like Oscar Hawes and Frank Tapley. When they were full, he would pick up the fish and load them onto a barge with a refrigerated box full of ice. (LEWM.)

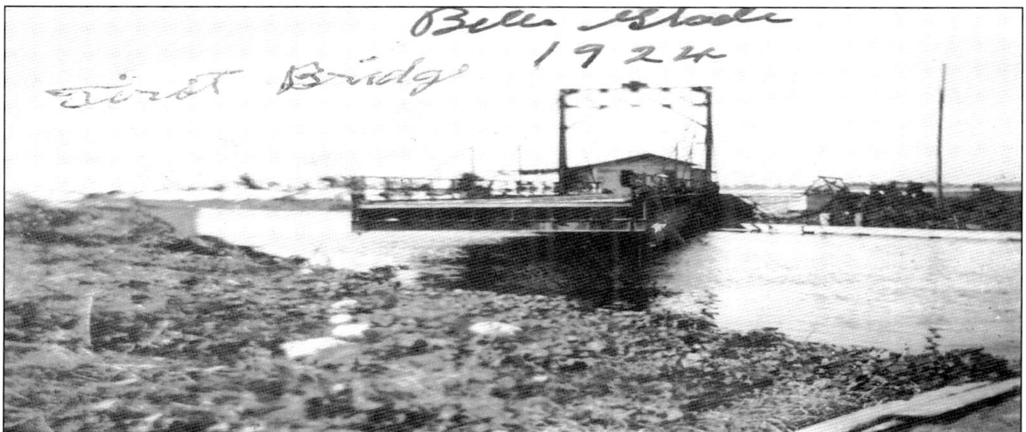

Before the first bridge in Belle Glade was built in 1924 there were only footbridges. Passengers and goods were ferried across the many waterways by boat. (LEWM.)

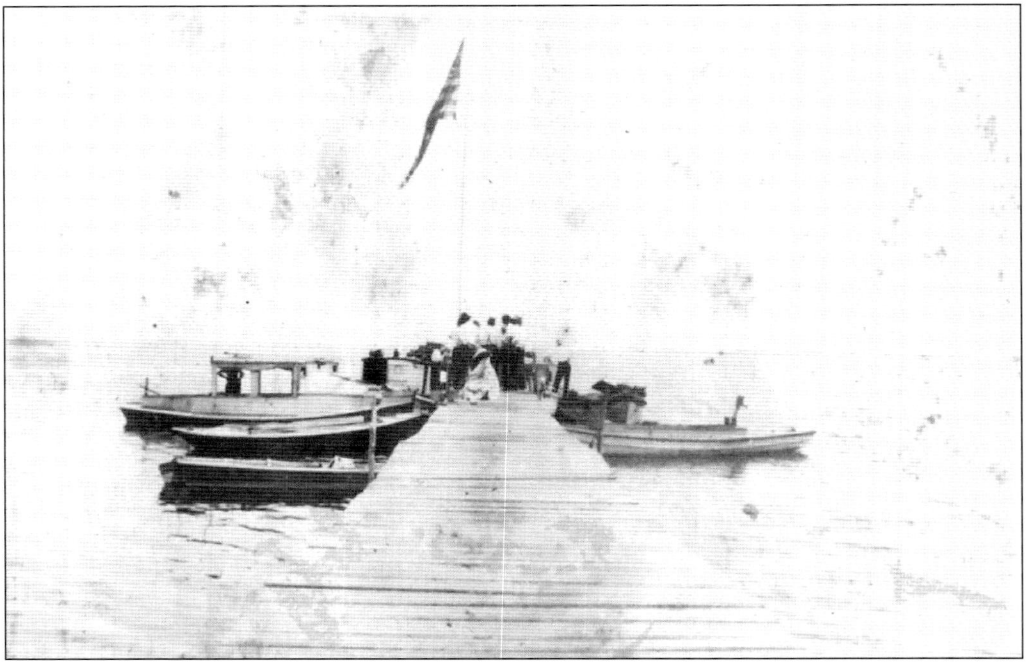

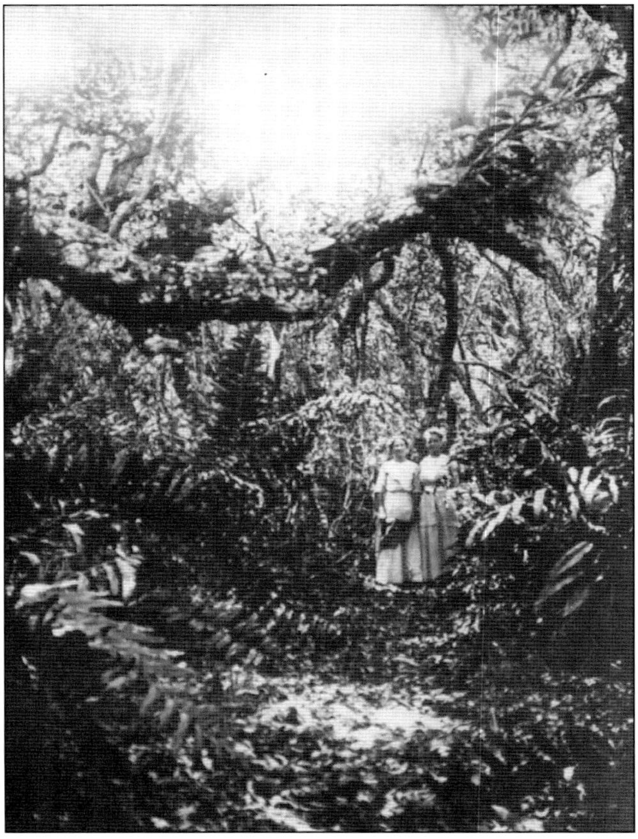

This scene is an early photograph of the dock at Mrs. King's Hotel in 1914. Events were ominous for the catfishing industry at this time. Sportfishermen competed with commercial catfishermen out on the lake. The rise in Florida tourism led to complaints by the sportfishermen that seining was destroying the game fish—namely, the abundant large mouth bass. In 1916, the commercial fishermen were hit with a four-month closed season. Gaming laws kept the nets to 1,000 yards of 3-inch mesh. (LEWM.)

This view of Lake Shore Swamp near Lake Harbor skirts the south shore of Lake Okeechobee. The women in the picture are not identified. (LEWM.)

Four

Boats and Bays

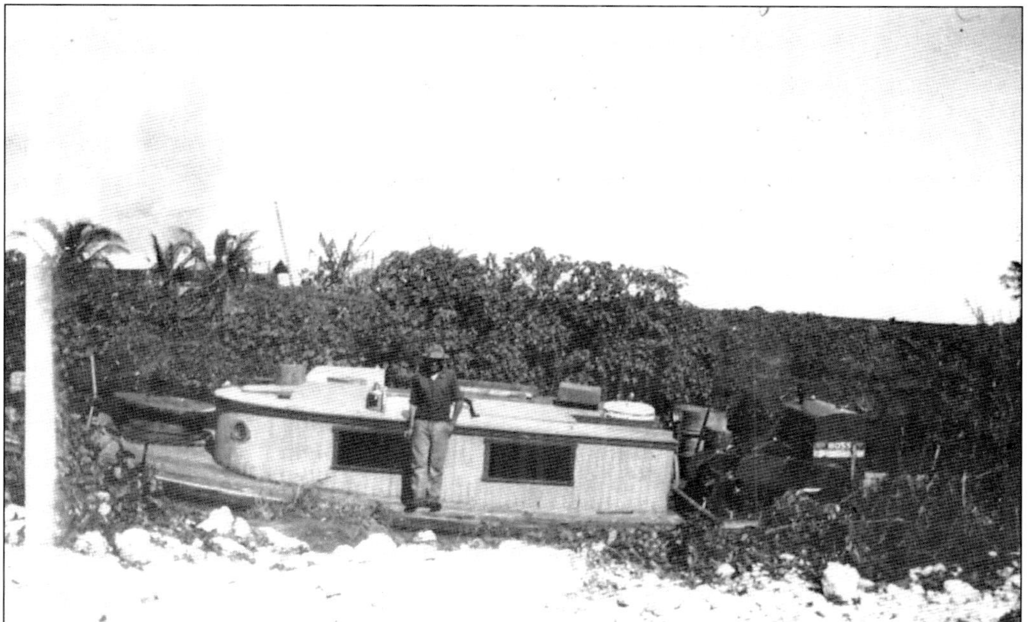

Bryan and Hamp Holloway, owners of the tugboat *Leviathan*, used it to guide barges in the canals and on the lake. The tug was operated by skipper Bill Hunt and Capt. Lawrence E. Will. In 1925, when seining was prohibited on all freshwater lakes, fishermen somehow convinced the authorities that Lakes Okeechobee and George were not freshwater. (LEWM.)

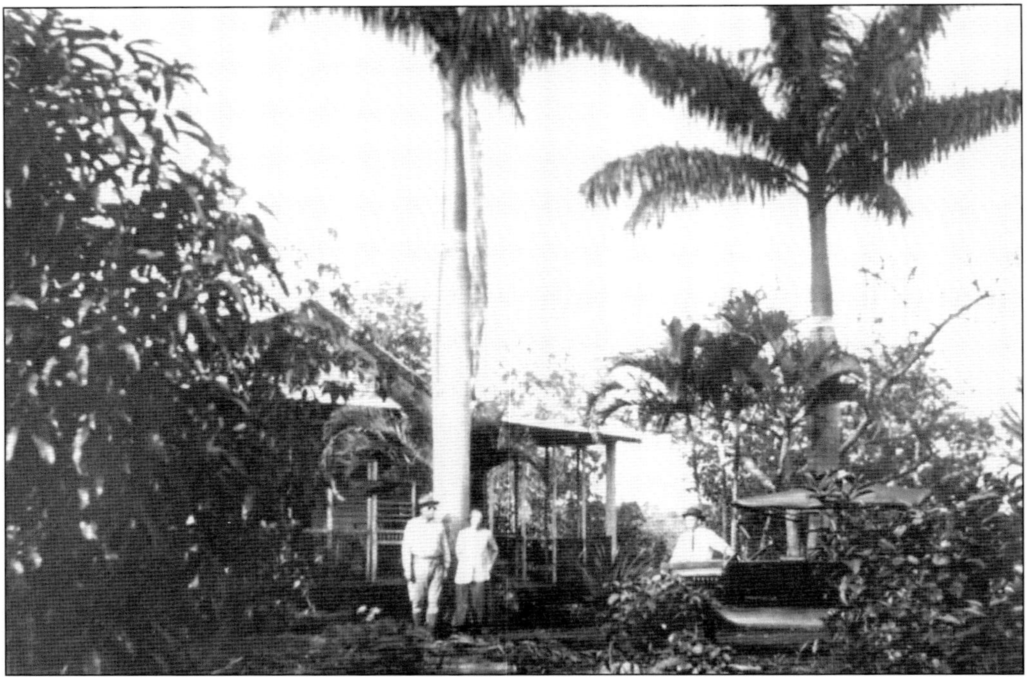

These folks are Mr. and Mrs. Madison M. Hall at Ritta in 1922. While the arrival of the railroad did not bring an immediate end to boat traffic, it hastened the end of river navigation, which had been the main form of transportation. (LEWM.)

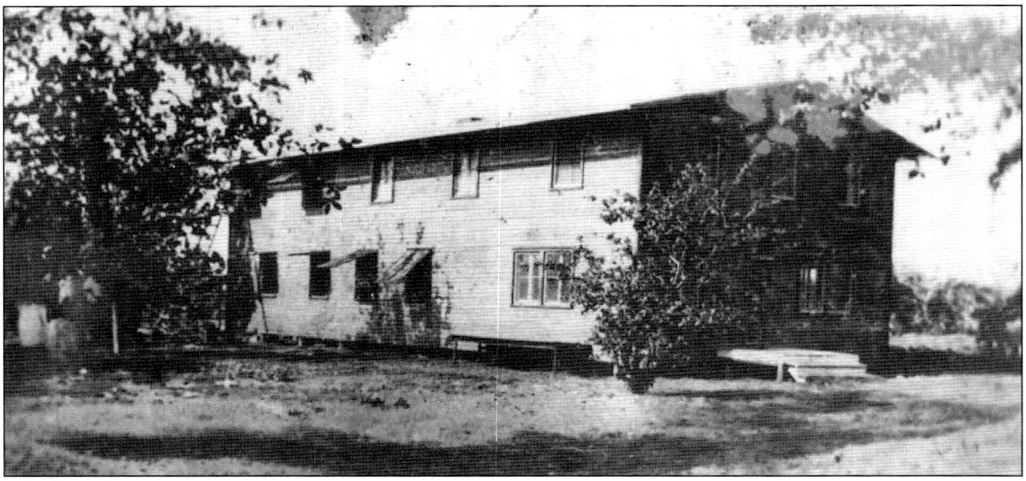

An important local landmark was the early Meyer Hotel in Belle Glade in 1921. Boatman Lawrence E. Will writes, "I stopped at Myer's Hotel and all the other landings, picking up passengers and crates and hampers along the way." He was serving the route between Belle Glade and Fort Lauderdale. He complained, "Since the farmers had a most unpleasant habit of dumping moon vines, old overalls, and shirts into the canal, you'd have to get overboard while stopped at Stein's Locks in Chosen, dive under her bottom in that chilly water with a sharp knife and whack and saw the cussed garbage from the propeller while the sun struggled to break through the clouds." Hotels like these sprang up in towns around the lake for the speculators and workers who came to this area in droves. (LEWM.)

Equipment required for farming included this buckeye ditcher at Belle Glade or South Bay. (LEWM.)

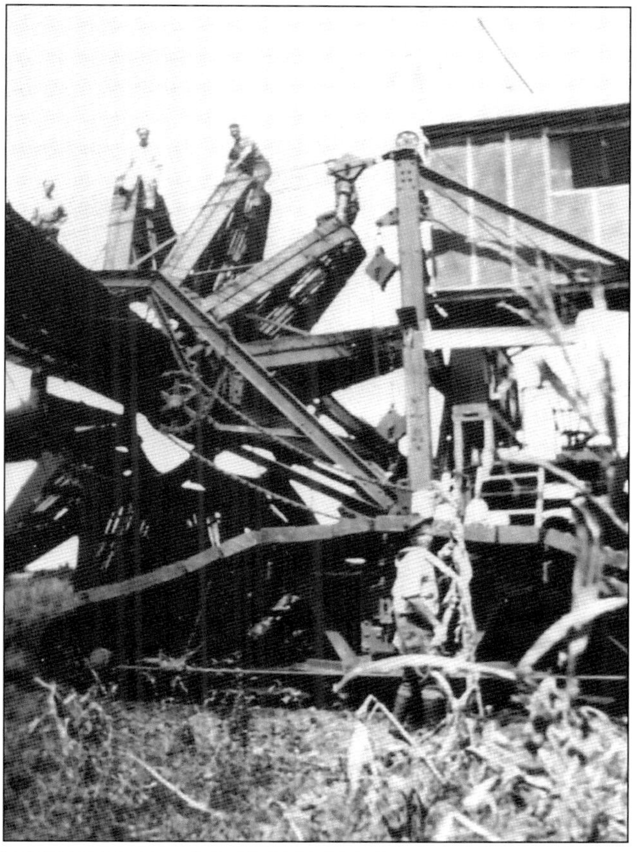

This Shawano tooth cultivator was marshaled for weeding young carrots. Beans and corn were also vegetable crops that were grown around the lake during this period. Pickers were given chips for each bushel they picked. These were turned in at the end of the day for cash or merchandise. (LEWM.)

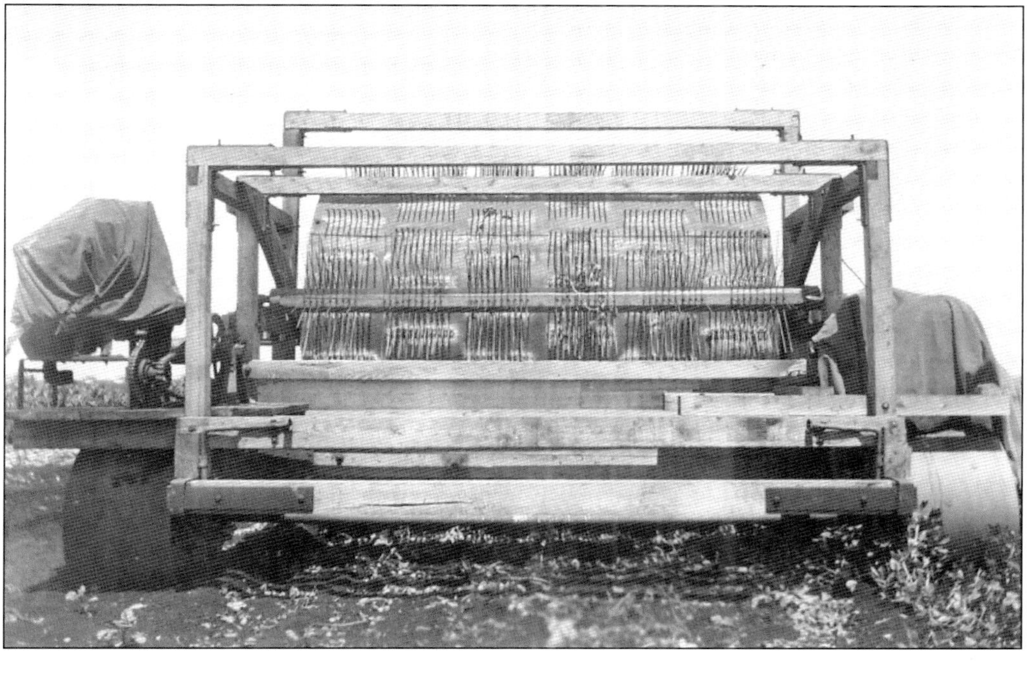

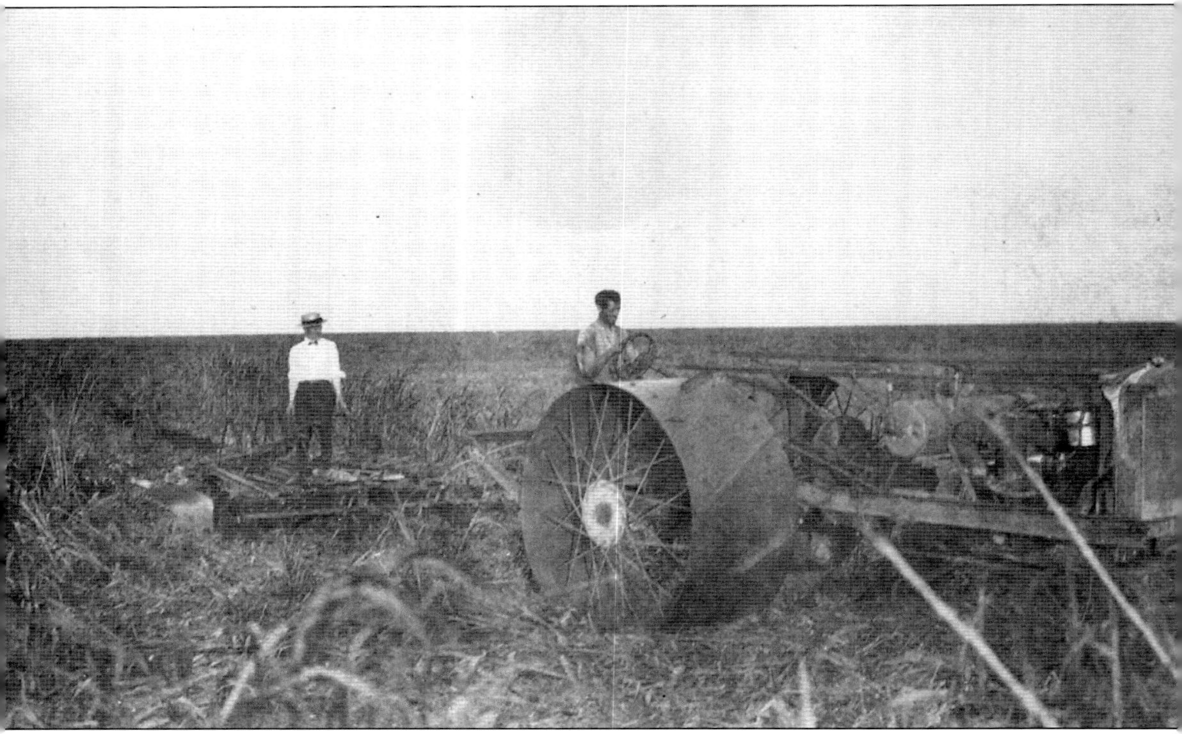

Machinery had to be adapted to the unique farming conditions in the Everglades. This is the first round-wheel tractor ever built to run over sawgrass land by Crams from Davie in 1914. (LEWM.)

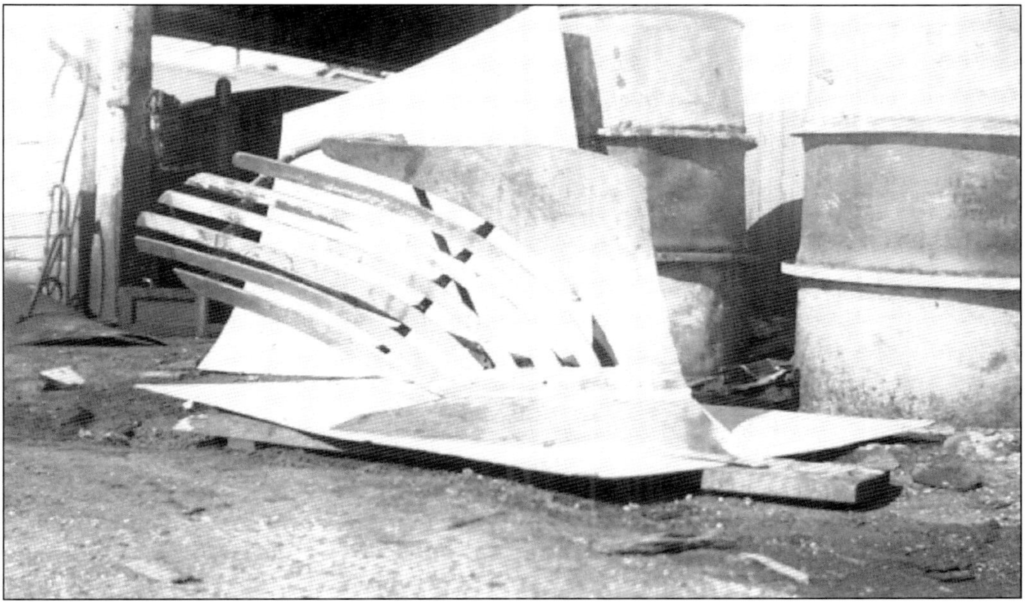

This slatted moldboard plow was developed and built by Pioneer Motor Sales Company of Belle Glade. Early equipment had to be specially constructed for the agricultural work necessary to farm the Lake Okeechobee fields. (LEWM.)

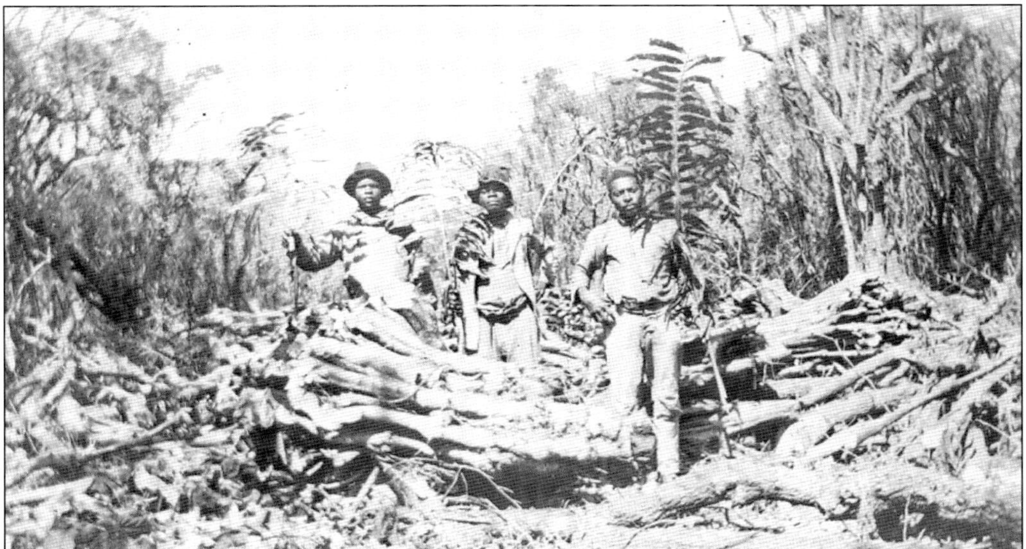

With a year-round growing season, inhabitants were kept busy clearing custard apple land for the road to Pahokee in 1920. Custard apple trees abounded in and around Lake Okeechobee. The local American Indians used them for food along with pumpkins and hearts of palm from the sabal palmetto, or "swamp cabbage." By 1,000 BC, an aboriginal population camped at Fort Center on Fisheating Creek near Lakeport. Findings from the area indicated the clan was one of the first to practice agriculture in Florida. These early people cultivated maize (corn) that could be stored to establish a dependable food supply. Pollen analysis revealed that these early tribes had also probably grown squash and beans. (LEWM.)

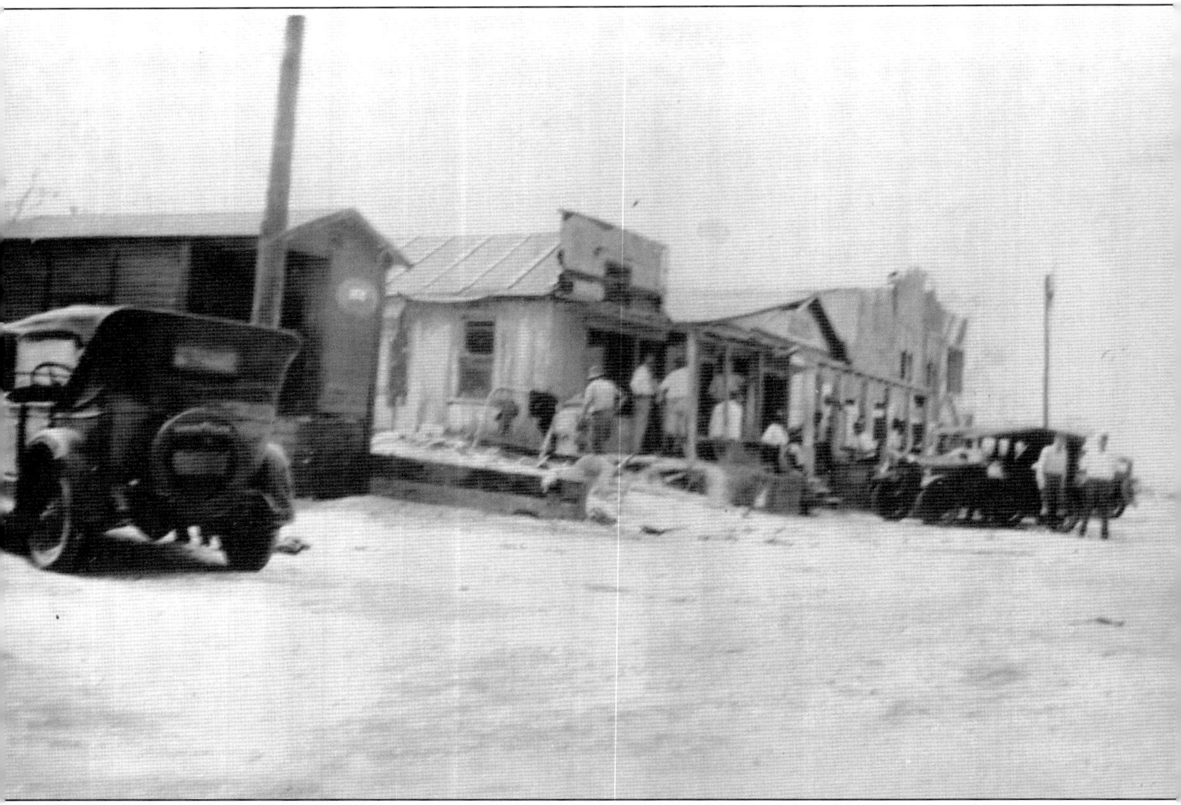

Pahokee means "grassy waters" in Miccosukee. These stores flank the south side of town at Lake Avenue and Main Street looking toward Lake Okeechobee in September 1928. The Pahokee docks were built along the lakefront. (LEWM.)

Five

Clewiston, "America's Sweetest Town"

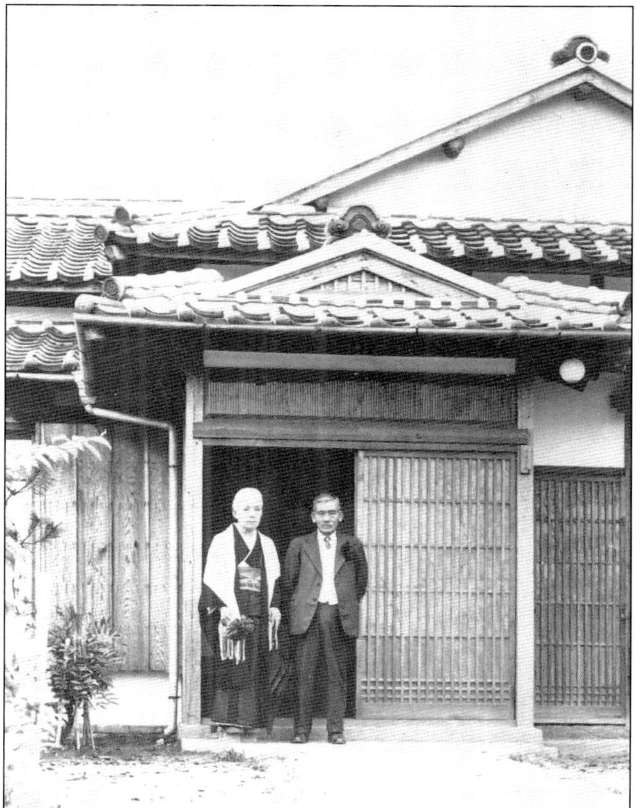

This 1924 photograph shows Papa and Madame Watenabe on the ridge of Lake Okeechobee in Clewiston. They were courteous hosts and let guests dress up in their Japanese costumes, which were kept in an old trunk. This was a prosperous year for the region. (CM.)

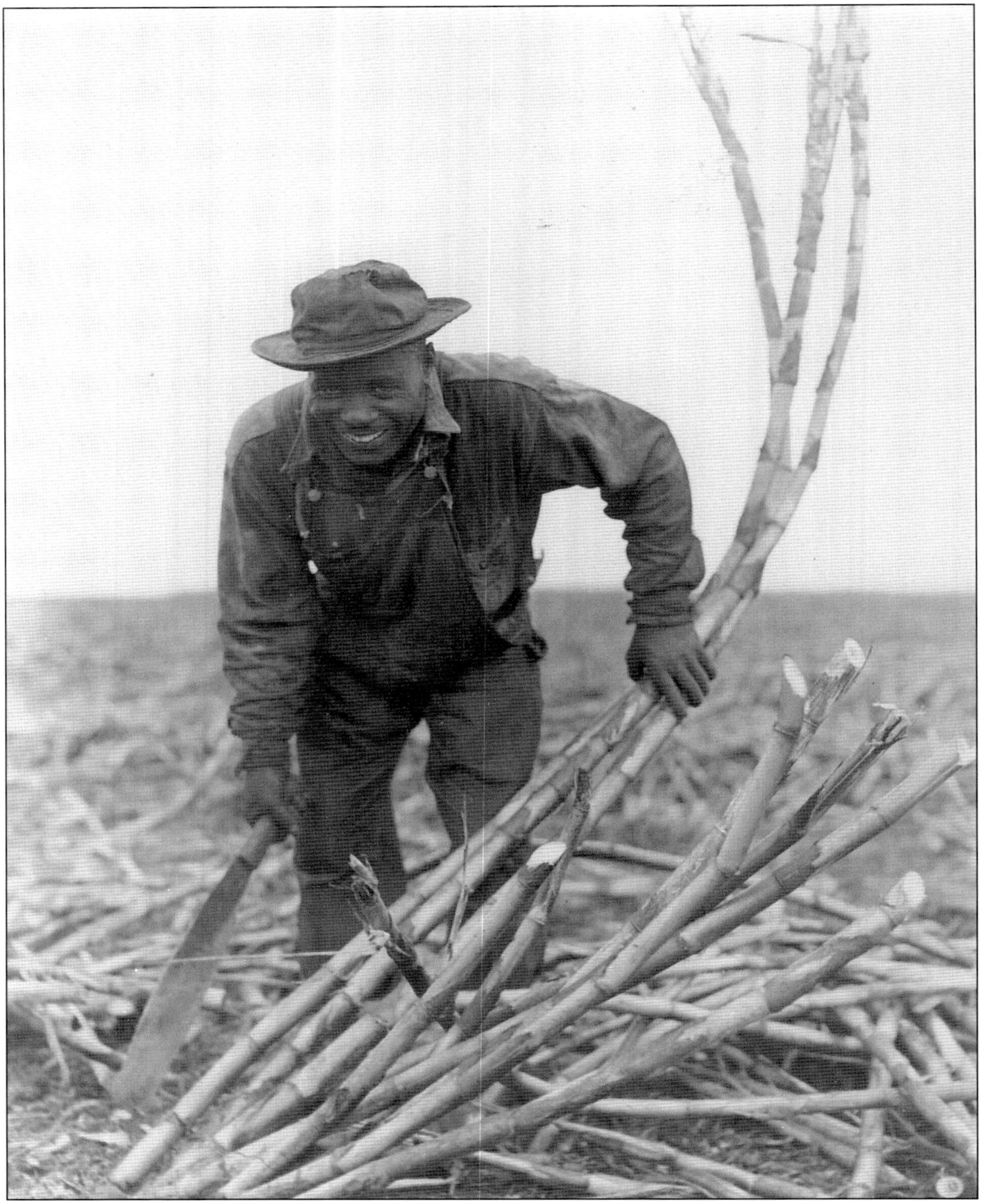

Toiling in the field were cane cutters, like this man who came from Jamaica for the sugarcane harvest season. (CM.)

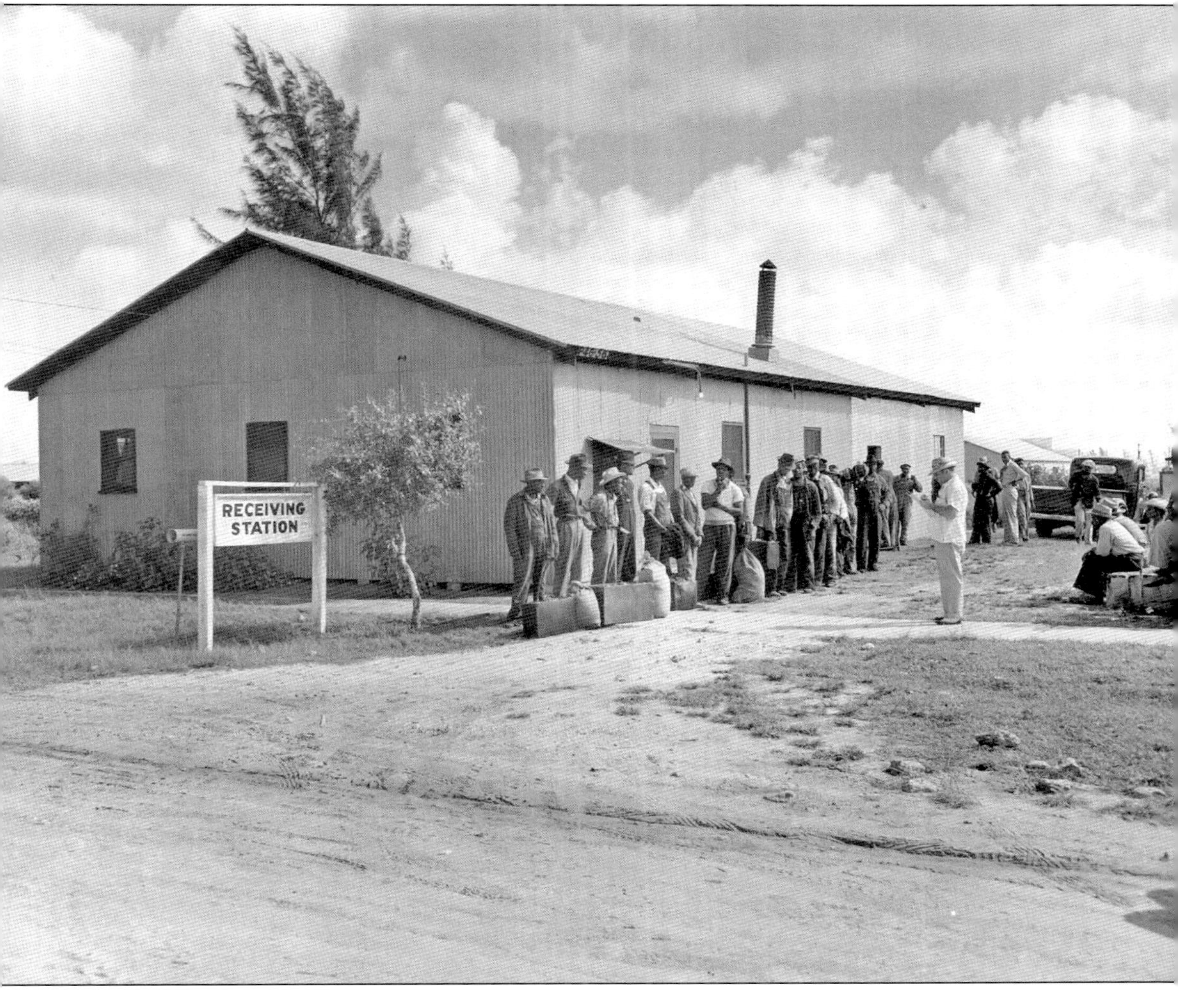

These sugarcane workers are shown lining up in front of the U.S. Sugar Corporation headquarters in Clewiston waiting to be hired for the season. (CM.)

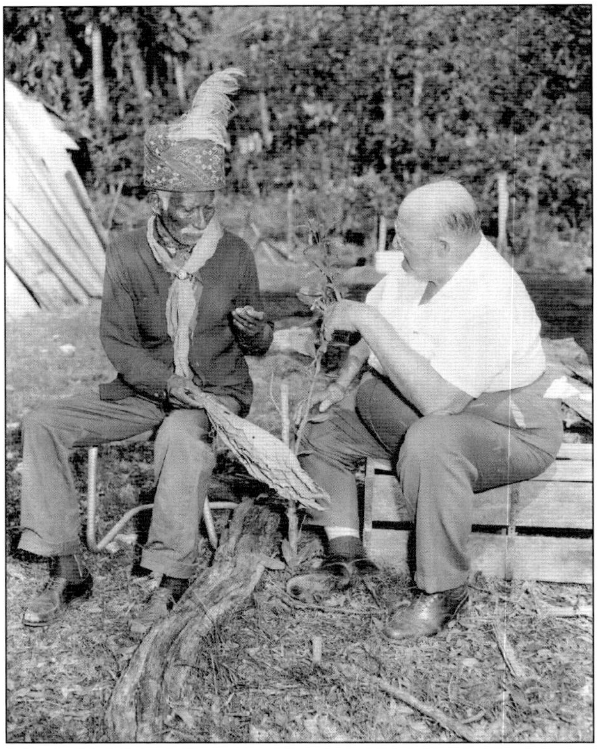

Billy Bowlegs III (left) is pictured here in 1962 showing a tobacco leaf that was still growing from seed given to him by his mother about 1874. Billy "shade cured" this tobacco. He is photographed here with Albert DeVane of Lake Placid, a friend of the Seminoles. About this time, Seminoles started smoke shops by selling tax-free cigarettes to tourists from stores. (Courtesy of the Florida Memory Project of the State Library and Archives.)

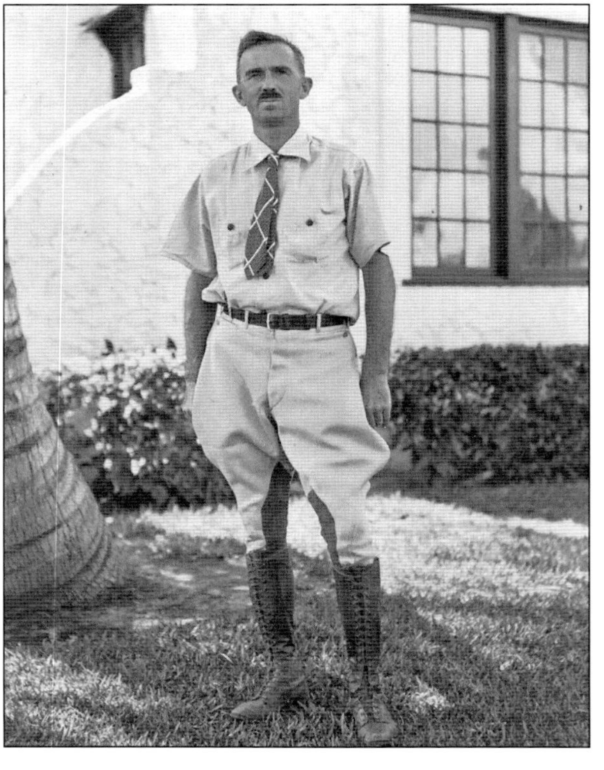

Shown here is William "Cap" Prewitt, a civil engineer. The 1937 Murphy Act passed by the state legislature brought about the greatest change between the past and the present by stating that all lands delinquent in taxes reverted back to state ownership. The land was then sold for the delinquent taxes and the governor of Florida, Fred Cone, signed the deed. (CM.)

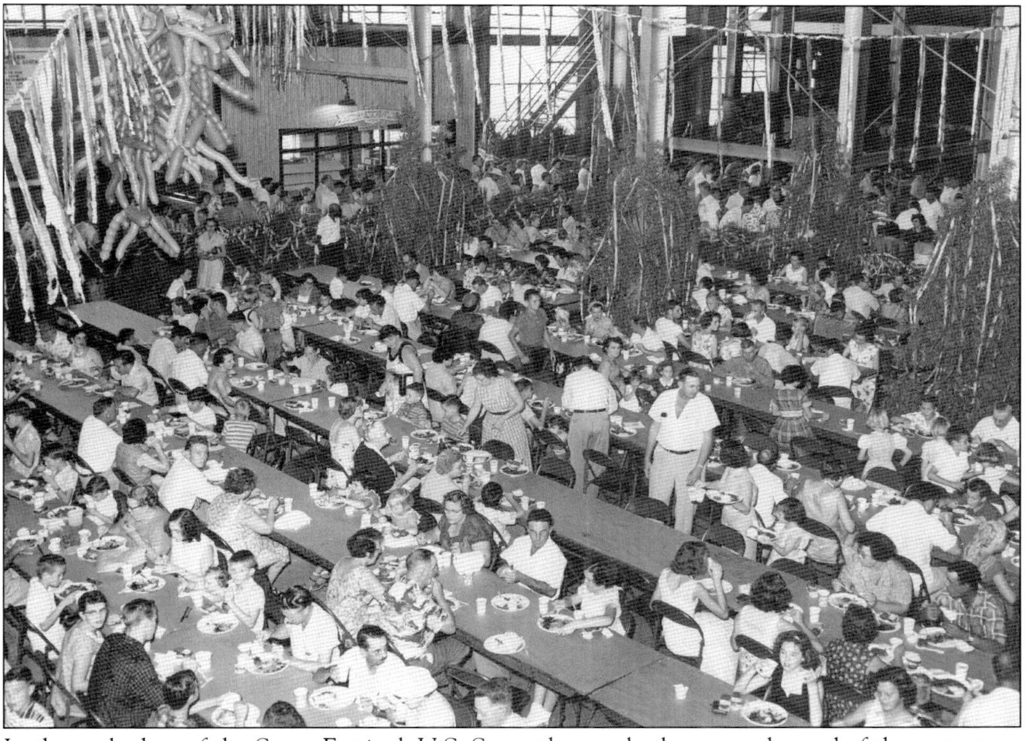

In the early days of the Sugar Festival, U.S. Sugar threw a barbeque at the end of the sugarcane harvest season in April for employees. Today the Sugar Festival Committee plans the event every year with the full support of U.S. Sugar and the city. Businesses also contribute to the celebration. The "Sweet Taste of Sugar" contest is a local cooking contest that awards cash prizes for the best pie, cake, brownie, candy, sweet creations, and bread recipes in the community. Other events include an antique car show, big-name musical entertainment, arts and crafts, food booths, nonprofit informational booths, a children's carnival, gospel singing, and children's dancing performances. (CM.)

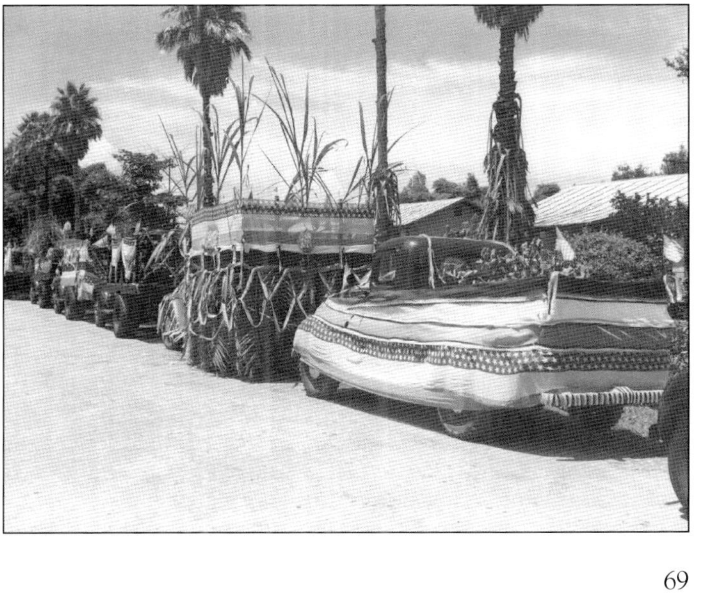

This is a typical float in the Sugar Festival Parade. The Sugar Honoree is elected every year as someone from the agricultural industry who has contributed to the community. This person is the grand marshal of the parade. A beauty contest is performed at the John Boy Auditorium and tickets are sold. In early April, judges are appointed to vote for Miss Sugar and for Miss Hendry County. These contest winners appear at the Sugar Festival and in the parade. (CM.)

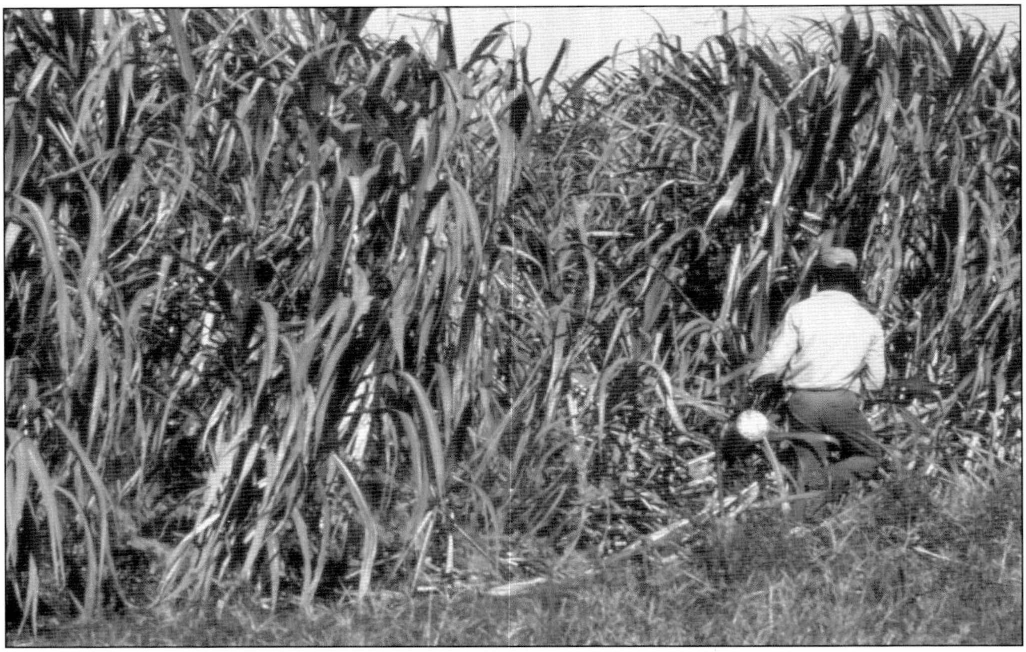

A worker starts a controlled burn, which is used in sugarcane harvesting. (CM.)

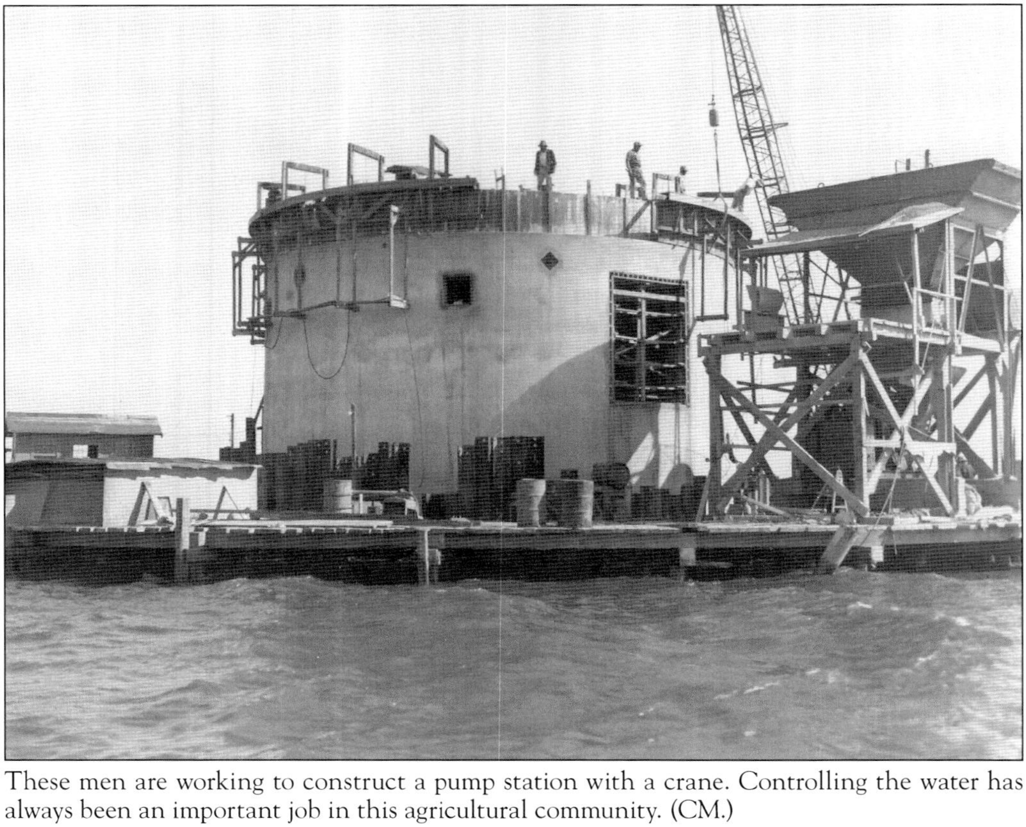

These men are working to construct a pump station with a crane. Controlling the water has always been an important job in this agricultural community. (CM.)

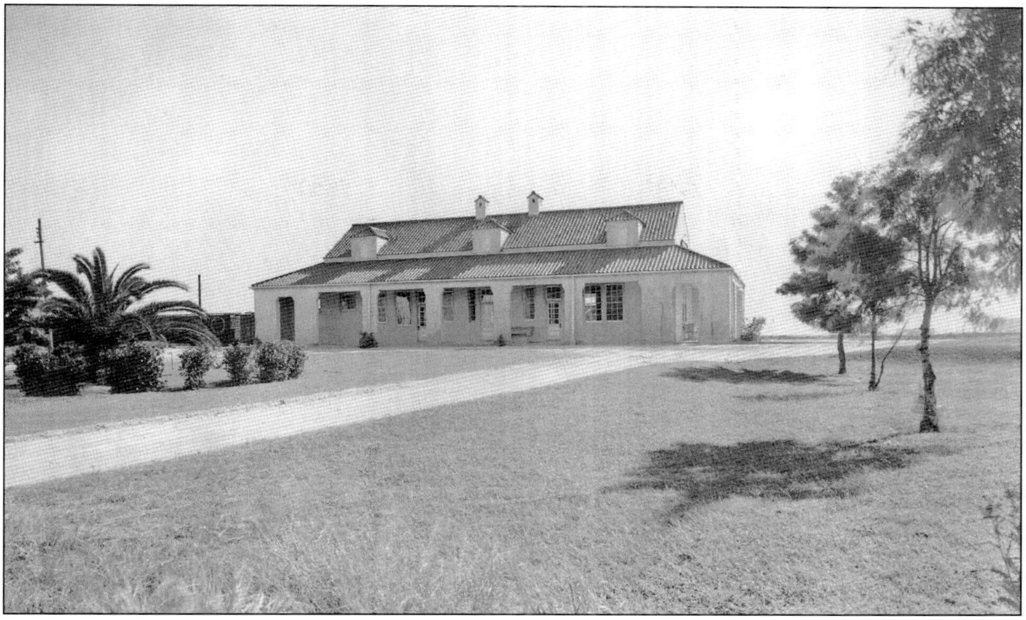

Here is the Atlantic Coast Line Railroad (ACL) passenger station in 1936. It was located at the south end of Central Avenue and Aztec Avenue. Marion Horowitz O'Brien, the first mayor of Moore Haven and one of the first woman mayors in the country, succeeded in bringing the ACL from Moore Haven to Palmdale in 1918. Her brother was a business associate of J. P. Morgan, vice president of the ACL railroad. This station was torn down during the 1970s. (CM.)

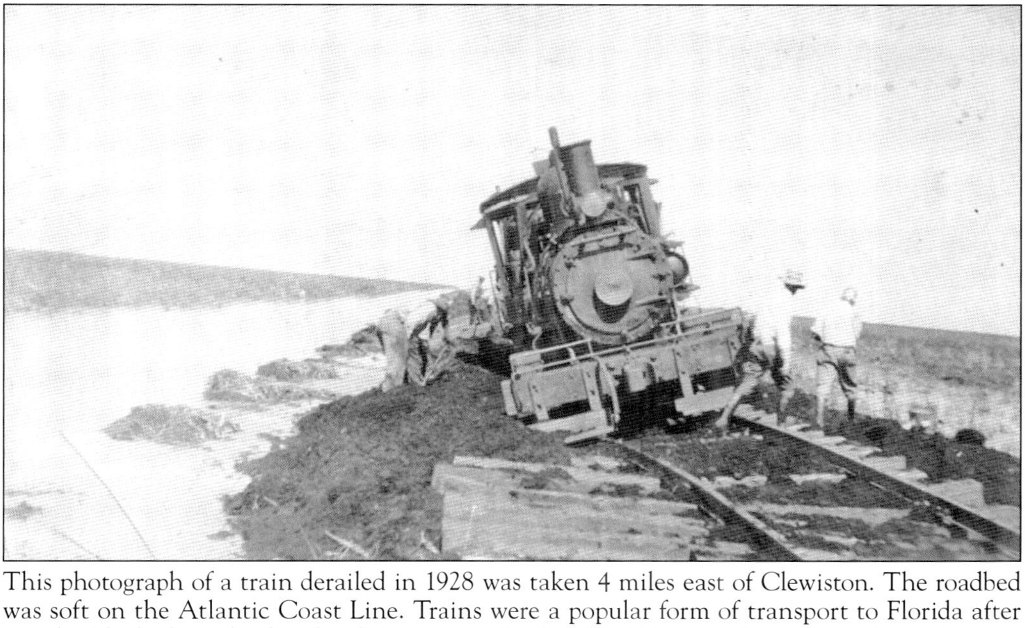

This photograph of a train derailed in 1928 was taken 4 miles east of Clewiston. The roadbed was soft on the Atlantic Coast Line. Trains were a popular form of transport to Florida after Hendry Flagler brought the Florida East Coast Railroad to Palm Beach. He extended it down to Miami because freezes hit the West Palm Beach area in 1894 and 1895. He also built the Royal Poinciana Inn and the Palm Beach Inn, which later became the Breakers Hotel on the Atlantic in 1901. (CM.)

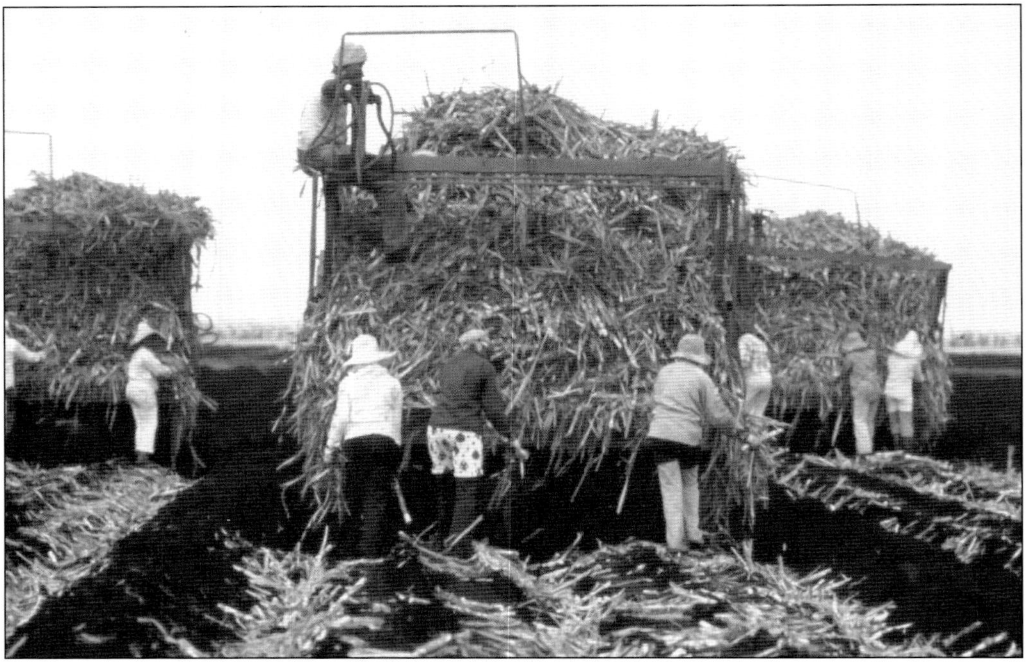

Sugarcane workers are tossing seed cane into the fields. After irrigation, sprouts appear from the cane stalks and take root. New cane can grow from the same roots for around five years. (FMP.)

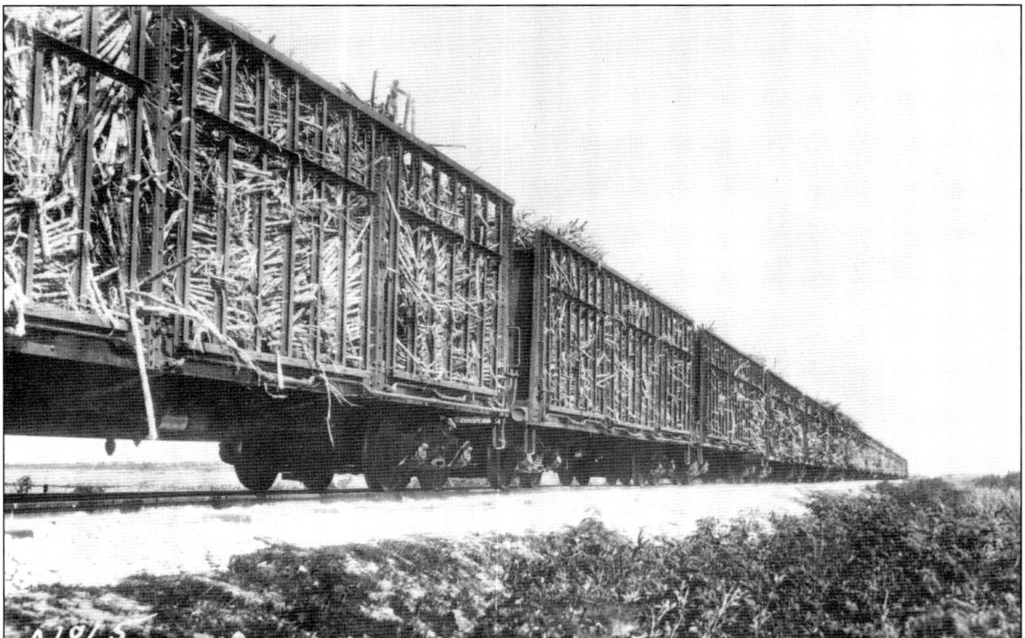

Railroad cars full of sugarcane are a common sight during harvest season. Starting in October, sugarcane is ready to be loaded into large trucks and moved to the processing plant, where sugarcane is processed and bagged to be distributed around the world. (FMP.)

Six

Sugarcane and Calamities

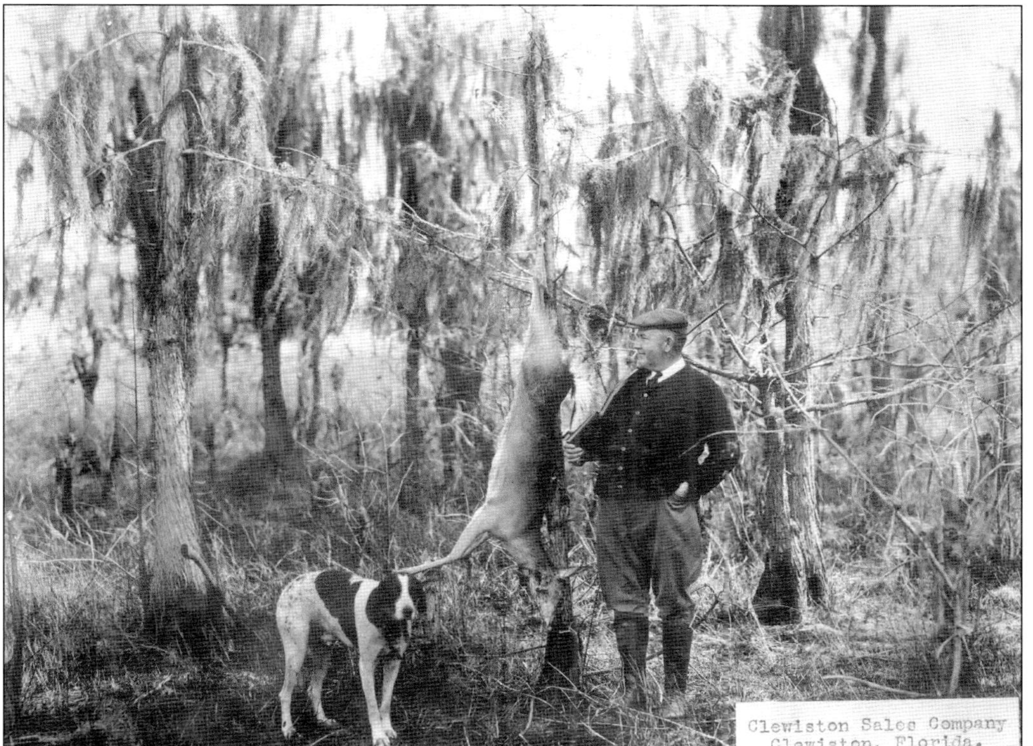

Deer were a common target for Glades hunters. This 1920s photograph shows a hunter with his dog next to the deer that he shot. (FMP.)

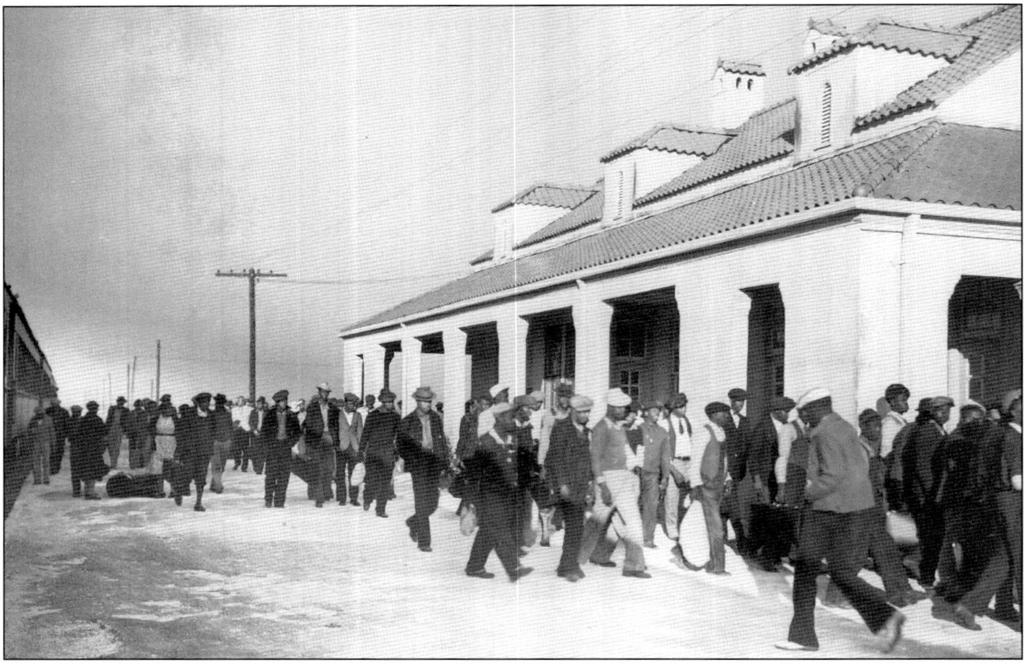

U.S. Sugar Corporation domestic labor recruitment workers departing from the train depot. The Mainland Sugarcane Program, locally referred to as the "Sugar Program," was enacted by Congress in 1937. Improved drainage systems and new strains of sugarcane seed brought about the successful raw sugar, which was produced and carried by rail to a refinery in Savannah, Georgia. In 1947, the Agricultural Stabilization and Conservation Service, a branch of the U.S. Department of Agriculture, sent Eugene H. Boyles to Glades County to supervise USDA programs in Glades, Hendry, and Palm Beach Counties. (CM.)

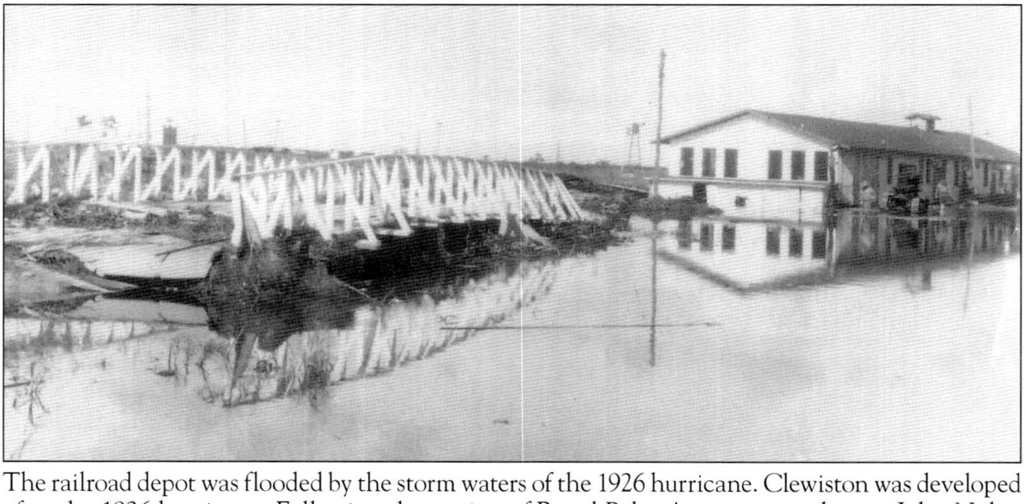

The railroad depot was flooded by the storm waters of the 1926 hurricane. Clewiston was developed after the 1926 hurricane. Following the paving of Royal Palm Avenue, city planner John Nolen suggested they pave Del Monte Avenue immediately, and that it should be a promenade. This was so that the city plan and its three most important design elements—the Civic Center north to the waterfront and what Nolen designated the Recreation Unit, the 1926 Clewiston Inn on Avenida del Rio, and Francisco Street—would be linked to each other. (CM.)

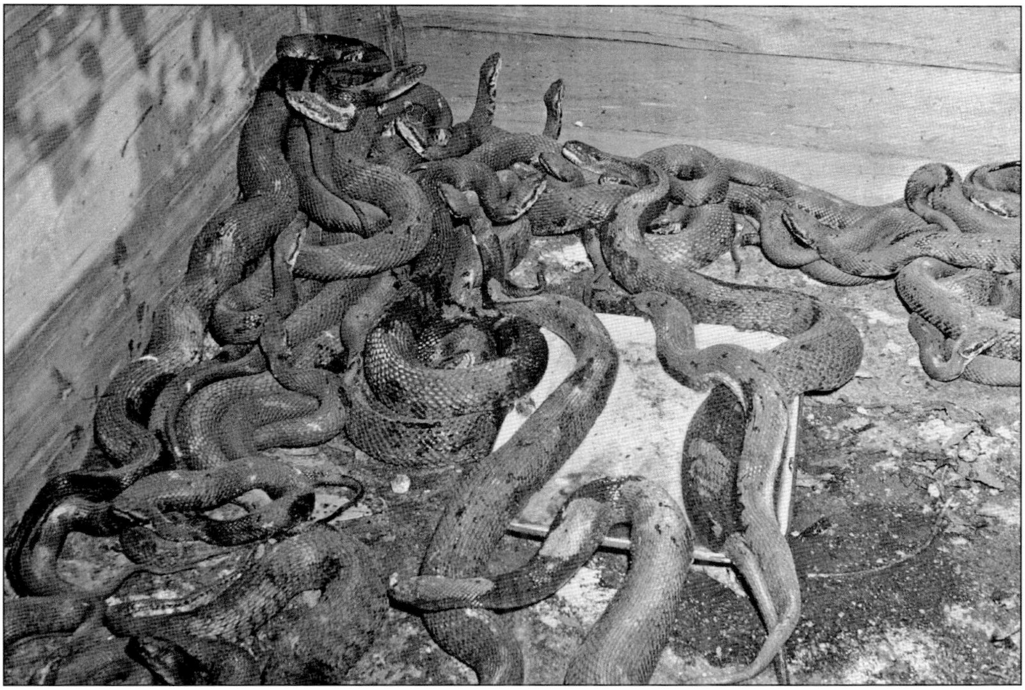

Water moccasins like these are a common sight, and they live along the banks of Lake Okeechobee. After the 1926 hurricane, snakes were swimming around the city, and several residents died from snakebites. Florida is the home of six deadly snakes: the eastern diamondback rattlesnake, the cottonmouth (water moccasin), the coral snake, and the dusky pygmy rattlesnake in South Florida and the timber rattlesnake and the copperhead in the Panhandle. (FMP.)

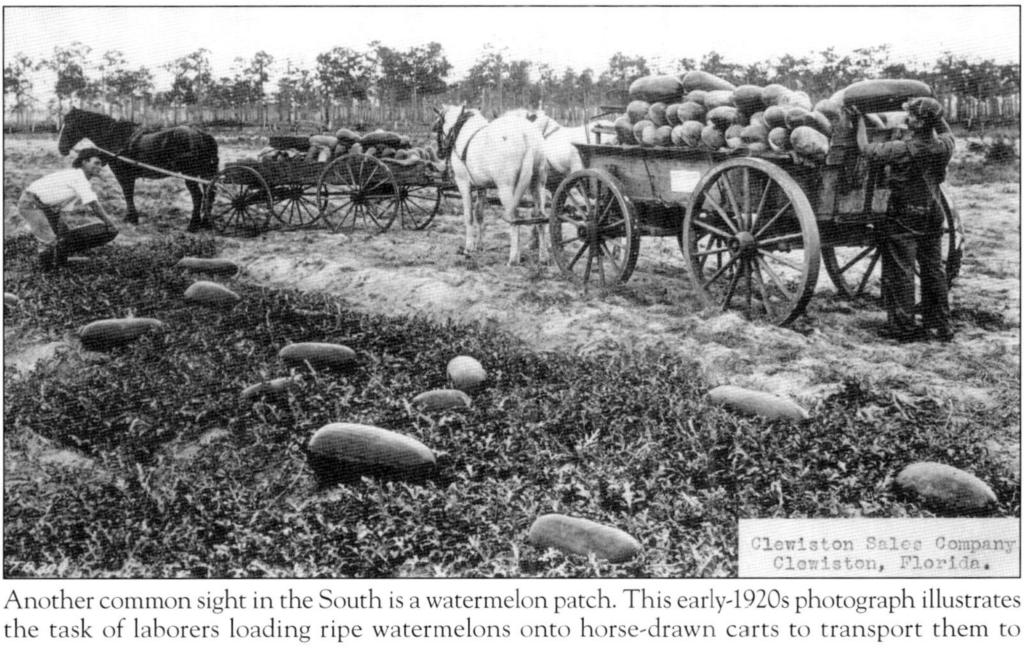

Another common sight in the South is a watermelon patch. This early-1920s photograph illustrates the task of laborers loading ripe watermelons onto horse-drawn carts to transport them to market. (FMP.)

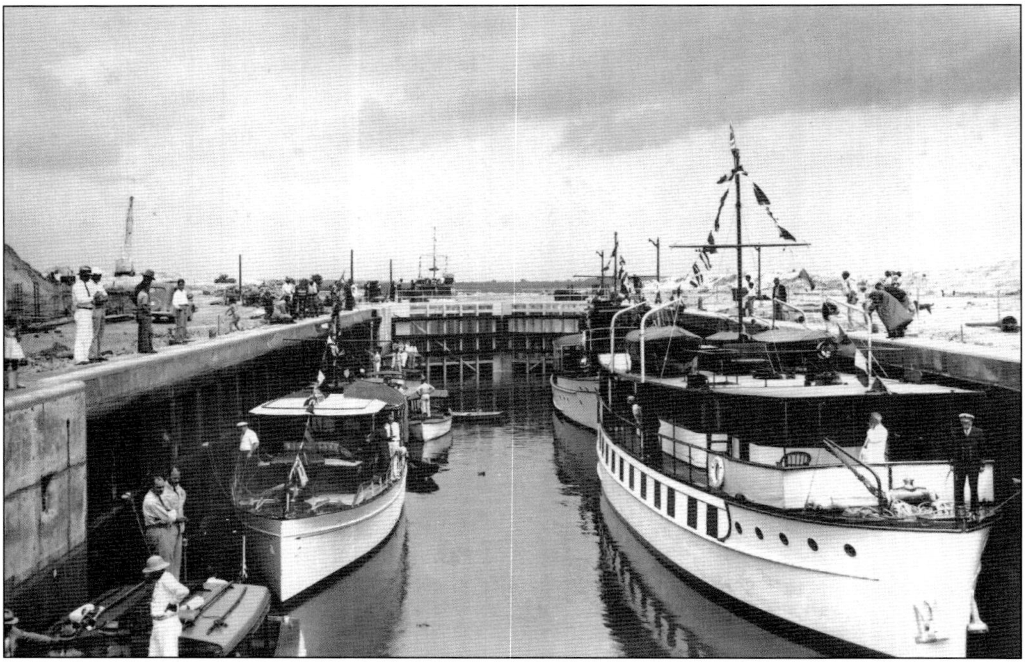

Hydraulic engineers constructed these sophisticated locks so that boats of many sizes and shapes could enjoy navigating through Lake Okeechobee. Every year, 25,000 craft of all kinds use this waterway across Florida. This is a view of the locks at Clewiston. (CM.)

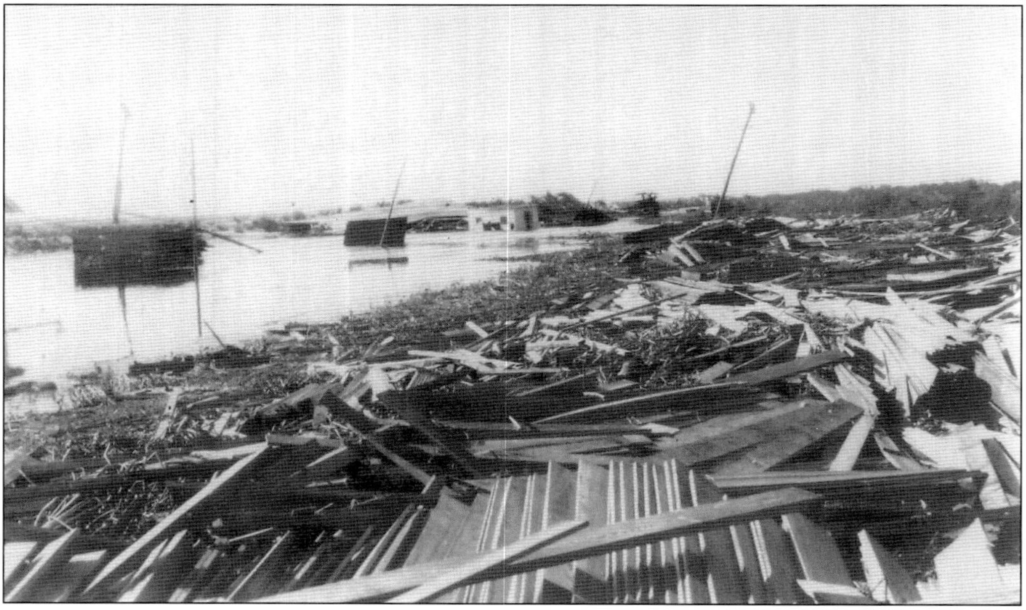

Lake airflow damage is apparent after the 1926 hurricane. Vance Whidden's grandparents, Mr. and Mrs. Willoughby Whidden, had come to the area in 1907, settling 6 miles northwest of Gator Slough, where they raised hogs, cattle, oranges, and vegetables and made syrup. Willoughby was a lay preacher on Sundays. Most of these early settlers came to the area to farm or fish but turned to other professions or moved away after the 1926 storm. (CM.)

This aerial view of Clewiston from 1947 or 1948 shows the lock and the rim canal of Lake Okeechobee. Photographer Sherman Fairchild was born in 1896 in Oneonta, New York. He was contracted by the government to develop a camera for aerial photography; such cameras already existed but produced highly distorted photographs due to slow shutter speeds that could not keep up with the movement of the flying plane. Fairchild developed a faster camera with the shutter placed inside the lens. After World War I, the army made his cameras the standard aerial camera. (FMP.)

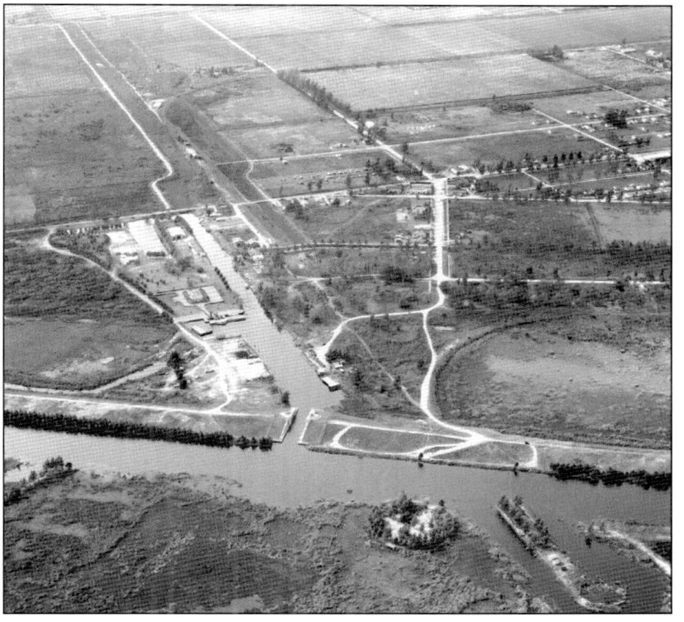

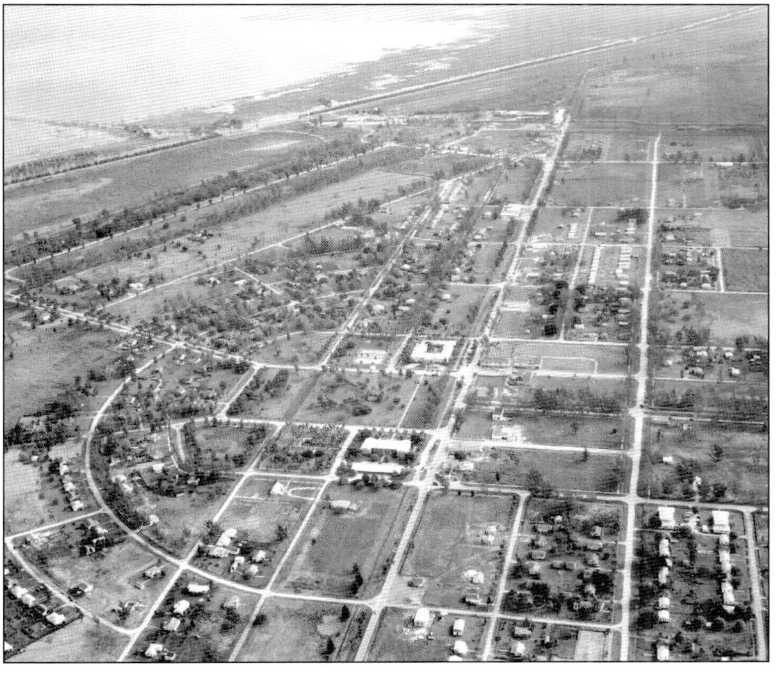

Clewiston bills itself as "America's Sweetest Town." Here is an aerial view or Crescent Avenue with Lake Okeechobee on the left. Clewiston was a planned community laid out by John Nolen, a city planner who also designed the city of Venice, Florida. He studied in England and then was hired to plat out the town. Notice the curved streets at left and verdant parks and trees for residents to have pleasing places to walk. (FMP.)

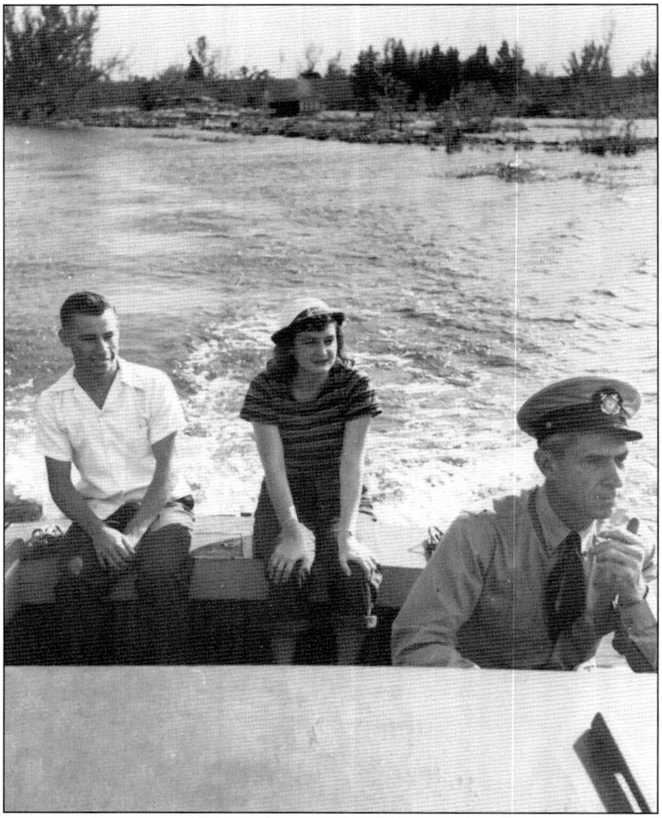

A boating group composed of Dean Heflin, June Espenlaub, and her father, George L. Espenlaub, a longtime Clewiston garage and service station owner, goes out to the old channel in 1946. Hoover Dike is in the background. (FMP.)

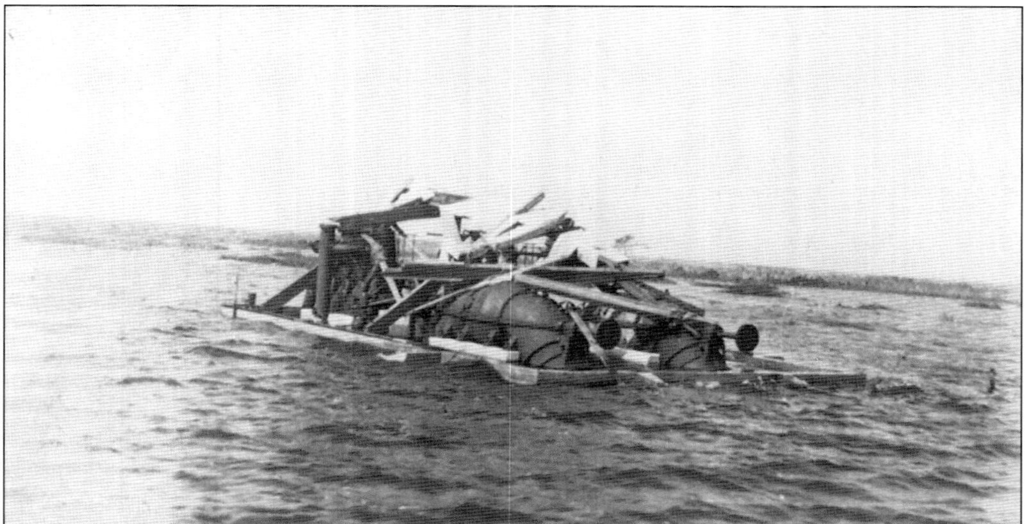

This photograph shows the destruction to the pump station after the 1926 hurricane. I. E. Scott and Dr. Draugh were walking to Dr. Draugh's house in Moore Haven after the hurricane waters had receded. They met an enormous alligator, at least 10 feet long, whom they observed "looked pretty well beaten." Since he had once had an eye shot out, he was known to the local fishermen as "One Eye Riley." (CM.)

Seven

Patchwork, Politicians, and Parties

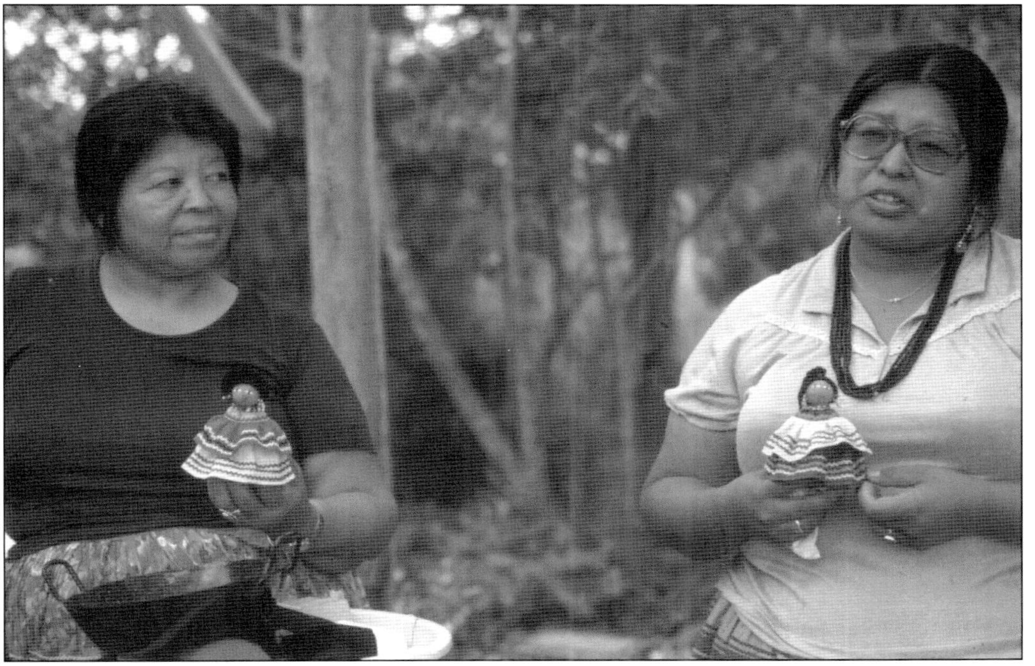

Traditional Seminole patchwork is recognized by American Indian tribes throughout the country. Florida Seminole jackets, skirts, and dolls have been handmade by tribal women at reservations in Brighton, Hollywood, Immokalee, and Big Cypress. Mary Billie (left) and Claudia John display their creations in this 1980 photograph taken at the Big Cypress reservation. Collectors of American Indian art prize these tribal crafts. (FMP.)

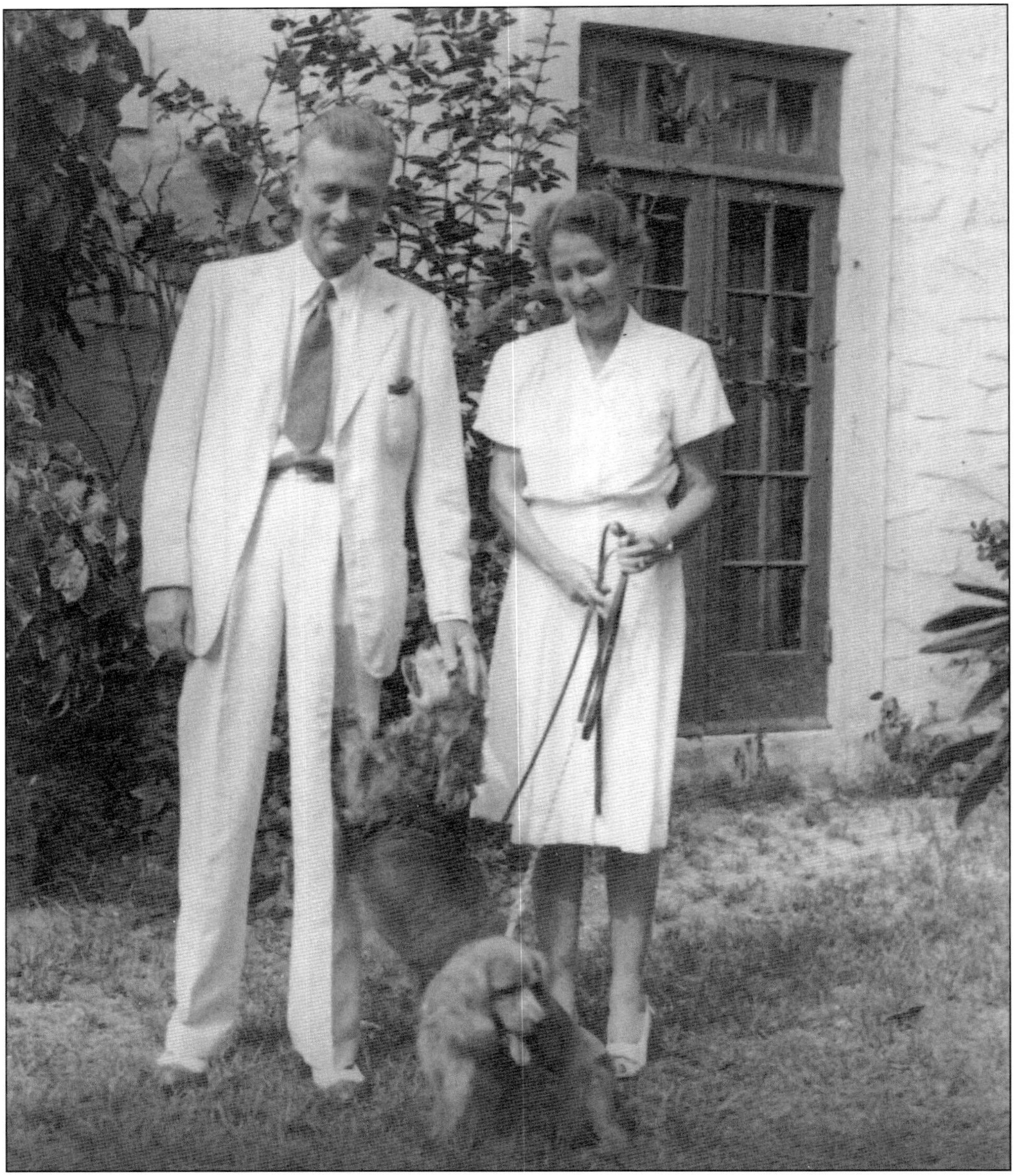

F. Deane and Elizabeth Bryant Duff are shown here with their dogs. In 1931, Duff, the first mayor of Clewiston, asked city planner John Nolen to revise the Clewiston General Plan by moving the central business district farther west along the primary state highway to Fort Myers. Nolen therefore designated Sugarland Highway as Clewiston's main business district. As a result of the heavy traffic, the business development continued to grow along the highway. In the 1920s, businesses had initially been planned to be located near Civic Park and along Central Avenue. These were the Southern Sugar Office building, the *Clewiston News* building, the Hopkins Building, and the Bond Street building. It was Nolen's intent to develop the main business district near the railroad and industrial canal. Early buildings sprouted up, such as the Alston Block, the Clewiston Motor Company (now Kelly's Tractor Caterpillar Agency), the 1926 Clewiston Inn (now gone), W. C. Hooker's big packinghouse, and J. J. O'Brien's bulk plant, built around 1925. (CM.)

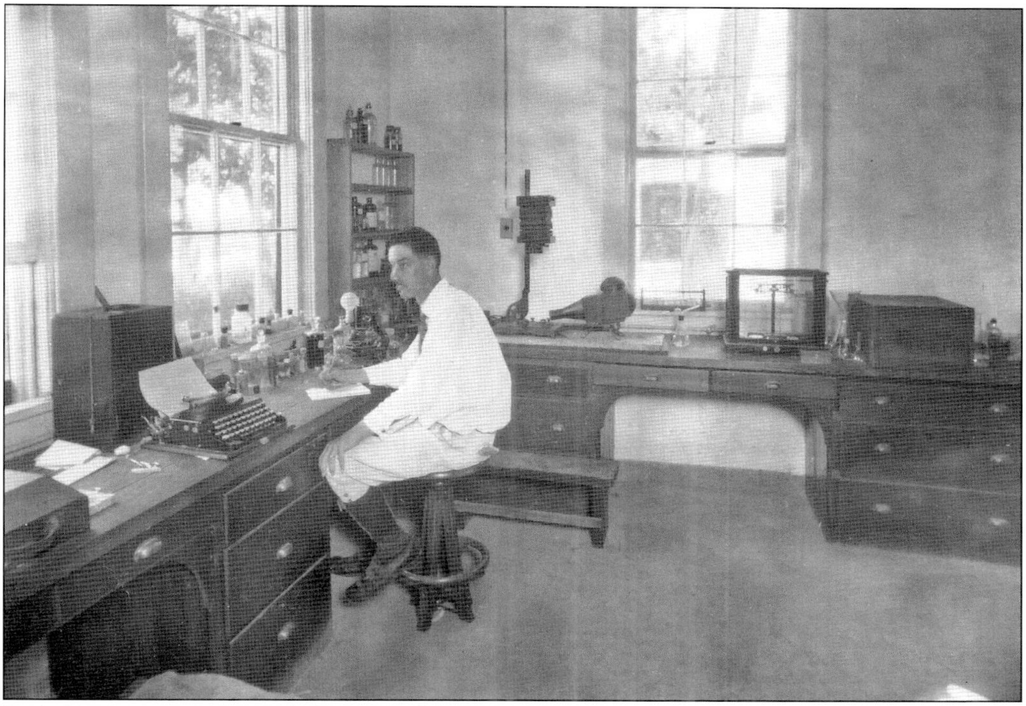

B. A. Bourne, assistant pathologist in charge of the USDA Sugar Cane Field Station laboratory, is pictured at work in Canal Point. (CM.)

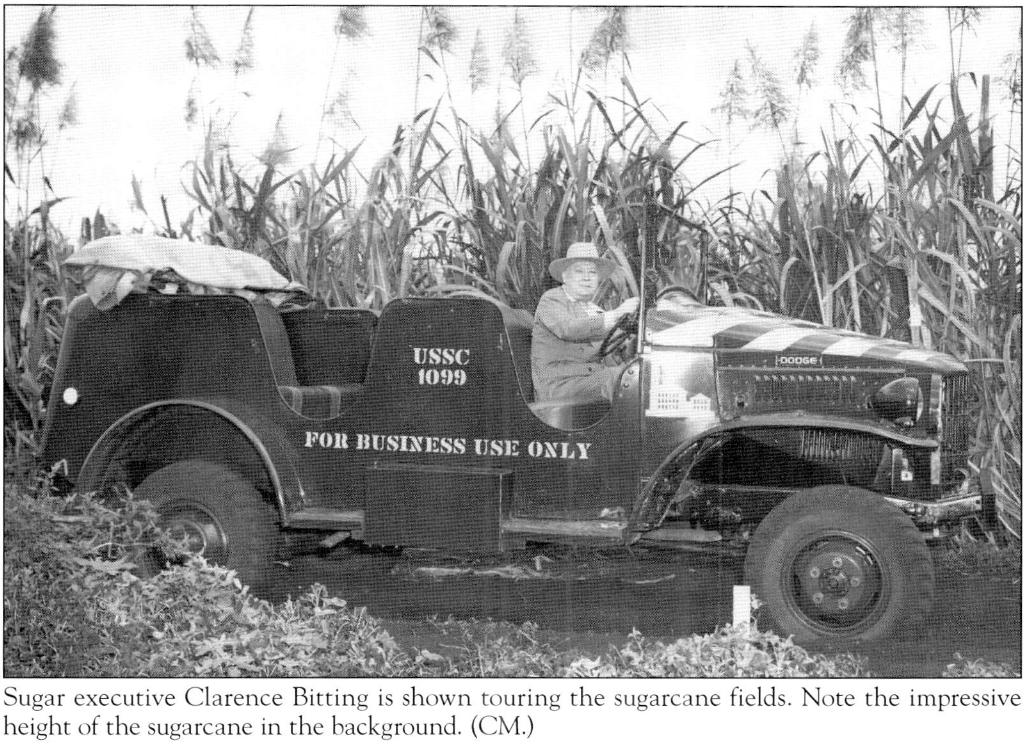

Sugar executive Clarence Bitting is shown touring the sugarcane fields. Note the impressive height of the sugarcane in the background. (CM.)

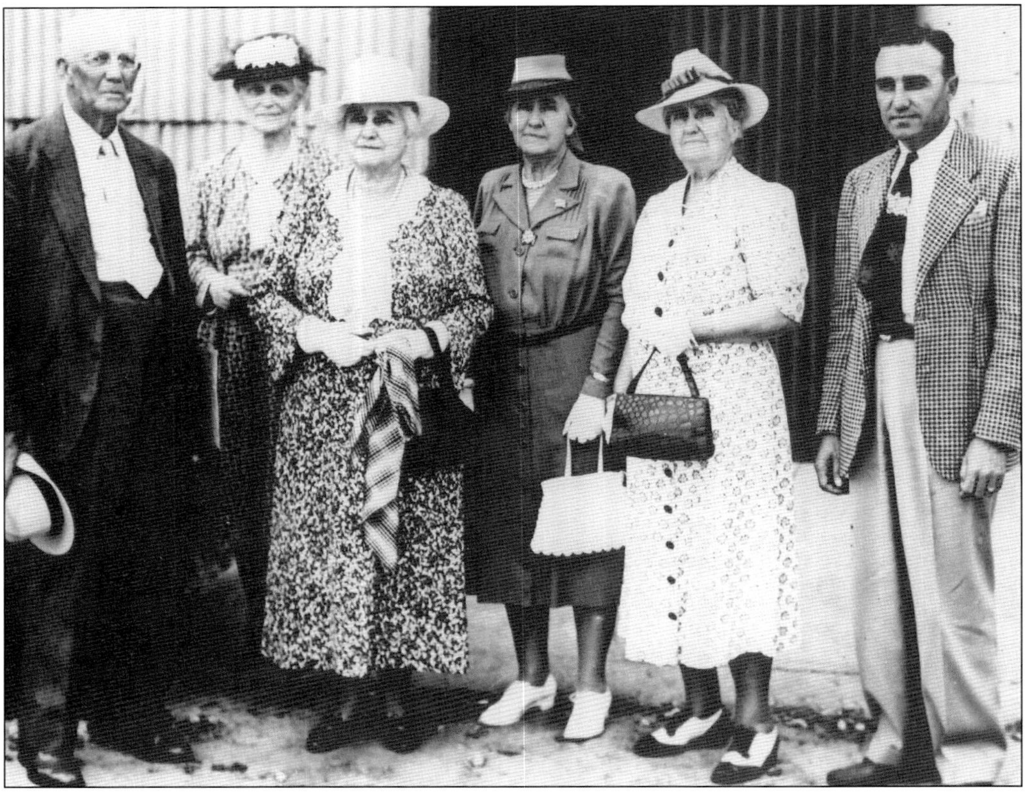

Mina Edison (wife of Thomas Edison) is pictured with her party at the U.S. Sugar Corporation mill in 1940. From left to right are a Mr. Nichols, Lucy Bogue (Mina Edison's secretary), Mina Miller Edison, Grace Hitchcock (sister-in-law of Mina Edison's sister), Mary Nichols, and S. L. Crocket of U.S. Sugar Corporation. (CM.)

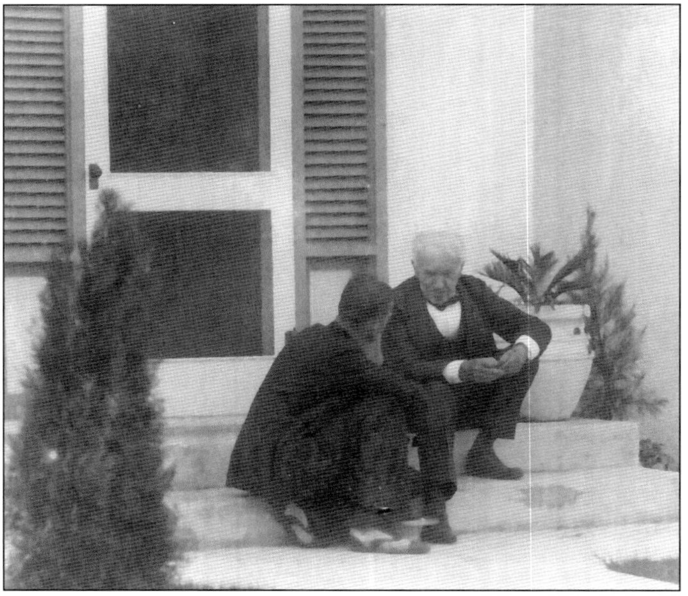

Thomas Edison chats with a neighbor during a visit to Clewiston. Henry Ford, Thomas Edison, and Harvey Firestone were winter residents of Fort Myers. The Firestone Tire and Rubber Company was founded in 1900 to supply pneumatic tires for wagons, buggies, and other forms of wheeled transportation common in the era. Firestone was quick to realize the huge potential in automobile tires and started mass-producing them for the Ford Motor Company. The three men often got together and were good friends. (CM.)

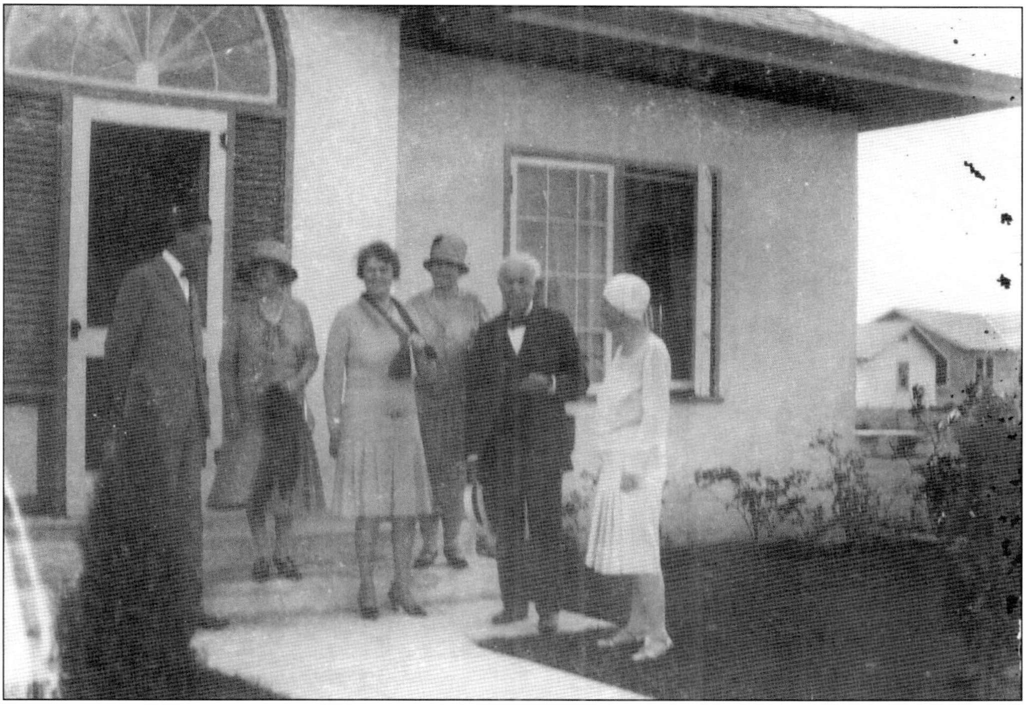

Henry Ford and Thomas Edison and their wives were guests at the home of F. L. Williamson during their Clewiston visit. Ford's Model T, nicknamed the "Tin Lizzie," was produced Ford Motor Company from 1908 to 1927. Henry Ford paid his workers $5 a day so that they could all afford to buy his cars. (CM.)

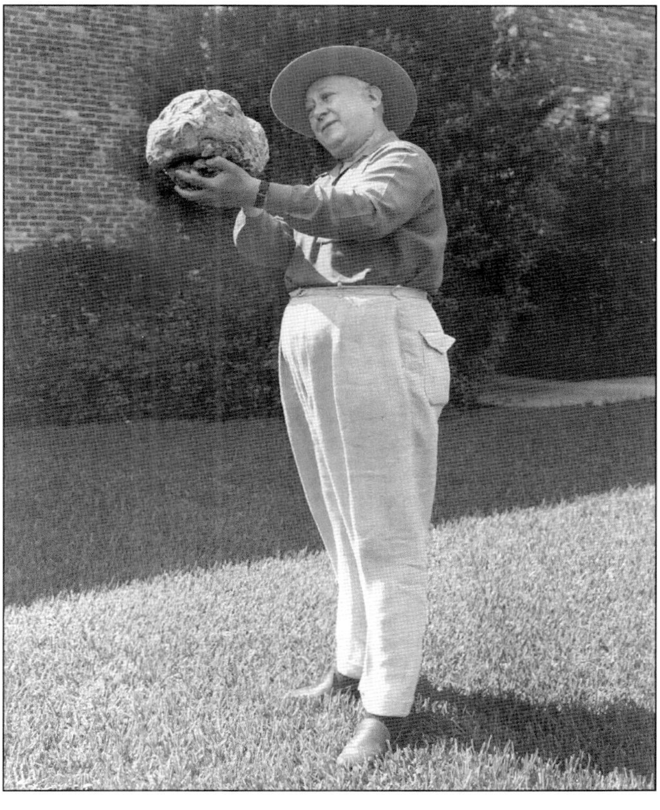

Clarence Bitting, chief operating officer of U.S. Sugar, shows off this huge sweet potato. U.S. Sugar's Sugar Festival in April was a harvest celebration to thank everyone for working seven days a week to ensure the best possible sugarcane crop in the shortest amount of time. (CM.)

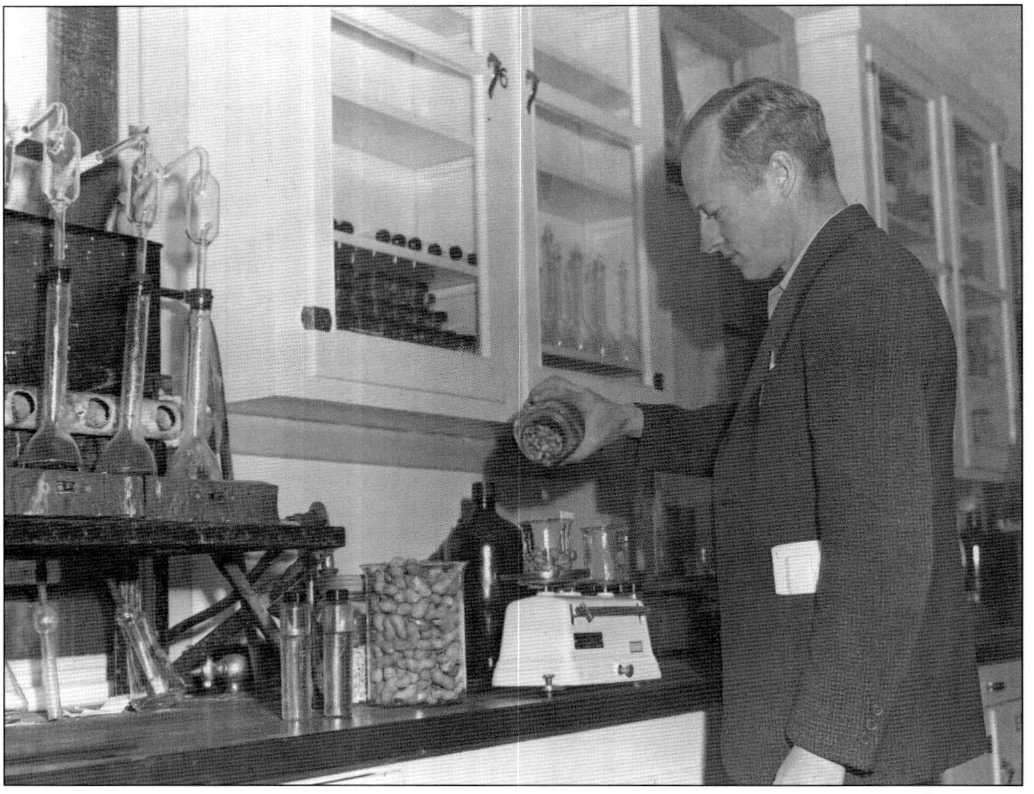

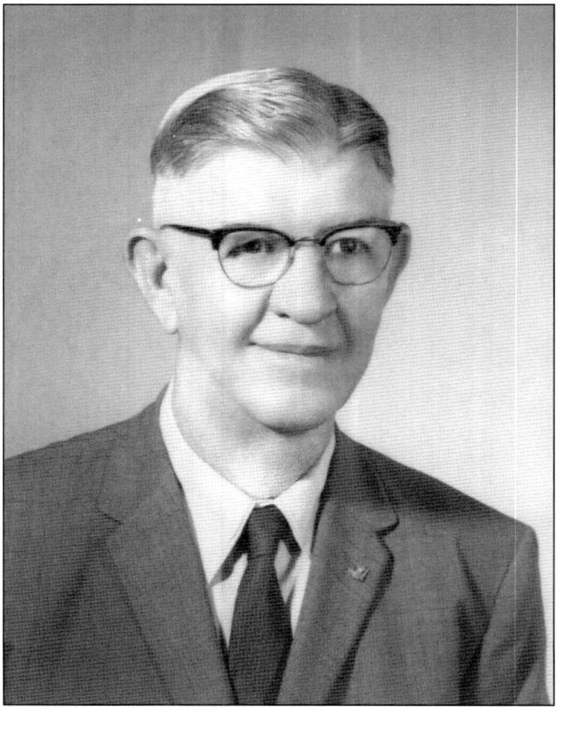

Peanut experiments were one of the areas of research at the Agricultural Research Laboratory of the U.S. Sugar Corporation. Scientist Dr. G. E. Gericke is shown here. (CM.)

W. C. Owen was a civil engineer who came to Clewiston in 1922 to oversee the drainage of the Clewiston town site. Owen became a member of the board of directors of the Clewiston Company. He played a leading role in the development of Clewiston for the rest of his life. The town renamed one of the city's main northwest streets for him following his death. His historic residence was one of the earliest homes built here and is qualified for listing on the National Register of Historic Places. (CM.)

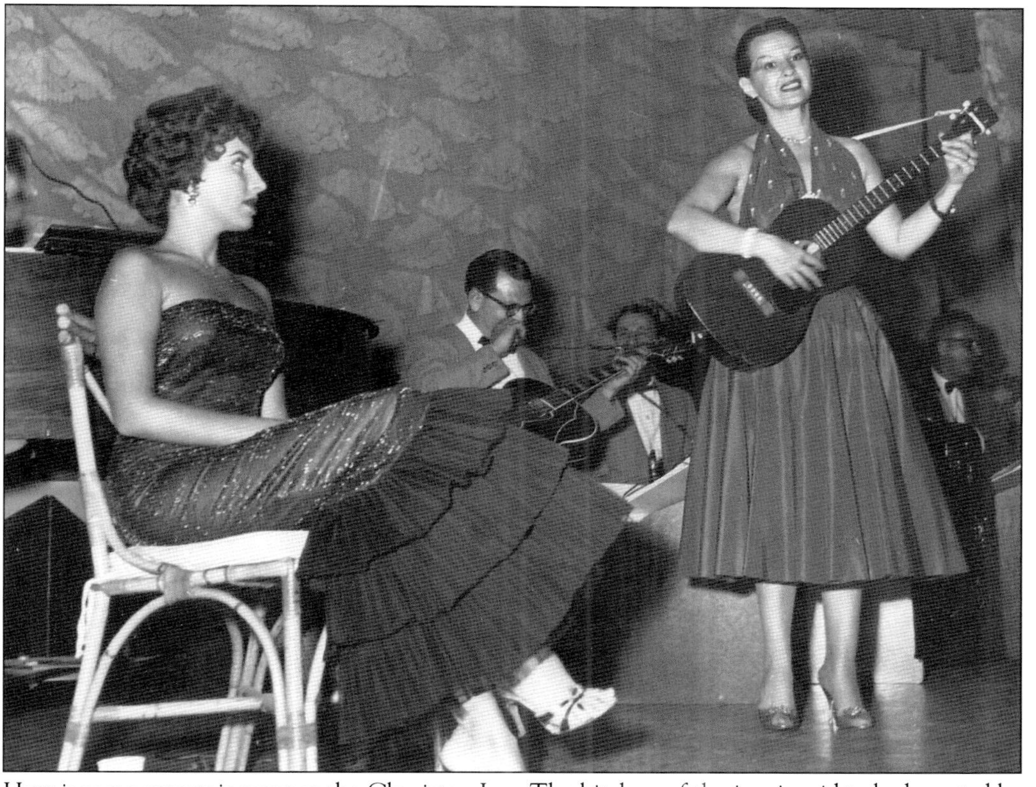

Here is some entertainment at the Clewiston Inn. The kitchen of the inn is said to be haunted by a small girl who may have been related to one of the workers. Room 218 has had reports of a "Lady in White" appearing to guests during the night. One night, two fishermen stayed in that room, and one of the men saw an apparition of a woman. It spooked him so badly that the men checked out immediately. Suite 255 was occupied by A. Conklin. After she died, the switchboard lit up for her room, even though the phone was removed. Sometimes guests hear books being banged around by the ghost. Another ghost is Clarence, a man in a brown suit who had been the dining room host for a number of years. Christa, the current manager, has had her hair tugged by a mysterious presence. Patrick Burns, a paranormal investigator, spent a weekend at the Clewiston Inn with a group of psychics and curious ghost hunters to record and photograph the hauntings. (CM.)

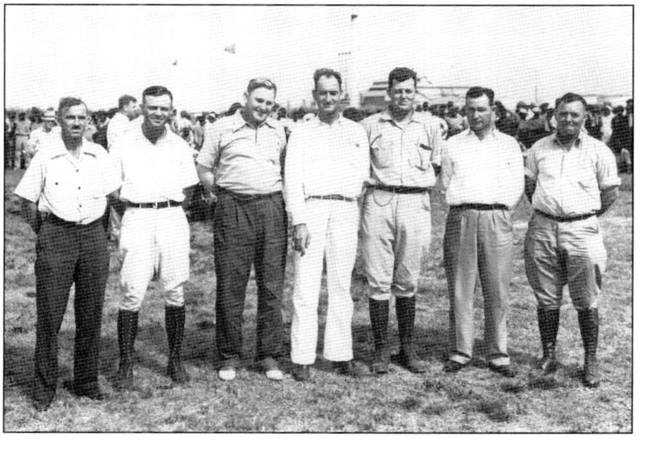

Pictured from left to right are U.S. Sugar field supervisors W. C. Prewitt, W. E. Bolton, C. L. McLendon, George A. Yor, Fisher Ange, Neal Williamson, and E. W. McLeod. (CM.)

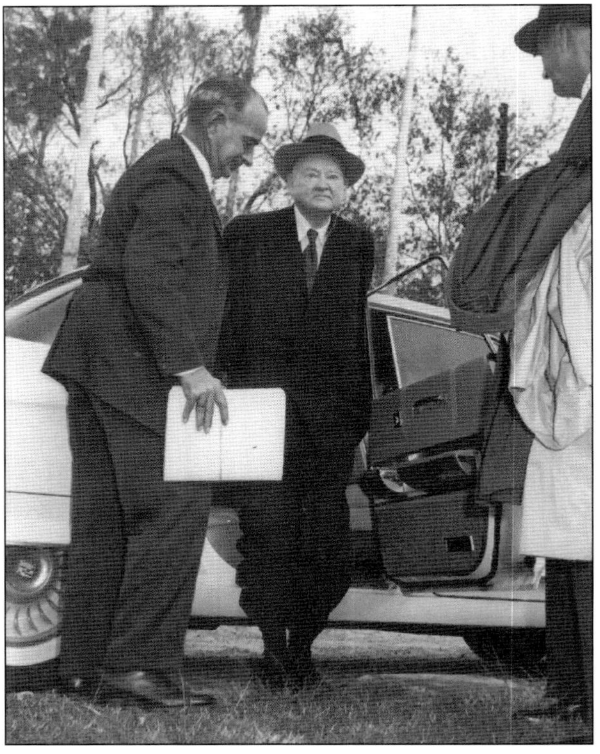

Pres. Herbert Hoover is shown arriving at the north entrance of the Clewiston Inn apartments. His term during the Great Depression made him a proponent of public works programs such as the Lake Okeechobee levee and the Hoover Dam in Nevada, started in 1931 and completed in 1936. (CM.)

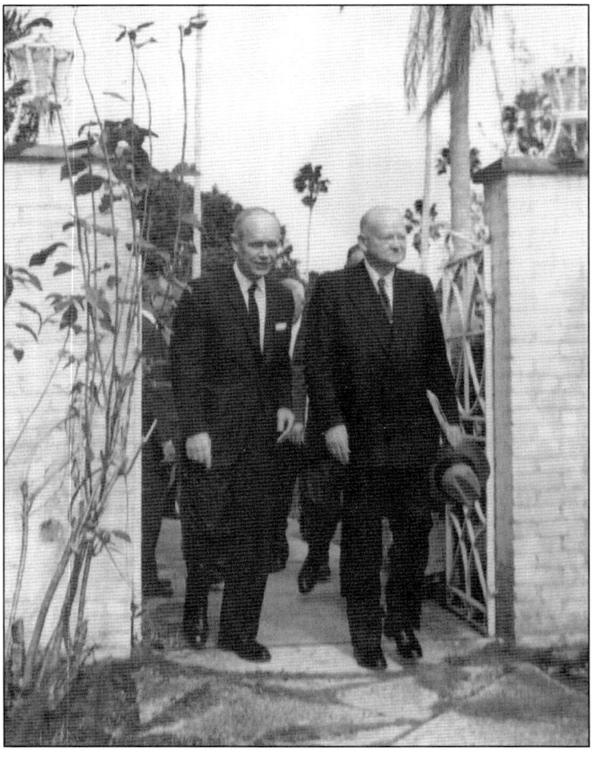

Here President Hoover (right) is purveying the Clewiston Inn's gardens. The historic Clewiston Inn, long a favorite dining place, has a valuable mural in the lounge of Everglades creatures such as Florida panthers, bald eagles, sandhill cranes, otters, raccoons, blue herons, bobcats, ducks, deer, owls, egrets, rattlesnakes, wild turkeys, and other native Florida species. It is presently valued at over a million dollars. The Clewiston Inn was listed on the National Register of Historic Places in 1991. It was found significant for business and social history for its role in the development of the town and as the hub of social activity since its construction. It also was found to be important as a rare local example of the Neoclassical Revival style and as the work of noted Florida architects L. Phillips Clarke and Edgar S. Wortman. (CM.)

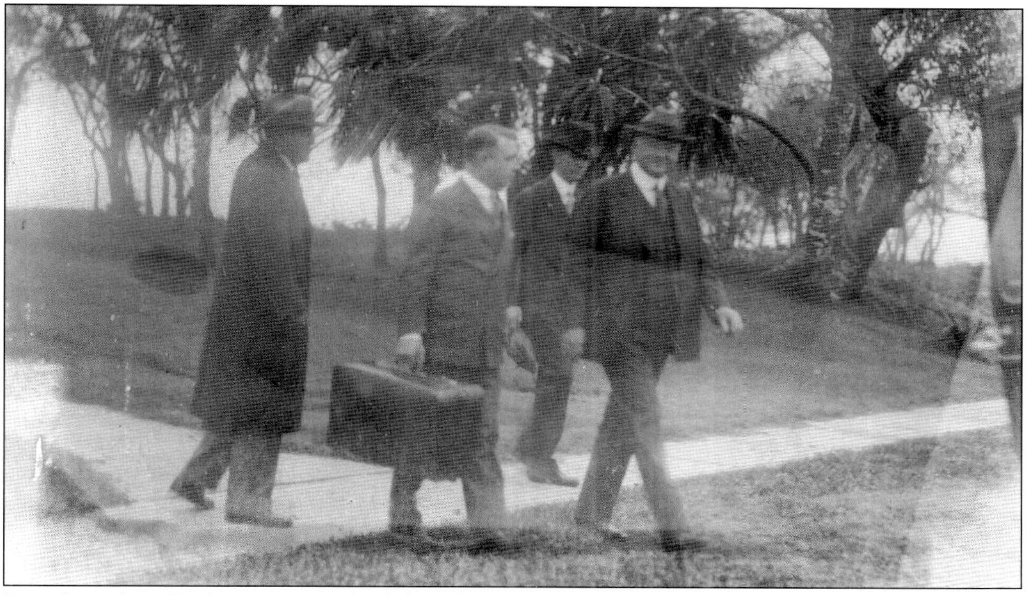

President-elect Herbert Hoover (right) and Bror G. Dahlberg (with briefcase) leave the Bishop house accompanied by two Secret Service agents. The Percy G. Bishop house at 325 East Del Monte Avenue was built in 1929 as the home of Percy G. "P. G." Bishop, who entered the sugar manufacturing business in Puerto Rico. He later became vice president of the Cuba Cane Sugar Corporation of Cuba. His Clewiston residence was designed by Palm Beach architect Clark J. Lawrence. Dahlberg was president of the Celotex Company of Chicago and saw great possibilities in growing sugarcane in the Everglades for the raw material bagasse, which was used to produce Celotex wallboard. He formed the Southern Sugar Company, which owned 100,000 acres. On January 14, 1929, sugar was produced, with the first sugarcane crop resulting in 745 tons of raw sugar. This was a miraculous discovery; however, it was short-lived. In 1929, the company was bankrupted when sugar prices dropped due to the Great Depression. (CM.)

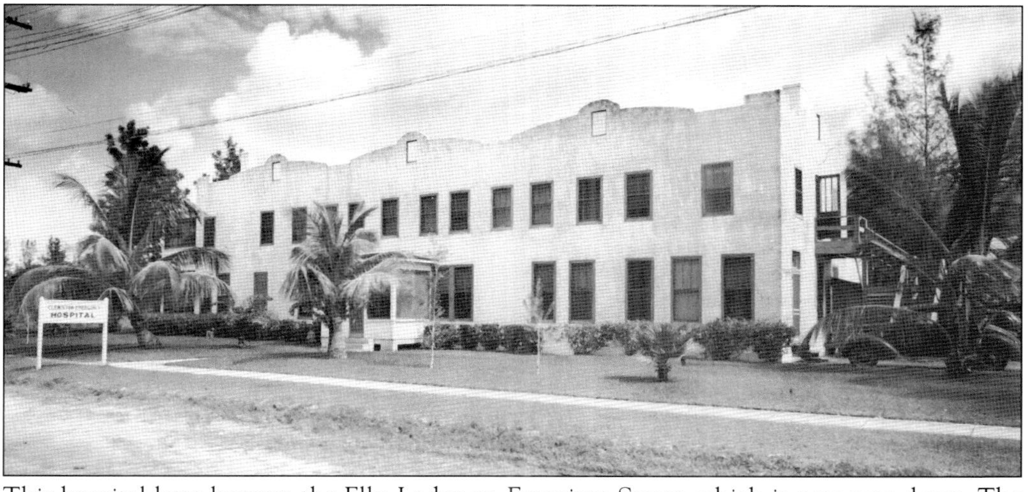

This hospital later became the Elks Lodge on Francisco Street, which is now torn down. The present Hendry Regional Medical Center is located on Sugarland Highway. The facility has a budget of $60 million and provides health care to Clewiston, Harlem, Montura, Moore Haven, and surrounding areas. (CM.)

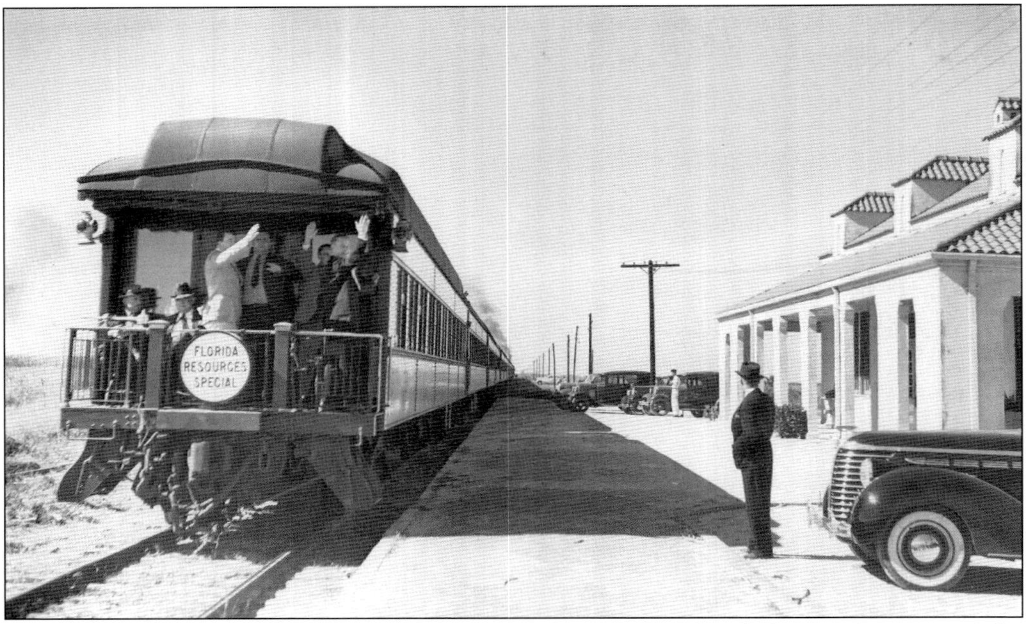

Florida governor Fred P. Cone designed a program to promote Florida by traveling around the state by train in 1938. Florida was called "the Garden of Eden" by a Chicago developer, a Mr. Fog. With the advent of the railroad, Florida attracted northern developers who advertised Florida as a "promised land full of adventure and dreams." (CM.)

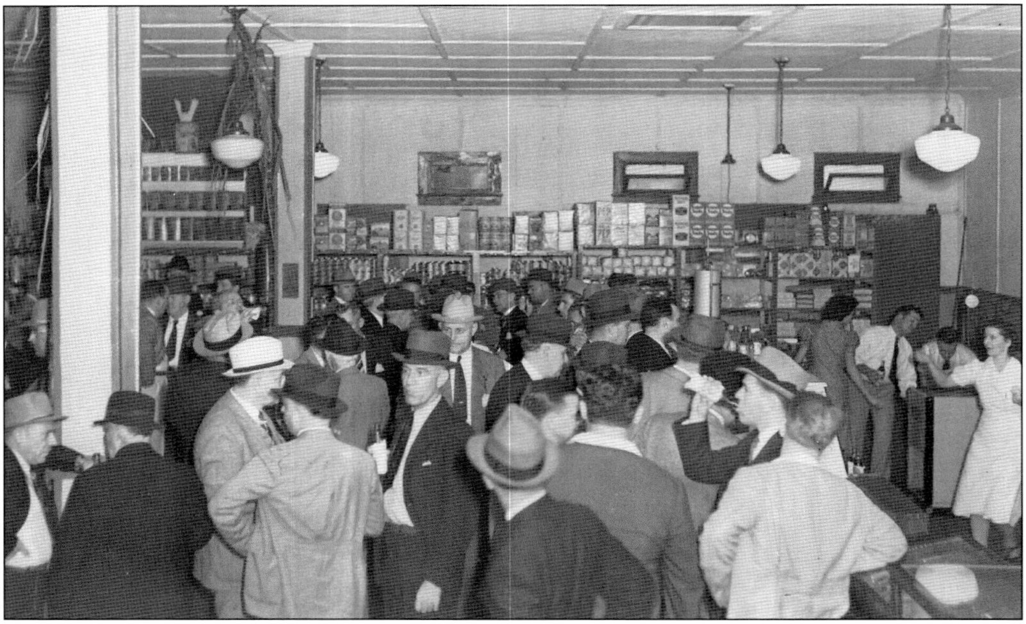

This party was held for U.S. Sugar executives in the early years of the company's history. Charles Mott, vice president of General Motors Corporation, purchased 60 percent of U.S. Sugar's stock. Another 10 percent of the stock was purchased by Clarence R. Bitting, a management expert and later chief executive officer. These two men organized the U.S. Sugar Corporation with land holdings in Glades, Hendry, and Palm Beach Counties. (CM.)

A sugarcane cutter is shown before automation of the harvest. The sugar program was unique in that it was the only USDA-controlled program that paid farmers a conditional payment to observe regulations set down by the U.S. Department of Agriculture. These regulations involved obeying established acreage quotas, observing wage rates, and employing no child labor. Funds to finance this program were generated by a tax on sugar; thus, the program paid for itself and returned a profit. (CM.)

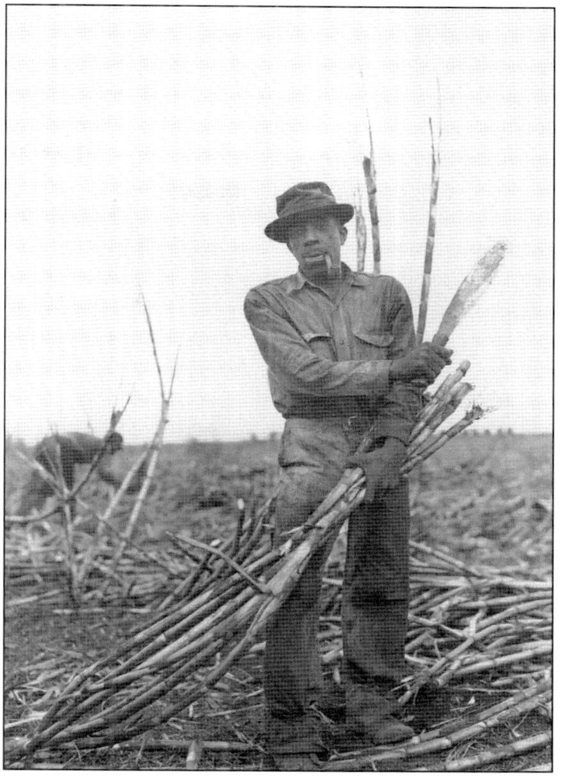

In this photograph of Shawnee farm workers, a woman is sorting the celery crop. Expansion of sugarcane growing had begun, and the U.S. Sugar Corporation took on some independent growers. In Glades County, these early independent growers were Roger M. Weeks, Click Farms, Inc., Moore Farms, J. E. Frierson, and Shawnee Farms. Most or all of the cane produced in Glades County at this time was in the Benbow area east of Moore Haven. (CM.)

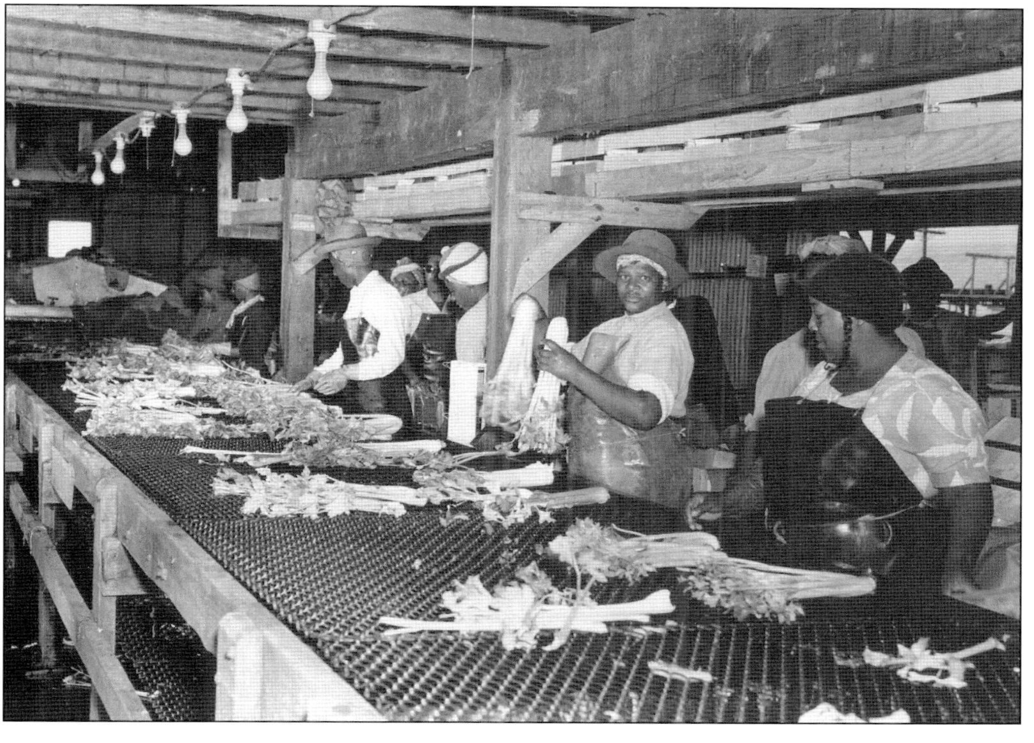

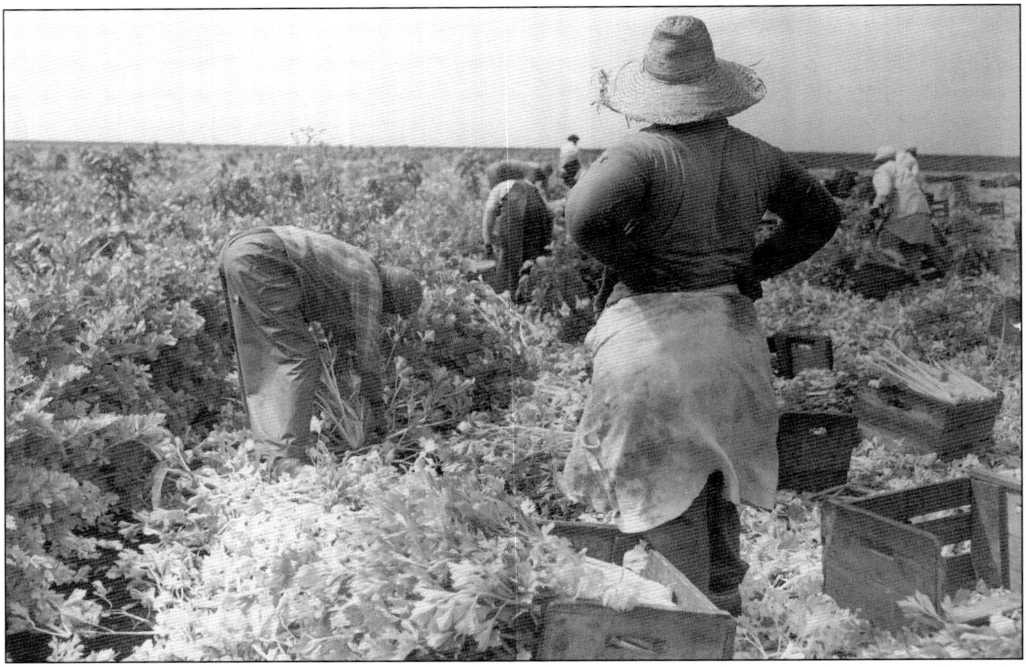

This scene shows farm workers picking celery in the field. Vegetable harvests occur mainly in the fall, winter, and spring in Florida's tropical climate. (CM.)

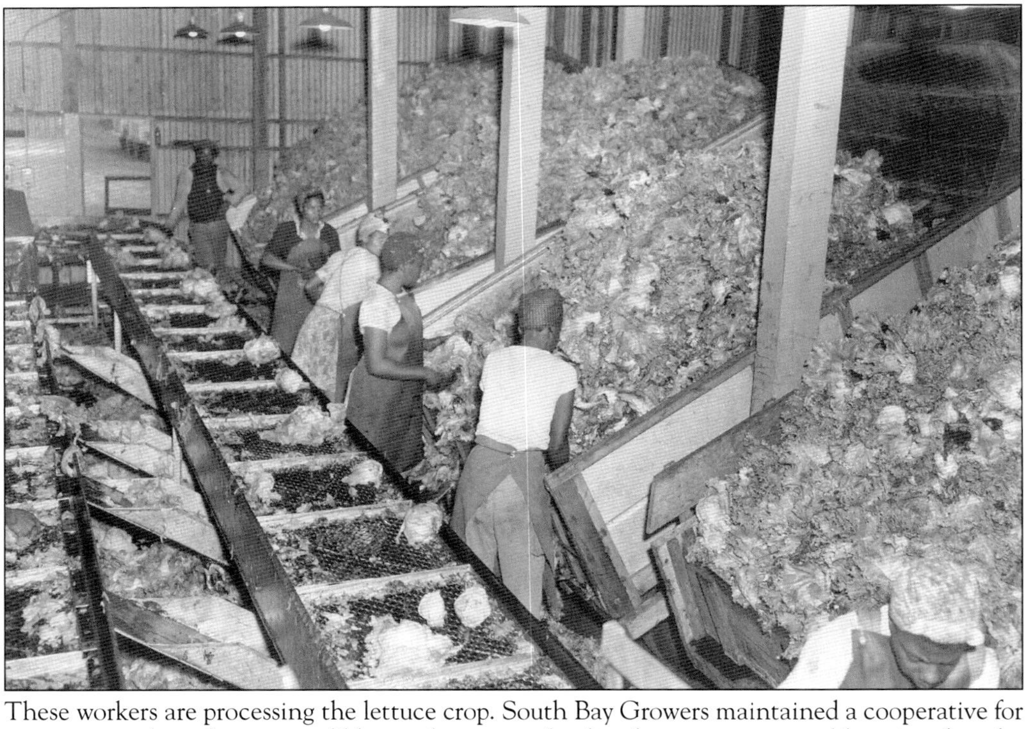

These workers are processing the lettuce crop. South Bay Growers maintained a cooperative for many years where farmers could bring their crops for distribution to a central location, but the facility is now closed. (CM.)

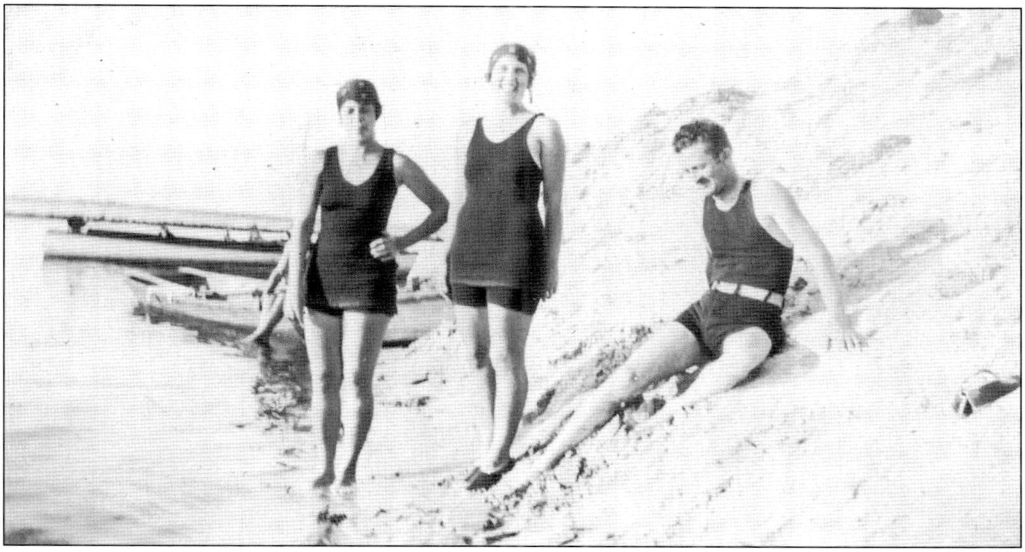

Bathing on the banks of Lake Okeechobee in 1926 are Charlotte (left), Lillian, and F. Deane Duff. A hole was dredged out of the sand in front of the Old Clewiston Inn. The resulting "Clewiston beach" was used for a swimming pool. (CM.)

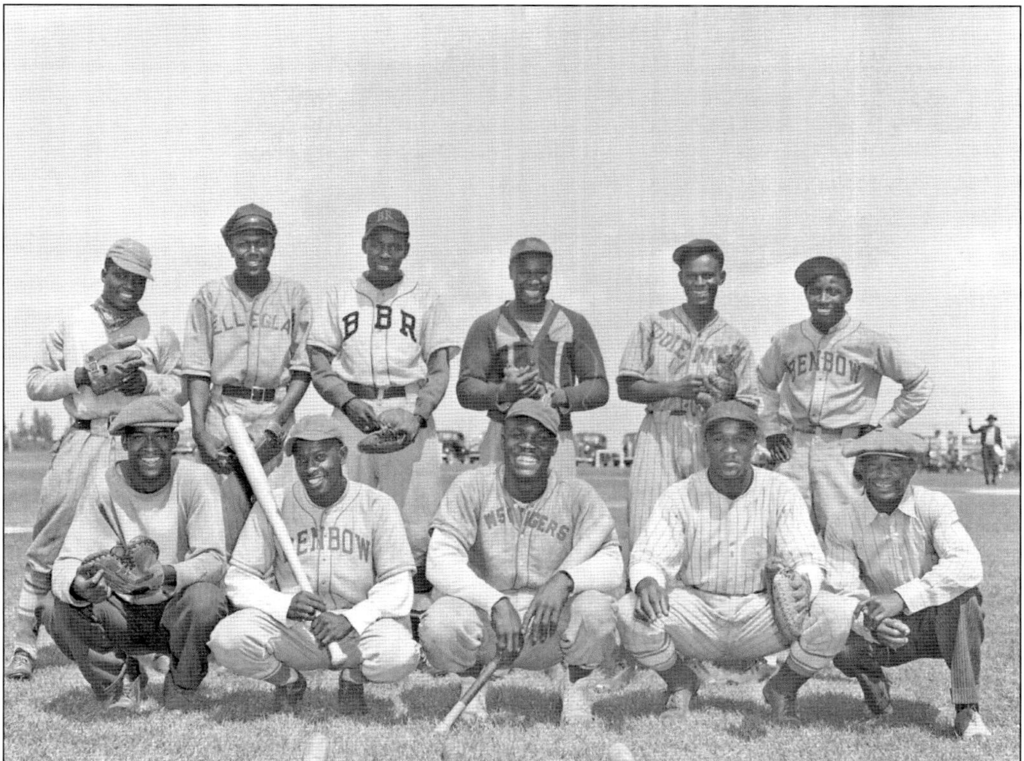

The Clewiston Tigers baseball team played teams from neighboring towns. Outdoor sports have always been popular in all the Glades communities around the lake. (CM.)

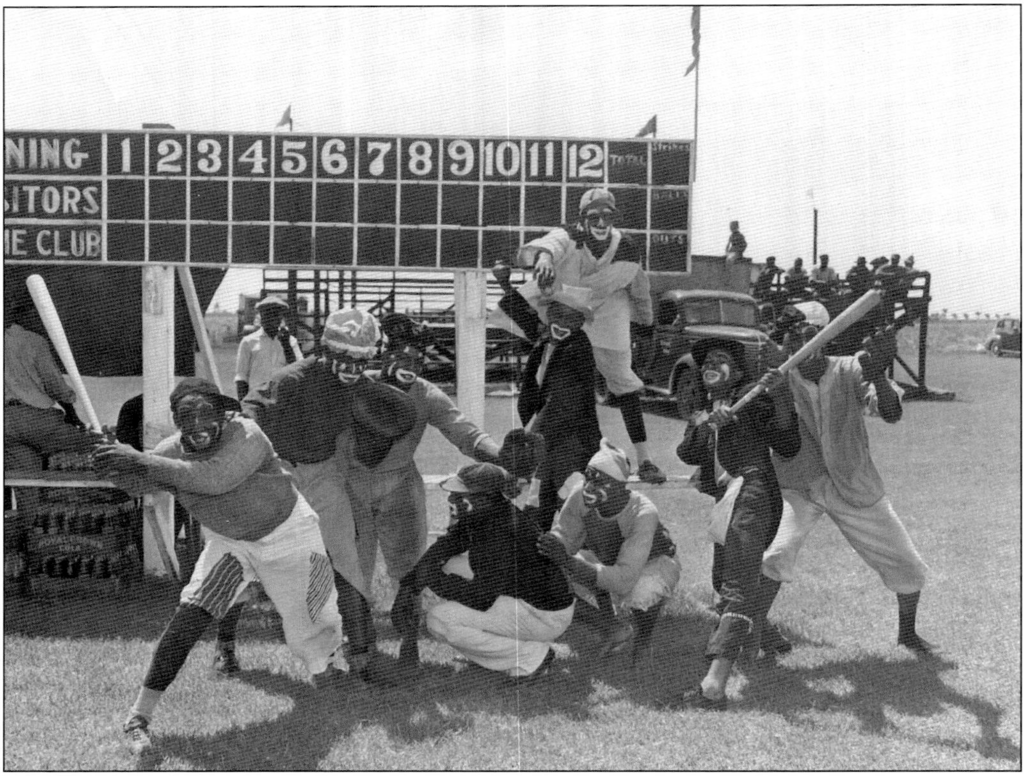

Belle Glade and Clewiston played sports events in friendly rivalry. Glades Central High School in Belle Glade has had more professional football players go on to the NFL than any other high school in the country. (CM.)

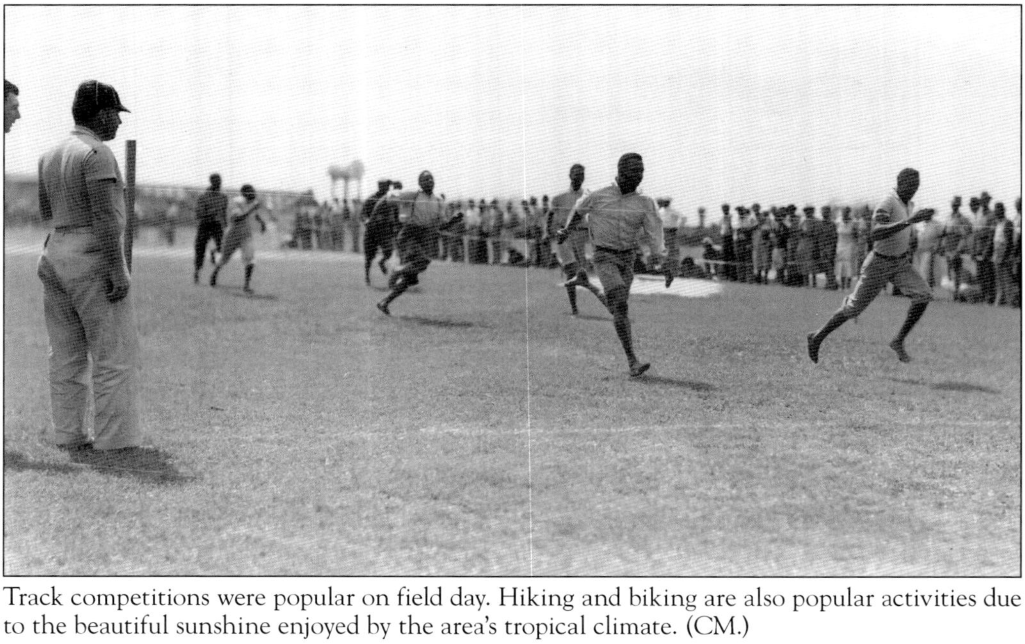

Track competitions were popular on field day. Hiking and biking are also popular activities due to the beautiful sunshine enjoyed by the area's tropical climate. (CM.)

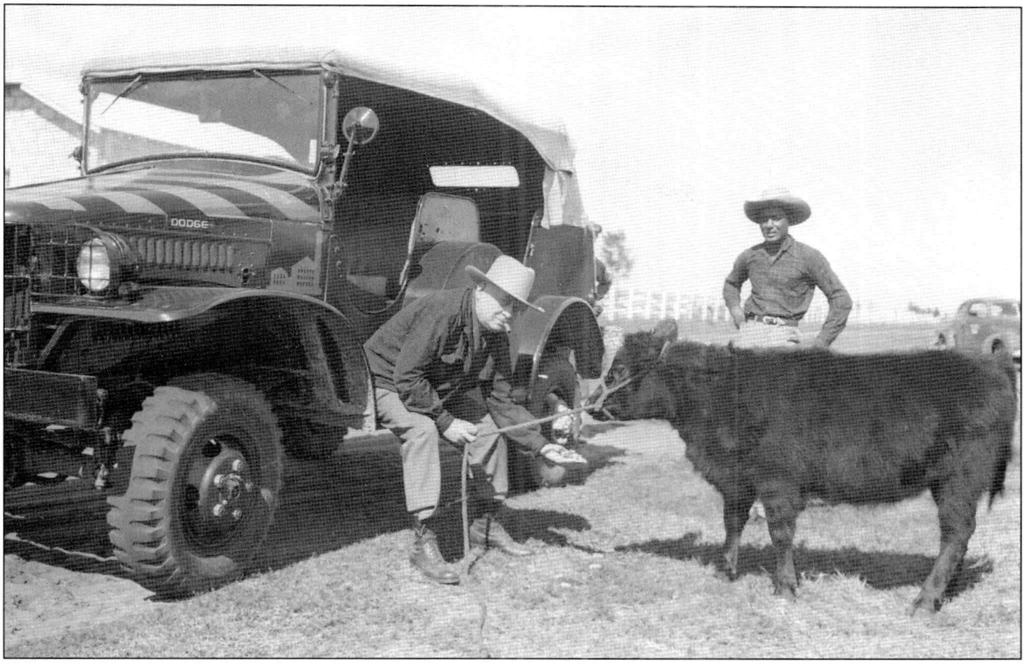

Clarence Bitting is shown making friends with a prized calf in Hendry County. Francis Asbury Hendry, called "the Cattle King of South Florida," moved with his family to the Caloosahatchee River valley to raise cattle after serving in the Confederate army during the Civil War. He sold cows to Cuba. Mixing purebred cows with his cattle, he slowly increased his herd to 50,000. Hendry named the town of LaBelle after his two daughters, Laura and Belle. In 1923, the state legislature named the county in his honor. (CM.)

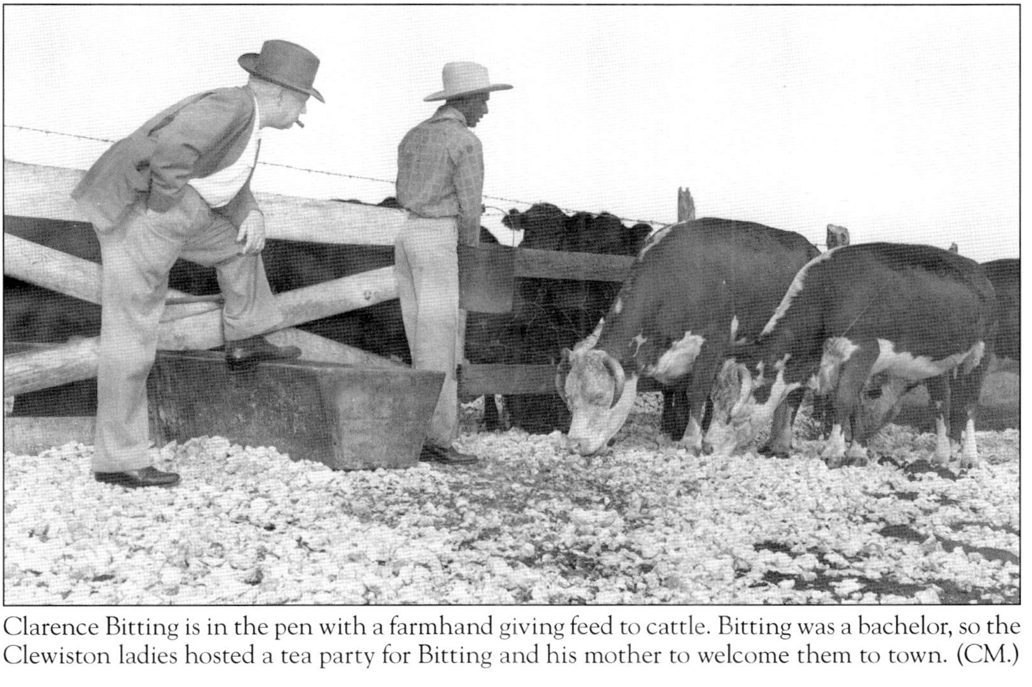

Clarence Bitting is in the pen with a farmhand giving feed to cattle. Bitting was a bachelor, so the Clewiston ladies hosted a tea party for Bitting and his mother to welcome them to town. (CM.)

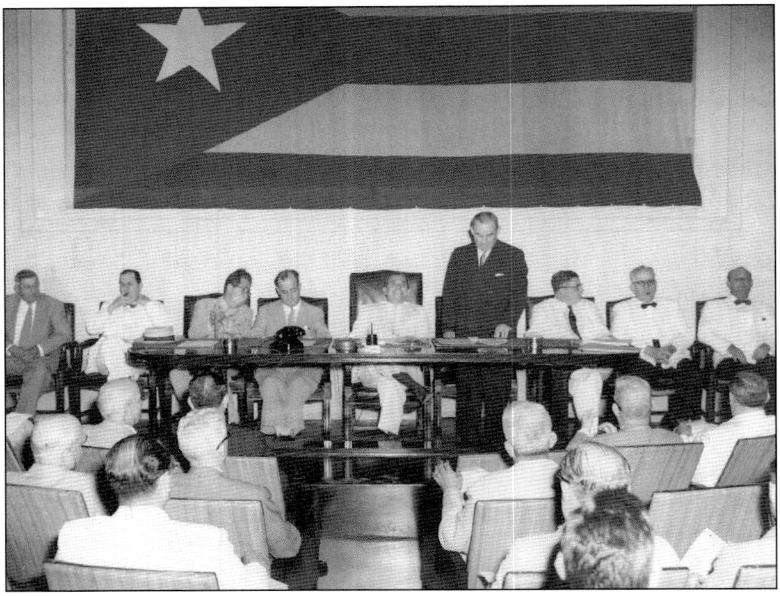

The U.S. Sugar delegation is pictured visiting Cuba. Percy G. Bishop came to Clewiston to serve as the operating vice president and mill superintendent of the Southern Sugar Company in the summer of 1928. He was previously vice president of the Cuba Cane Sugar Corporation. (CM.)

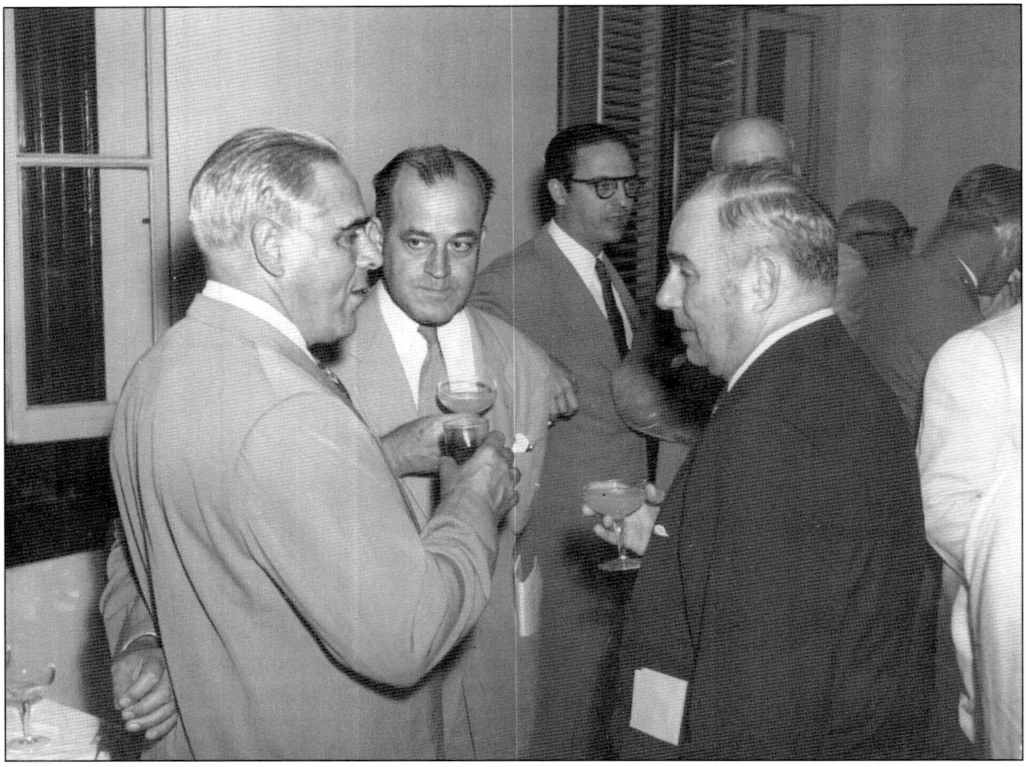

U.S. Sugar executives discuss business with Cuban plantation owners. Cuban president Fulgencio Batista bought and sold sugar to the United States. When Fidel Castro took over Cuba in 1959, many Americans lost their sugarcane holdings. (CM.)

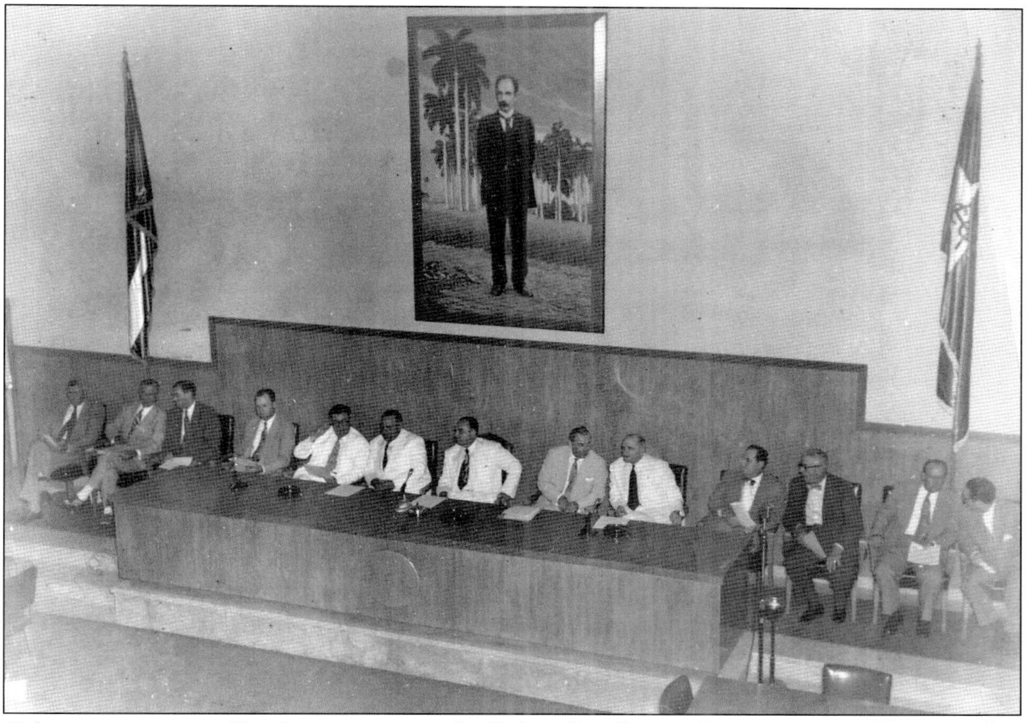

Cuban government officials meet prior to the Cuban Revolution. Sugarcane growers migrated to South Florida after Castro took command. One of the largest Florida growers is the Fanjul family, owner of Florida Crystals. (CM.)

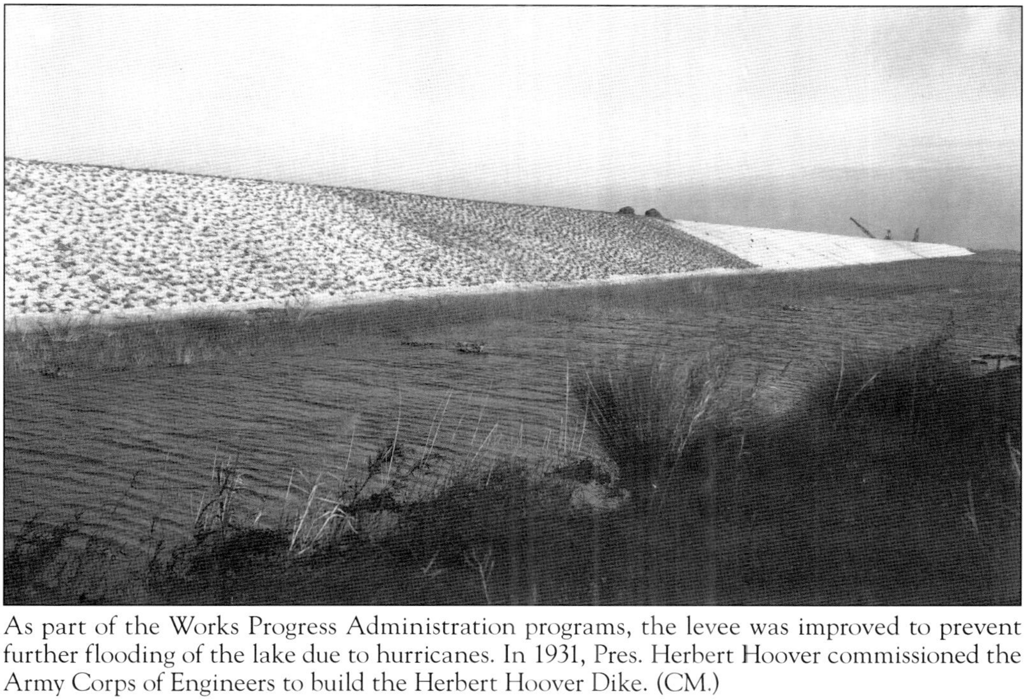

As part of the Works Progress Administration programs, the levee was improved to prevent further flooding of the lake due to hurricanes. In 1931, Pres. Herbert Hoover commissioned the Army Corps of Engineers to build the Herbert Hoover Dike. (CM.)

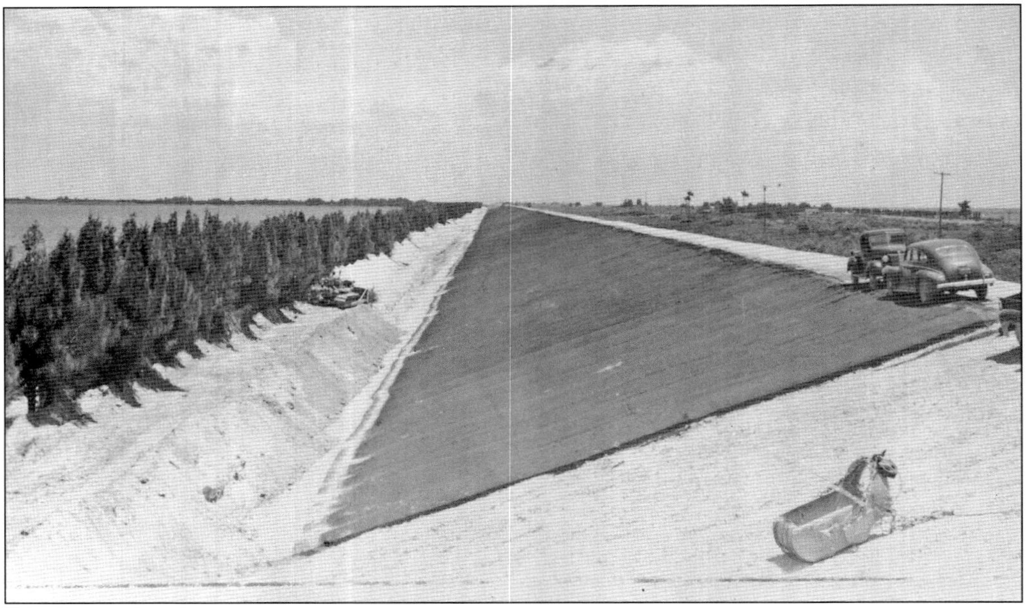

This photograph shows the completed Herbert Hoover Dike in 1933. Hoover was not reelected in 1932, mainly due to the Great Depression. (CM.)

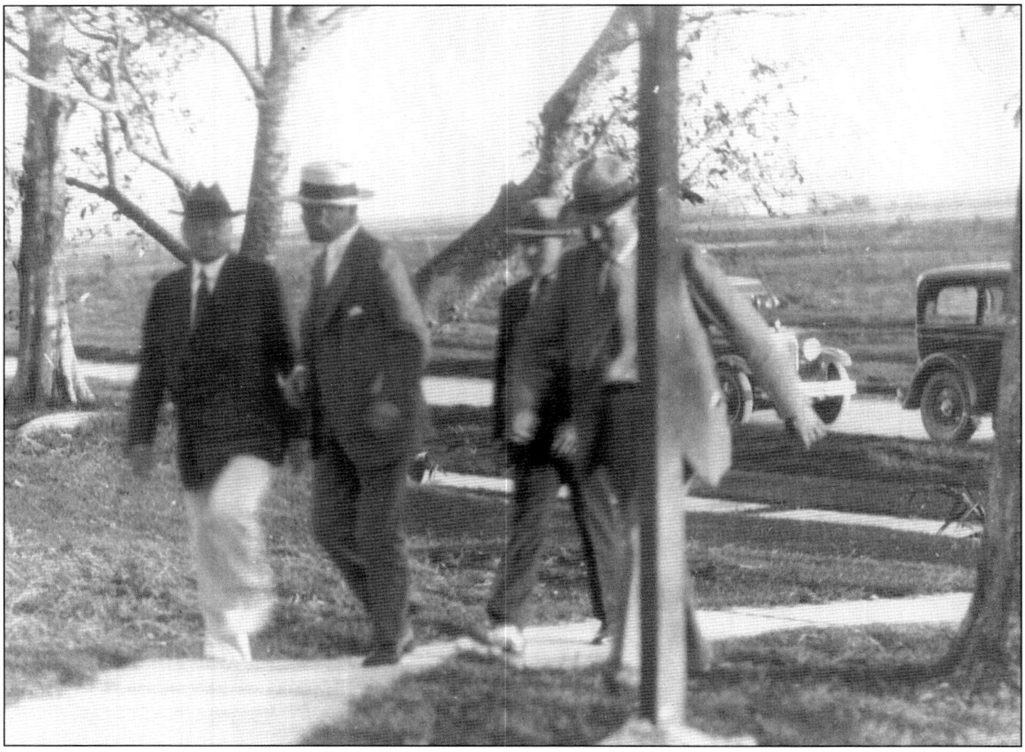

President-elect Herbert Hoover makes an overnight visit to Clewiston in January 1929. The historic Clewiston Inn was owned and operated by the U.S. Sugar Corporation until it was purchased by Yasser Kahn and Floyd Salkey in 2007. (CM.)

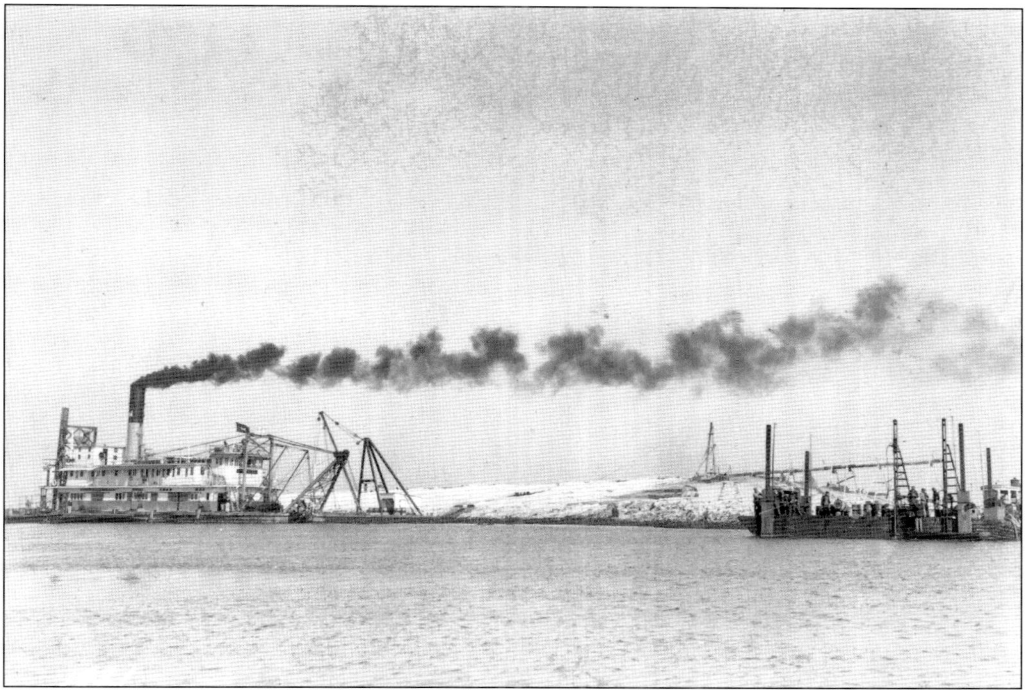

Construction in December 1934 is highlighted in this general view of the dredge called *Gulfport* and the levee. Continual maintenance of the lake is now under the jurisdiction of South Florida Water Management and the Army Corps of Engineers. (CM.)

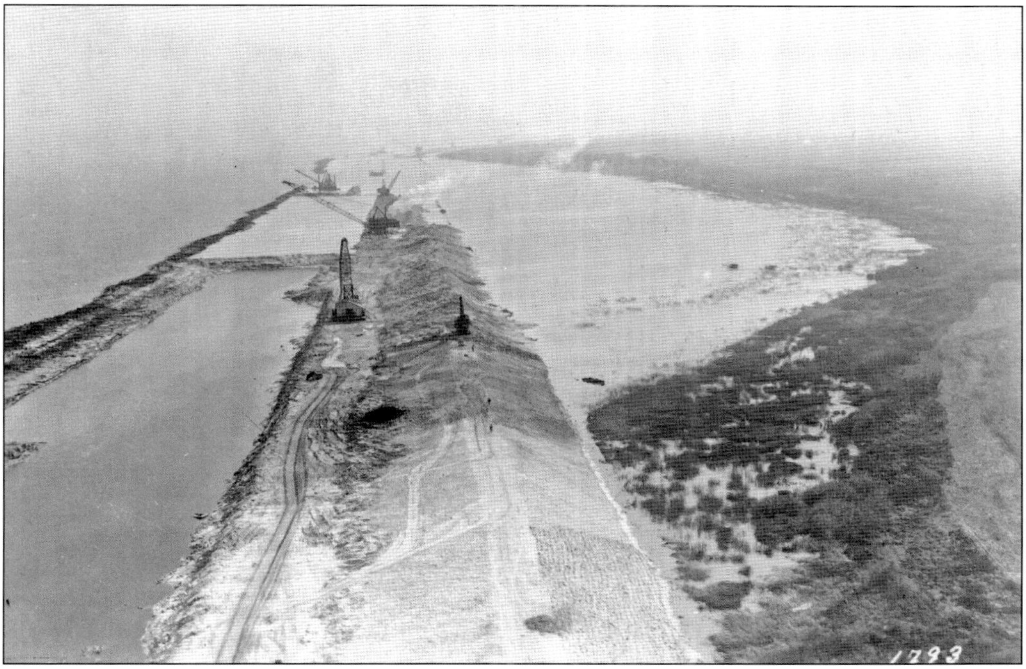

This is a view of the levee to the southeast of the lake in December 1934. Due to its shallow water, the lake fills up with vegetation. (CM.)

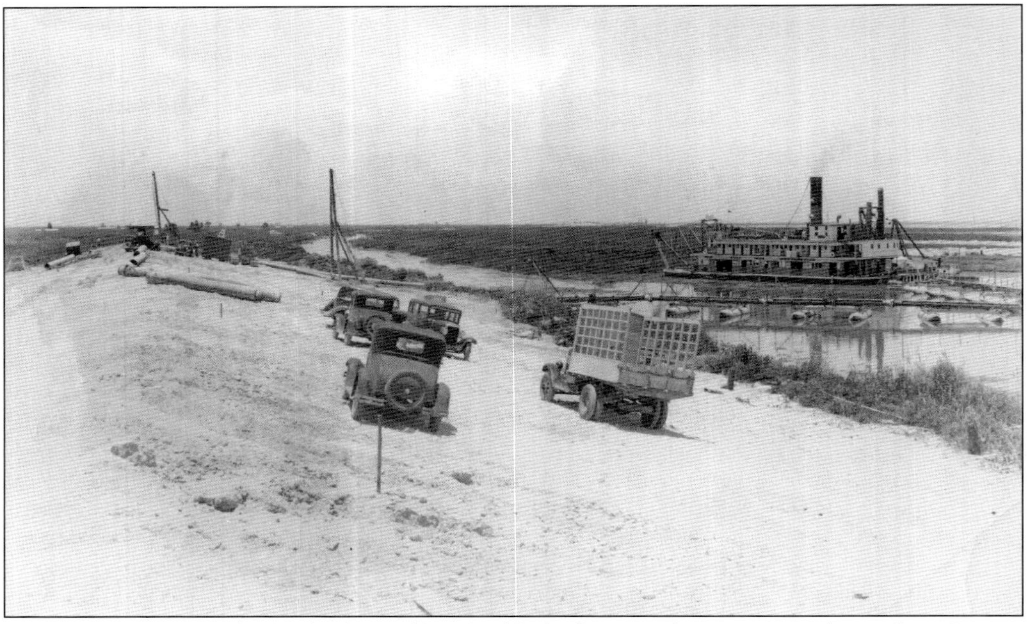

In this 1935 photograph, the dredge *Gulfport* builds the levee in the view to northwest from Station 712+50. Another dredge, the *General*, can be seen in the background at right center. (CM.)

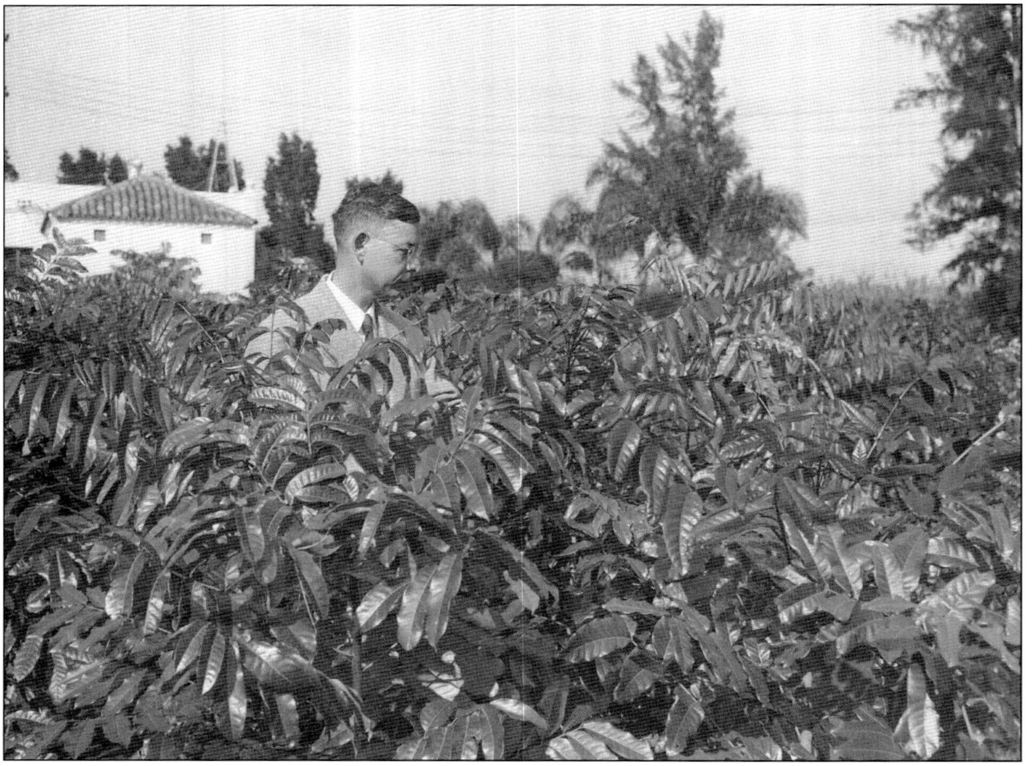

Dr. B. A. Bourne conducts scientific experiments at the Agricultural Research Station in Belle Glade. The University of Florida now runs this facility. (CM.)

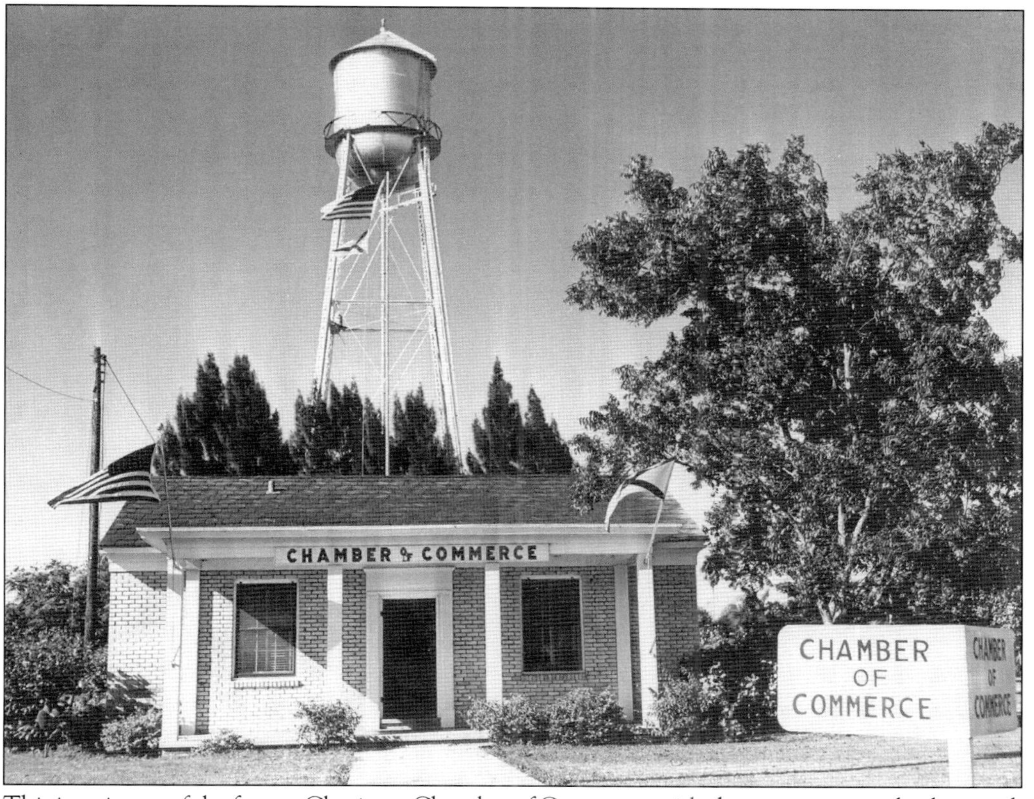

This is a picture of the former Clewiston Chamber of Commerce with the water tower in background. Today's chamber of commerce is housed in the Clewiston Museum. "Butch" Wilson, the museum director, has collected a vast assortment of memorabilia related to Clewiston's rich history. The colorful displays range from butterflies to mastodon tusks. (CM.)

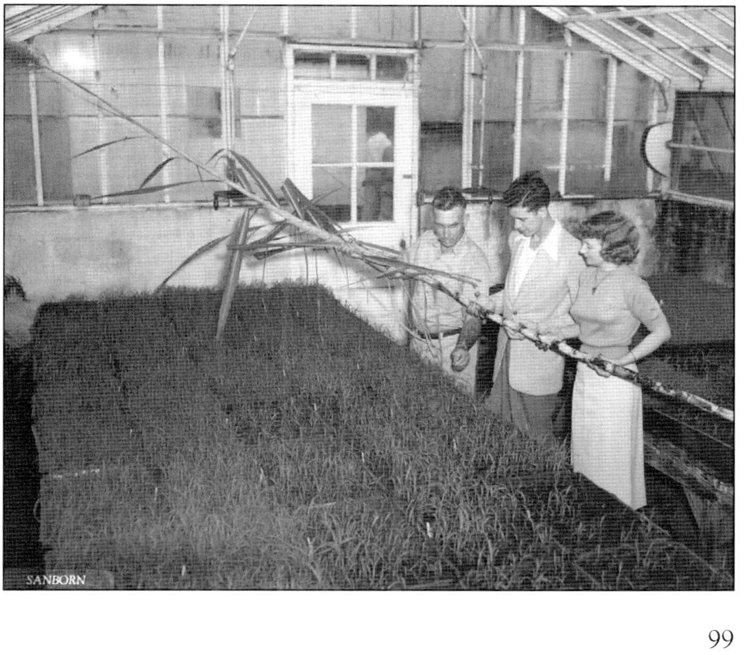

People are examining sugarcane varieties in this greenhouse. Geneticists constantly experiment to produce improved strains of sugarcane. (CM.)

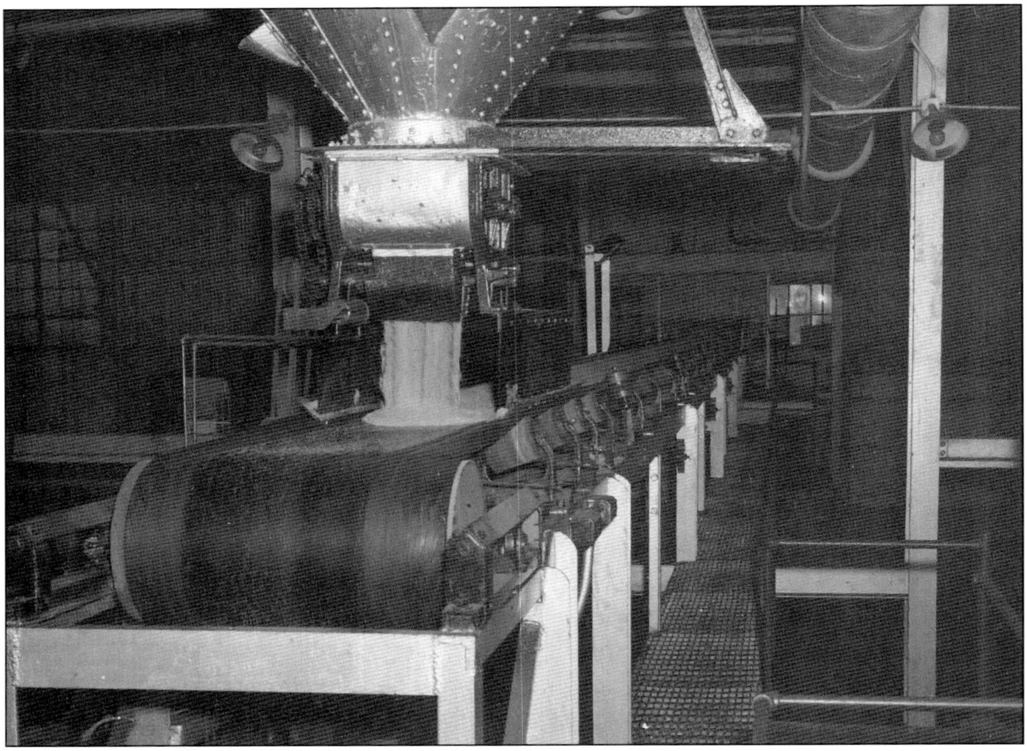

This large structure is the U.S. Sugar refinery plant. A $160-million renovation took place in 2008, and the plant facility was automated and upgraded. (CM.)

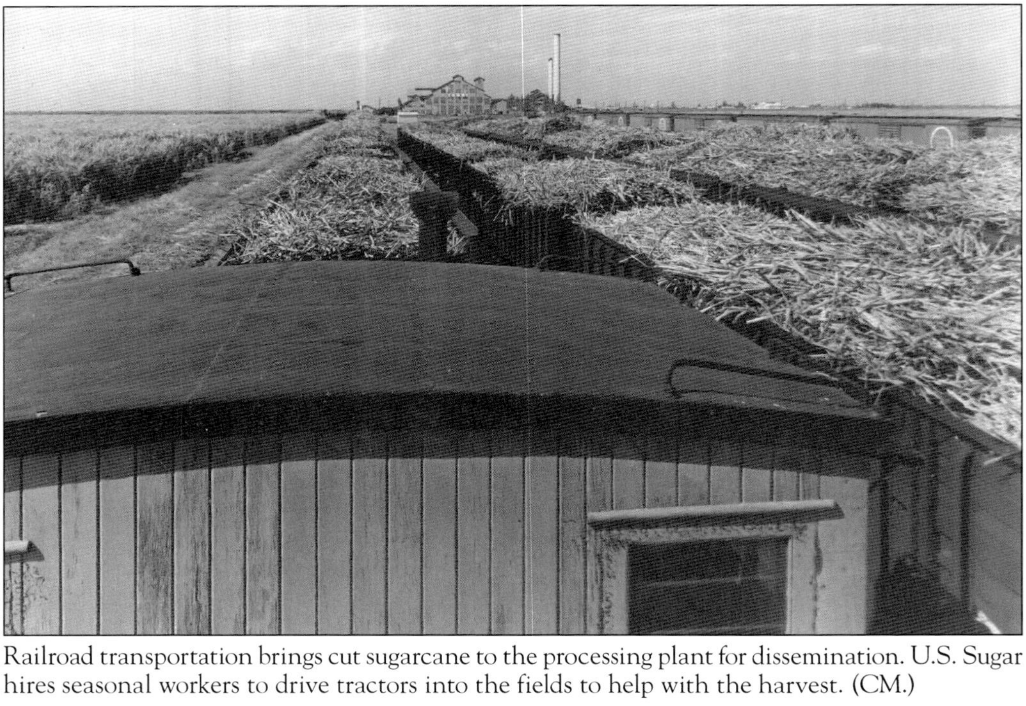

Railroad transportation brings cut sugarcane to the processing plant for dissemination. U.S. Sugar hires seasonal workers to drive tractors into the fields to help with the harvest. (CM.)

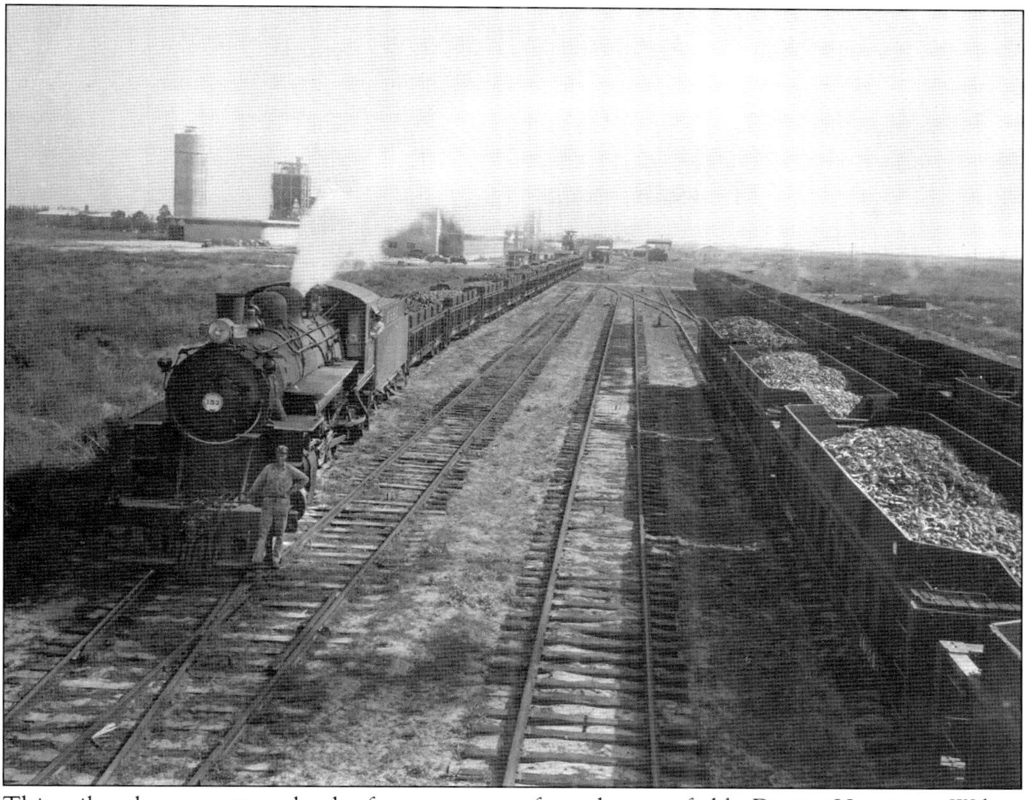

This railroad transports carloads of raw sugarcane from the cane fields. During Hurricane Wilma in 2005, two railroad engines, weighing several tons each, were blown along the tracks by the force of the storm. (CM.)

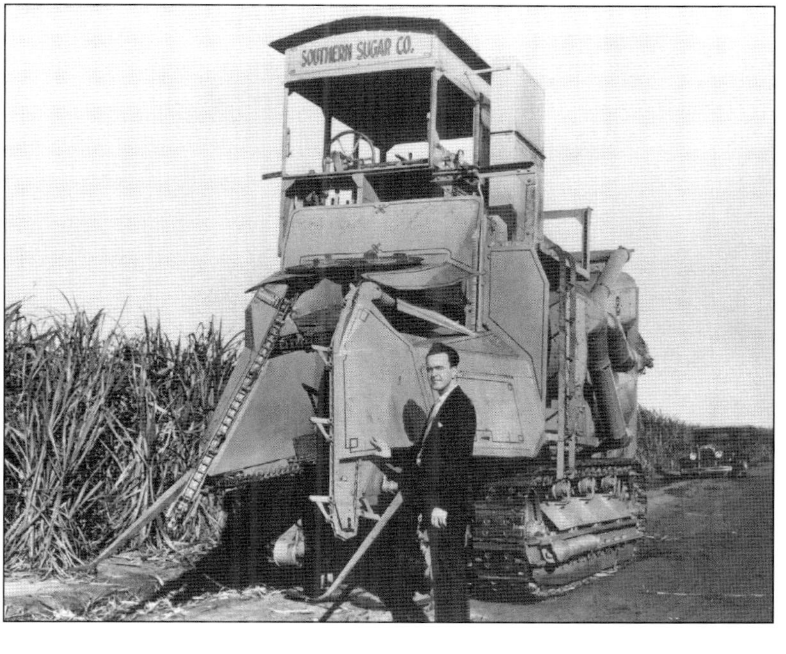

Field mechanics are constantly called upon to keep the farm machinery working. This picture shows an early cane harvester. Cranes are often used to extract tractors from canals or muck where they become stuck when rainy conditions prevail. (CM.)

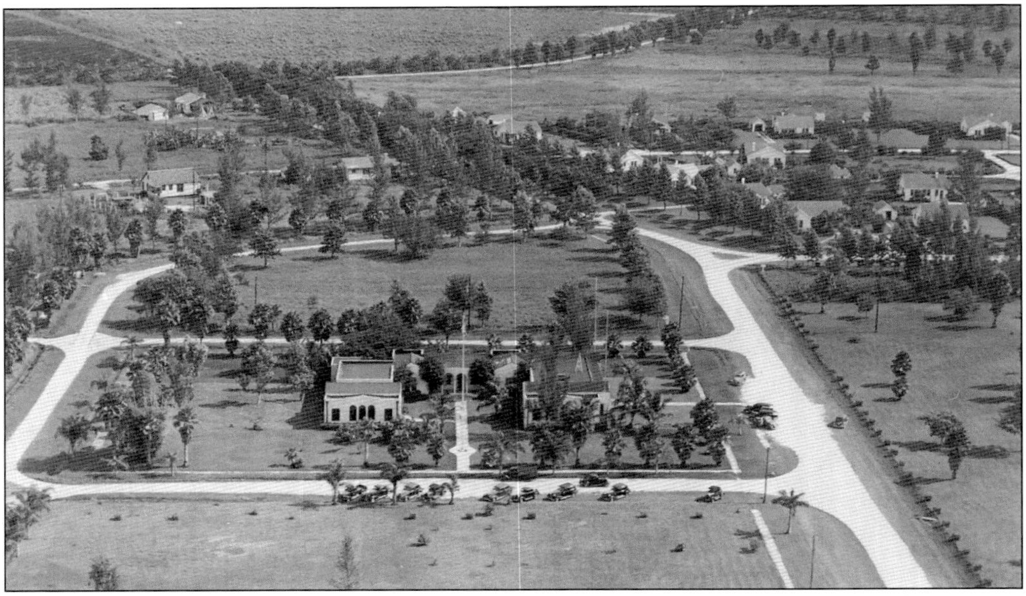

The lake area around the U.S. Sugar Corporation is one of the top 10 birding sites in the country, home to more than 300 species. The Audubon Society conducts lectures and field trips along with the Big "O" Birding Festival, which is held annually in Moore Haven or Clewiston for bird enthusiasts from around the country. Larry Lucky, a Glades County property appraiser, leads an "owl hoot." Many egrets, herons, limpkins, brown pelicans, anhingas, hawks, and great horned owls flourish in the marshy swamps around the lake. Exotic species such as the fulvous whistling duck and the mottled duck, the black-necked stilt, the roseate spoonbill, woodstork, least bittern, crested caracara, snail kite, short-tailed hawk, and barn owl can be spotted fishing or nesting. Five Great Florida Birding Trail sites are within the region. Stormwater Treatment Area No. 5 (STA5) and the Dinner Island Ranch and Okaloacoochee Slough State Forest and Wildlife Management Areas are in Hendry County. Fisheating Creek East and West Wildlife Management Areas are in Glades County. (CM.)

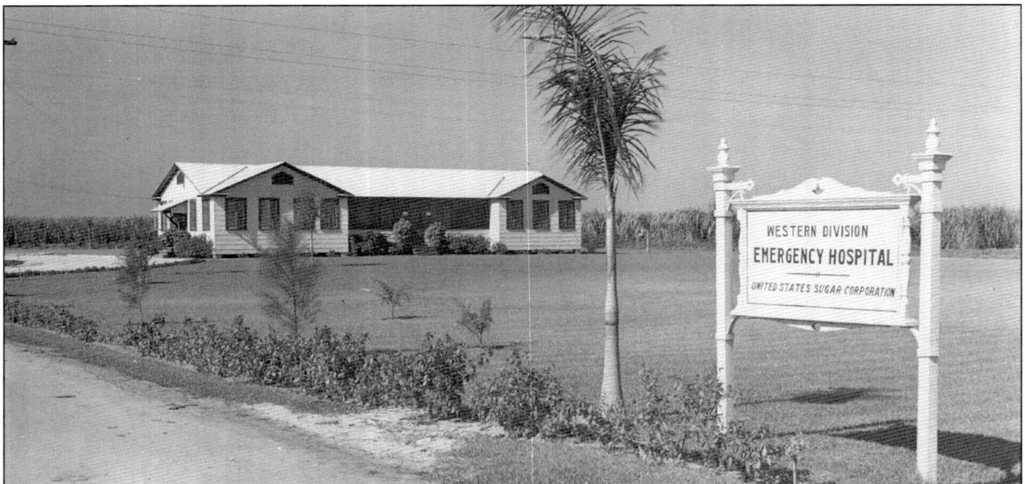

Medical care was provided by the Western Division Emergency Hospital. Similar medical facilities were provided in the Eastern Division. (CM.)

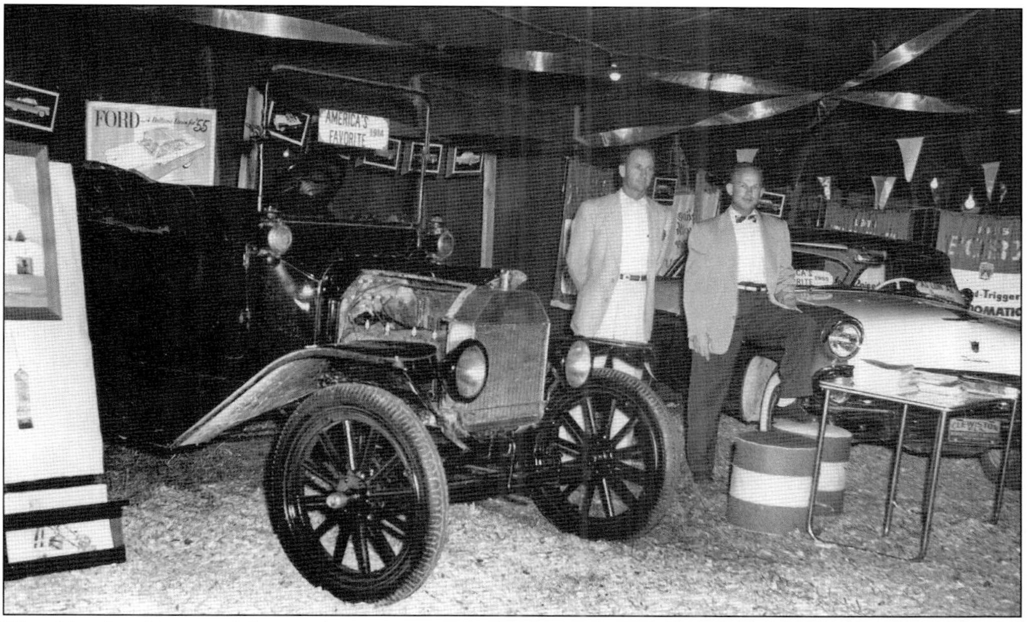

The Hendry County Motors showroom is showcasing the newest Ford model in 1955. The new model, at right, is compared with the always-popular Model T from 1914. (CM.)

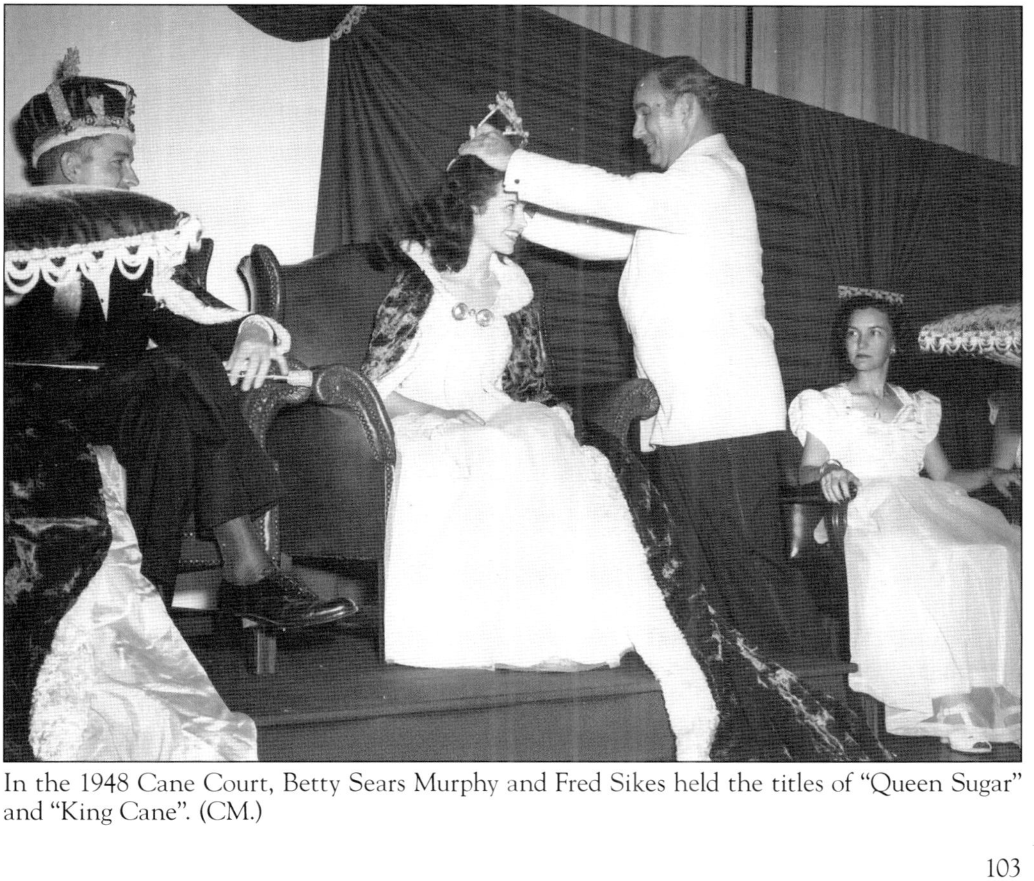

In the 1948 Cane Court, Betty Sears Murphy and Fred Sikes held the titles of "Queen Sugar" and "King Cane". (CM.)

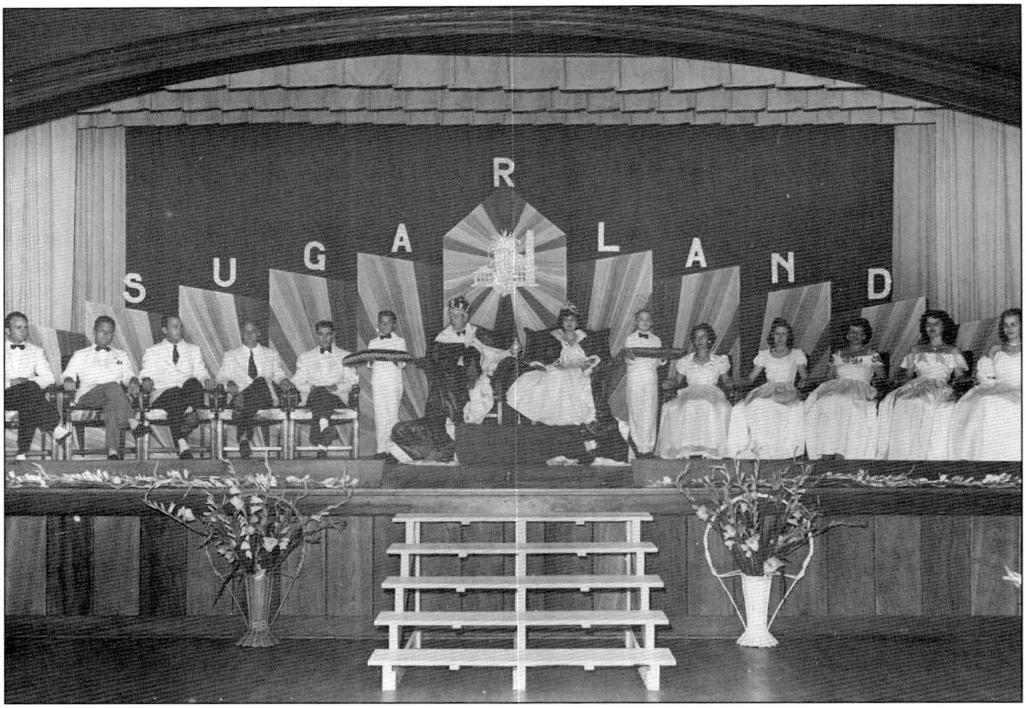

In the 1948 Cane Court, the princes were, from left to right, James Brannon, Clyde Egley, Earl Maxon, Frank Mueller, Frank Rodriguez, and Nick Schiffli; the princesses were, from left to right, Barbara Devane Hammock, Ann Morrison, Irene Shackford, Joan Walker Hooker, Lily Merle Waldron, and Mary Ruth Wilson. (CM.)

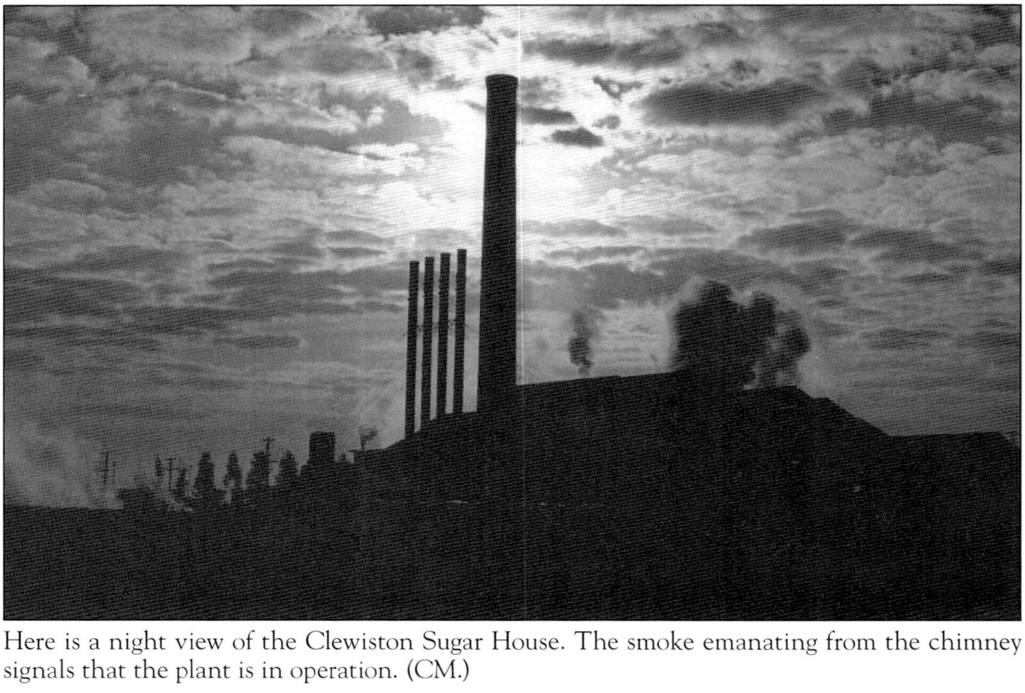

Here is a night view of the Clewiston Sugar House. The smoke emanating from the chimney signals that the plant is in operation. (CM.)

Eight

Prisoners, Planes, and Prize Catches

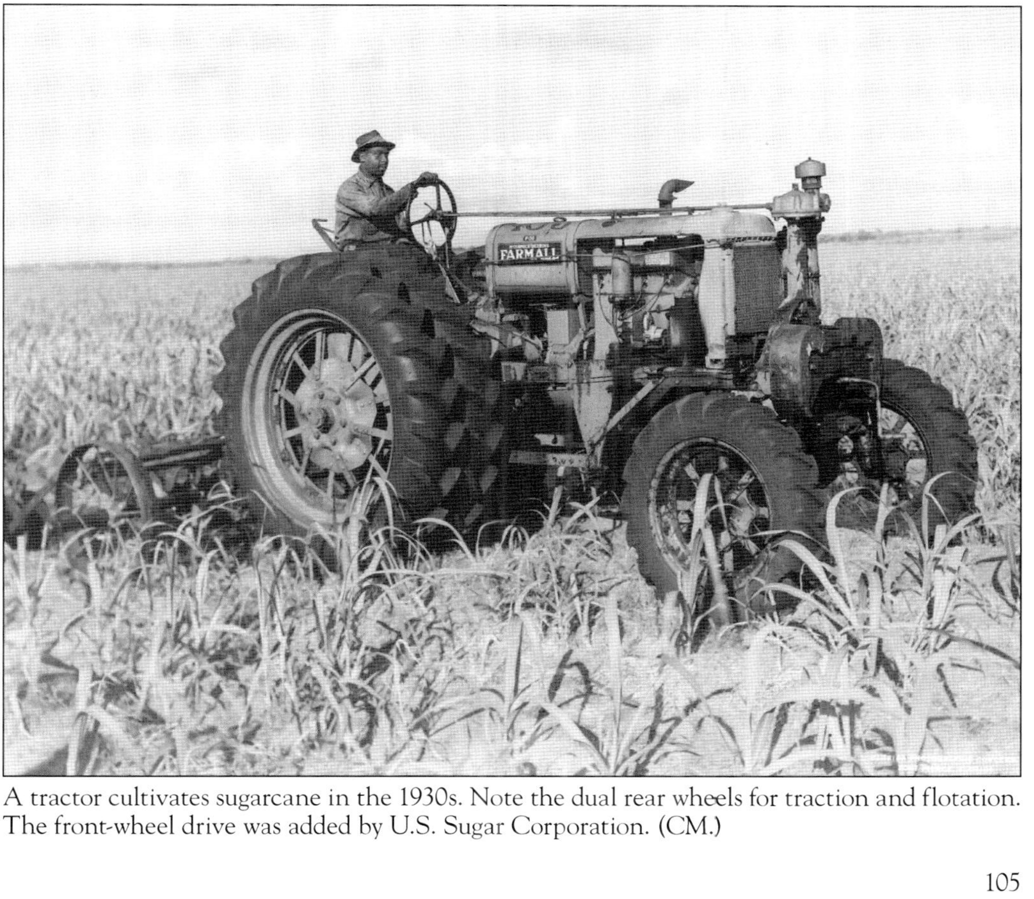

A tractor cultivates sugarcane in the 1930s. Note the dual rear wheels for traction and flotation. The front-wheel drive was added by U.S. Sugar Corporation. (CM.)

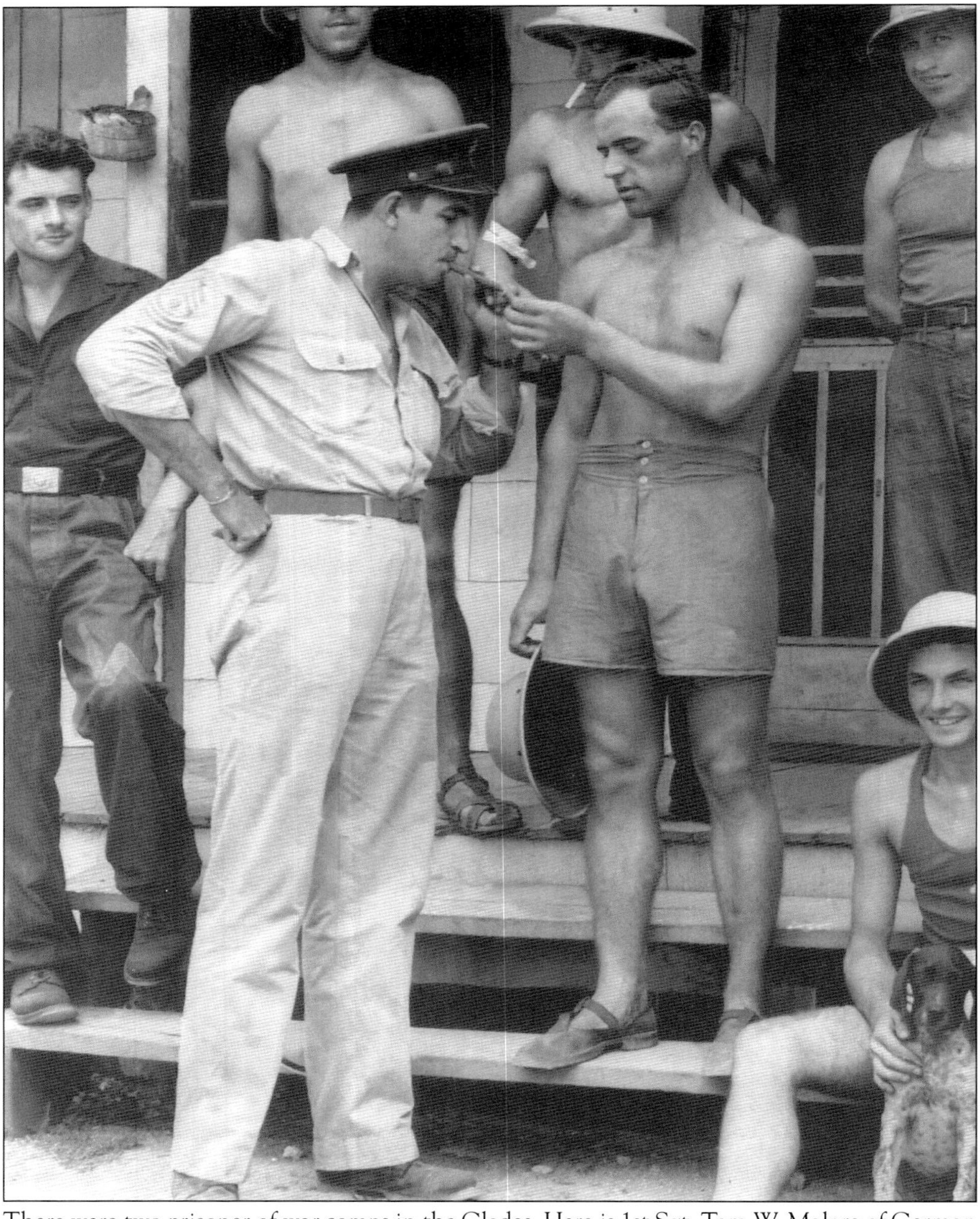

There were two prisoner-of-war camps in the Glades. Here is 1st Sgt. Tom W. Malore of German Prisoners of War Camp at Liberty Point in 1944. One camp was in Belle Glade, and the other was in Clewiston near Uncle Joe's fishing camp. Some of the prisoners were artists. They passed their time by decorating the walls of their barracks. These murals were lost when the POW camp was torn down. (CM.)

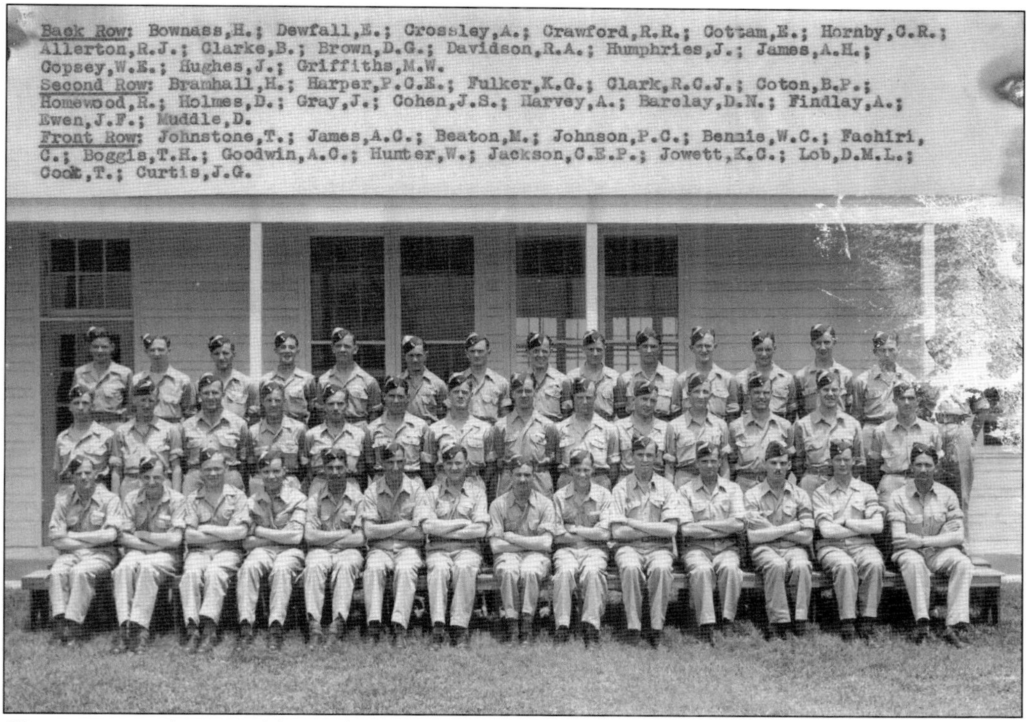

Clewiston was the site of the Embry-Riddle School of Aviation. This World War II school was set up to train fighter pilots from England and the United States in Florida and Tennessee. (CM.)

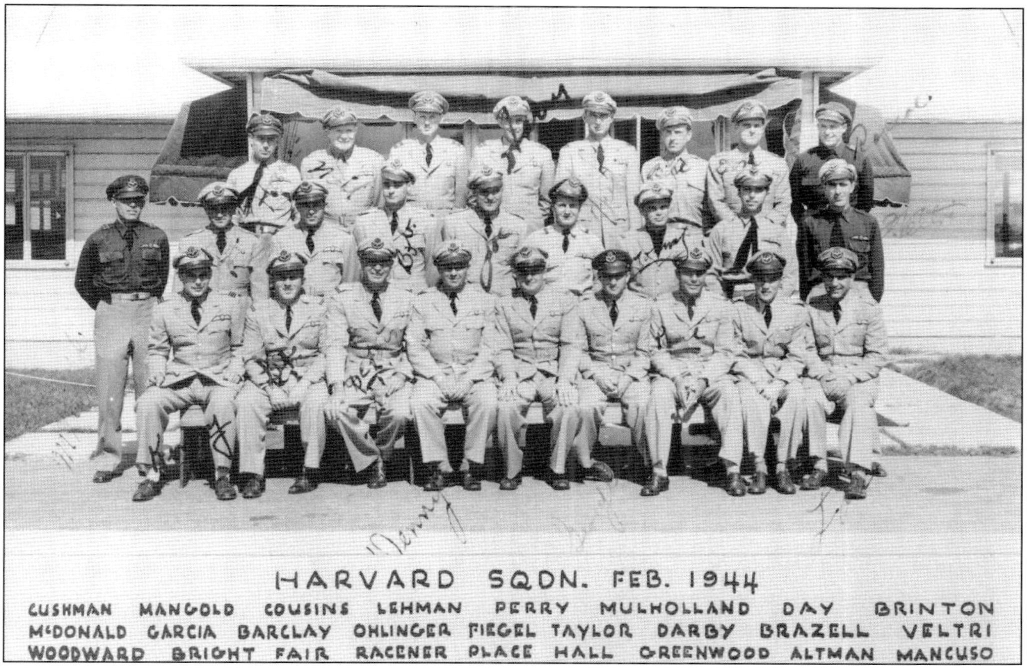

This World War II U.S. Air Force unit photograph of Harvard Squadron was taken in February 1944. Airmen practiced in South Florida and were then shipped overseas. (CM.)

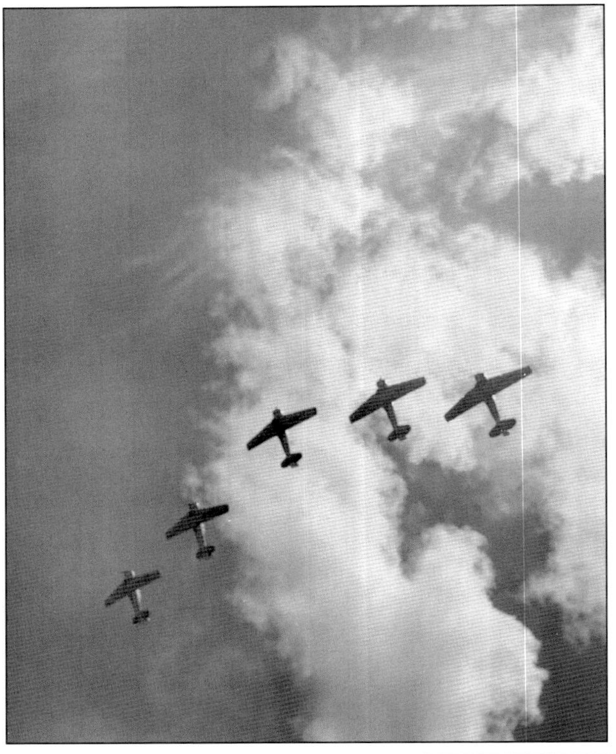

This airplane formation is seen flying over Riddle Field. Paul Riddle formed flying academies to train airmen from England and the United States for World War II. One of these was in Clewiston and another was in Arcadia. Walter Vaughn, whose father, Harry Vaughn, built the Clewiston Library while president of U.S. Sugar, remembers playing in a music concert when he was a child for the benefit of these airmen. (CM.)

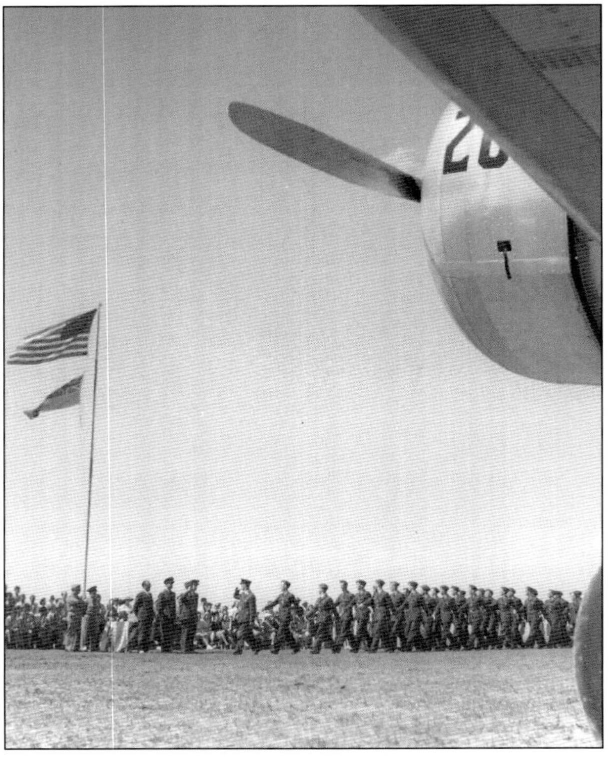

These Royal Air Force troops and U.S. trainers were stationed at Riddle field. Reunions are held in Clewiston for the soldiers who served here during World War II. (CM.)

This portrait of G. W. Tyson, commander of Riddle Field, was obtained from a book of photographs donated by Larry and Jean Tyson of Corona del Mar, California. The book was given to the family after the death of G. Willis Tyson on August 19, 1943, by the Riddle-McKay Aero College. Larry and Jean presented the book to the Clewiston Museum in person on March 26, 1990. (CM.)

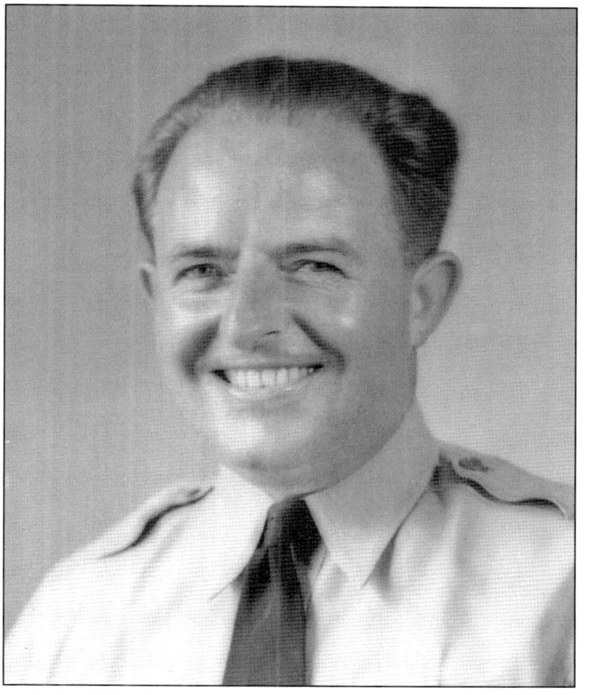

Sen. Claude Pepper led this late-1940s congressional farm tour from Miami to the U.S. Sugar Corporation. (CM.)

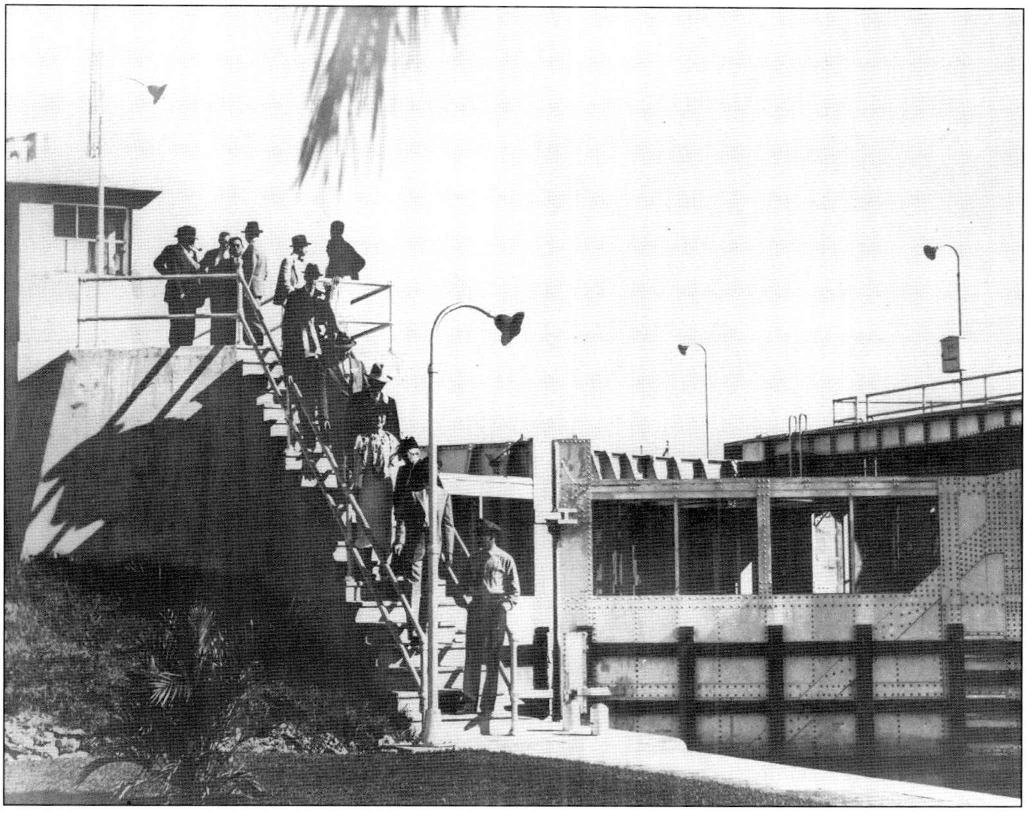

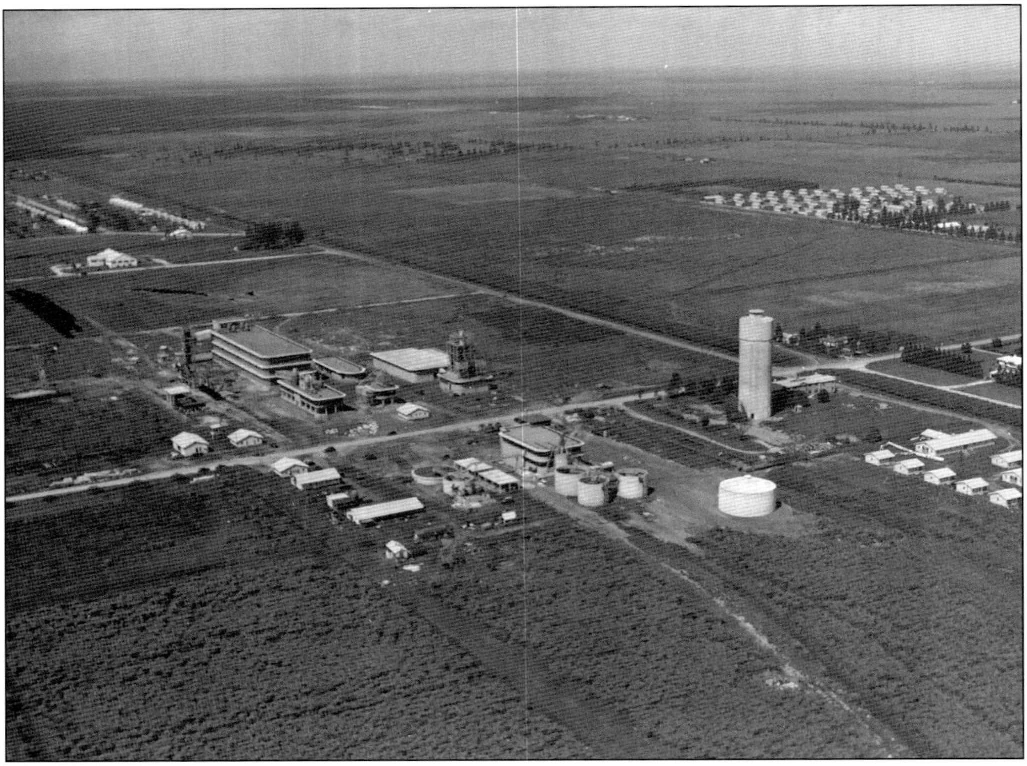

This is another aerial view of U.S. Sugar Corporation. The nickname "America's Sweetest Town" is derived from Clewiston being the company's headquarters. (CM.)

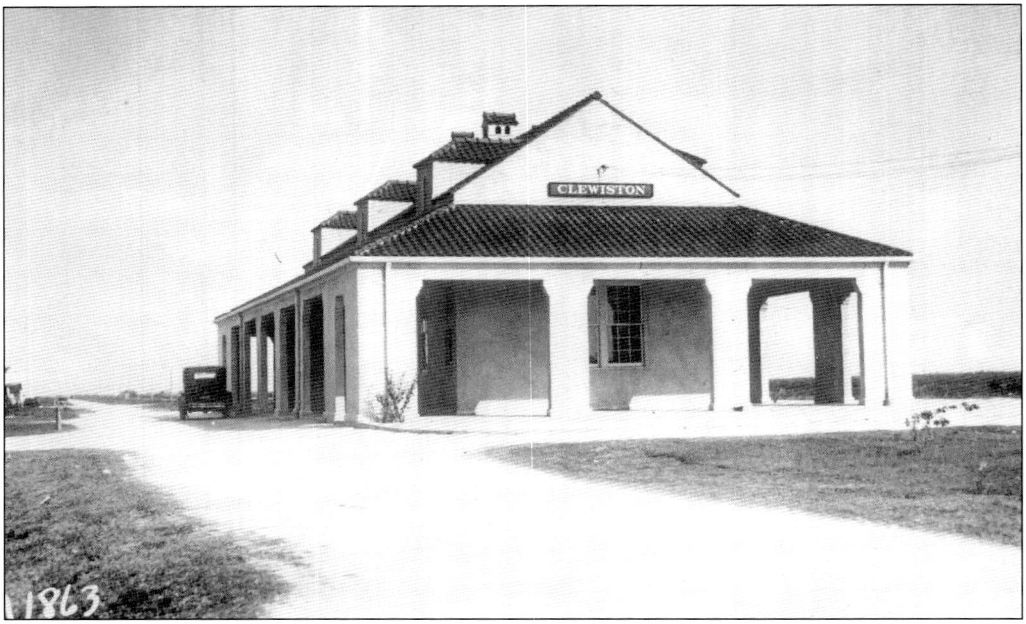

The Clewiston railroad station is shown here. In 1920, this building was the train depot for the Atlantic Coast Line Railroad Company. It has since been torn down. (FMP.)

Lake Okeechobee catches are held up by Coach Ferrari, a Clewiston High School physical education teacher. Both commercial and recreational fishing were important parts of the local economy and still draw sportsmen and women to the area. (CM)

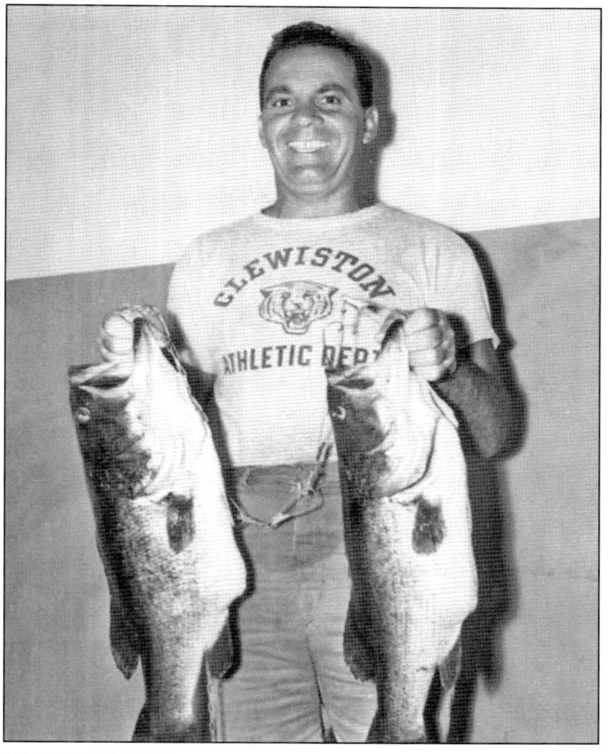

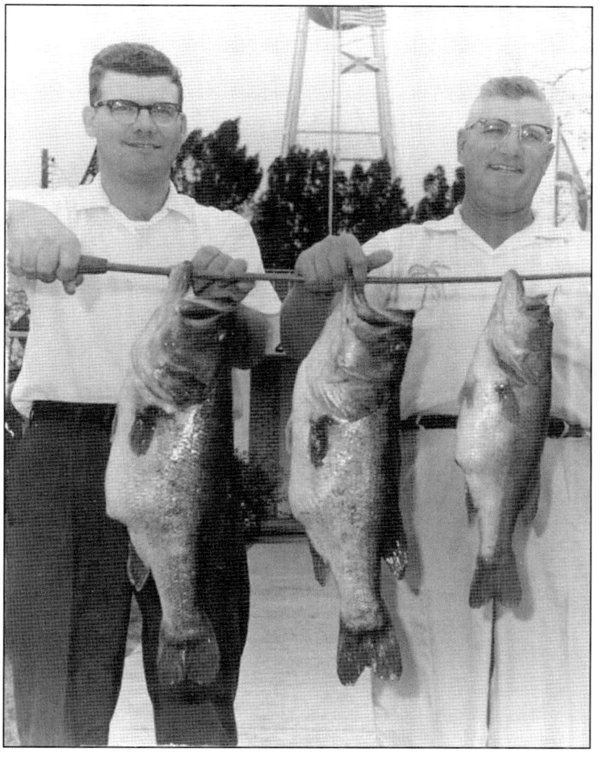

Fish camps still abound in the towns around Lake Okeechobee, such as Johnson's Fish Camp, shown here. Both commercial and recreational fishing were important parts of the local economy. Sportfishing continues to attract men and women to this scenic area today. (CM.)

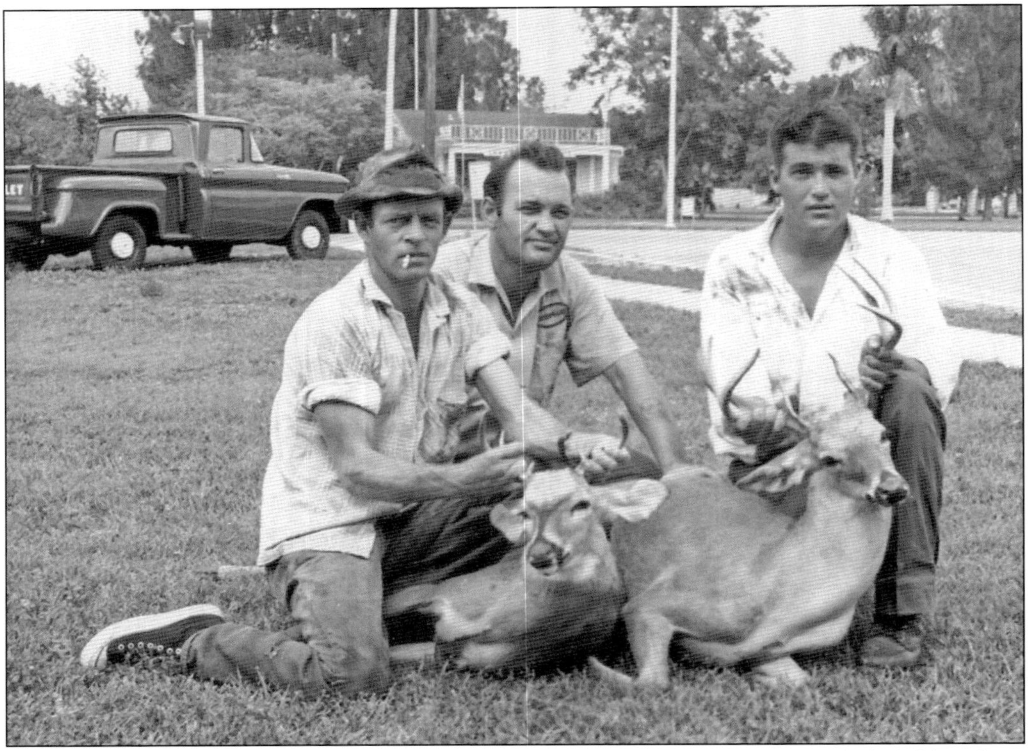

Local hunters can track buck, wild turkeys, duck, game, and wild boar in the lush fields. These hunters show off their catch near the present-day Clewiston Museum. The old chamber of commerce building is in the background. (CM.)

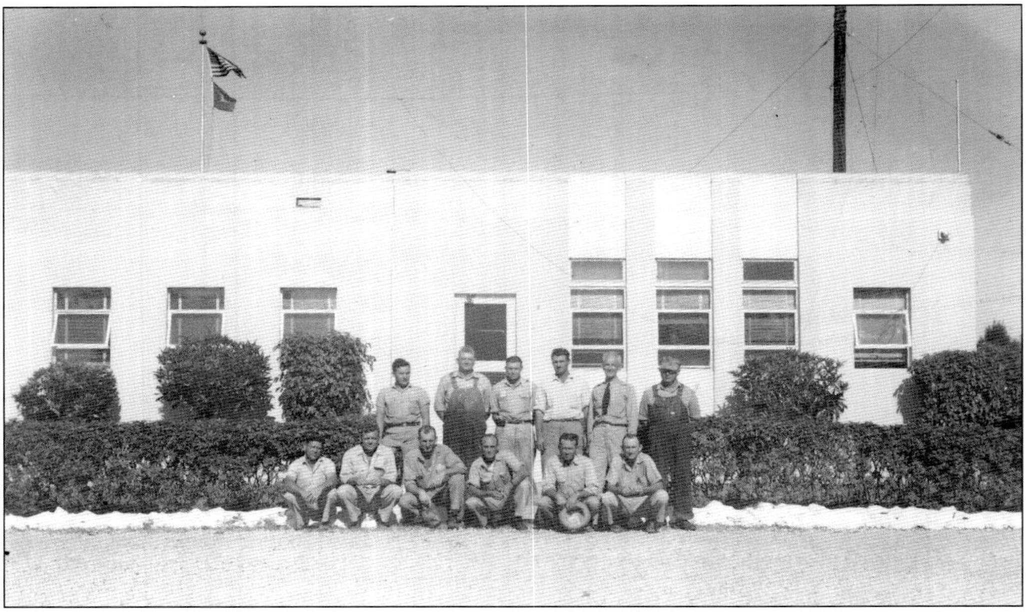

This Army Corps of Engineers photograph, taken on April 18, 1946, shows personnel from the Clewiston sub-office next to Rudd's Fish Store on Route 27, Sugarland Highway. (CM.)

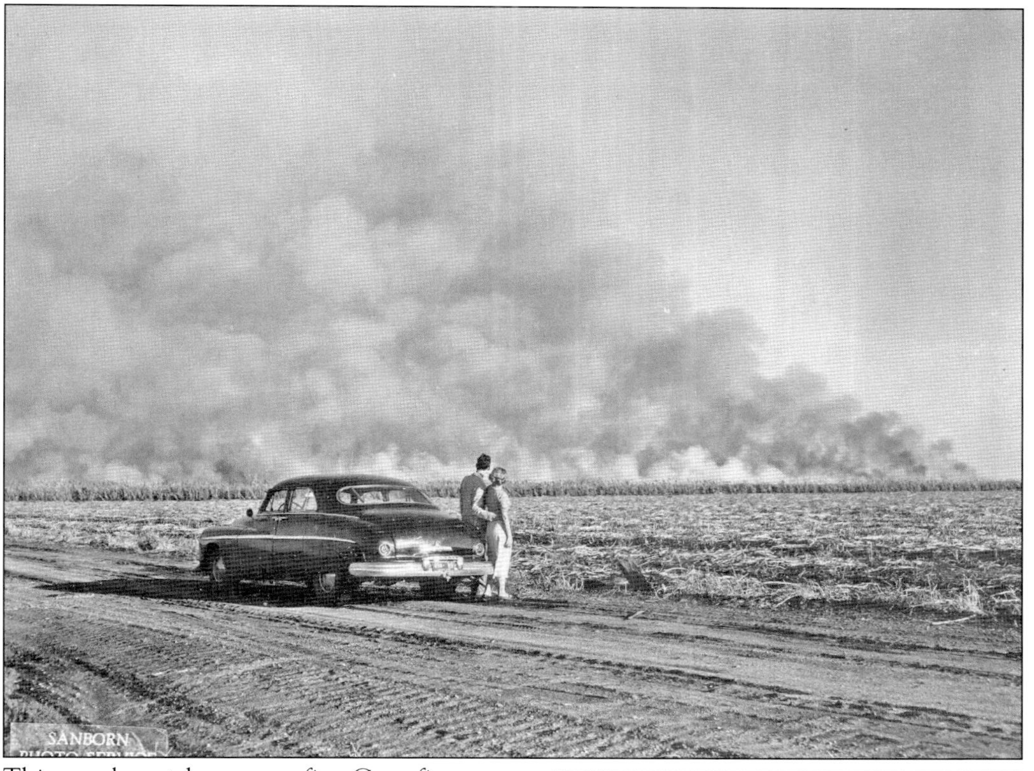

This couple watches a cane fire. Cane fires are set in a controlled burn to make harvesting the sugarcane more efficient, as burning the dried cane leaves boosts the quality and quantity of the sugar and makes harvesting and processing the sugarcane easier. (CM.)

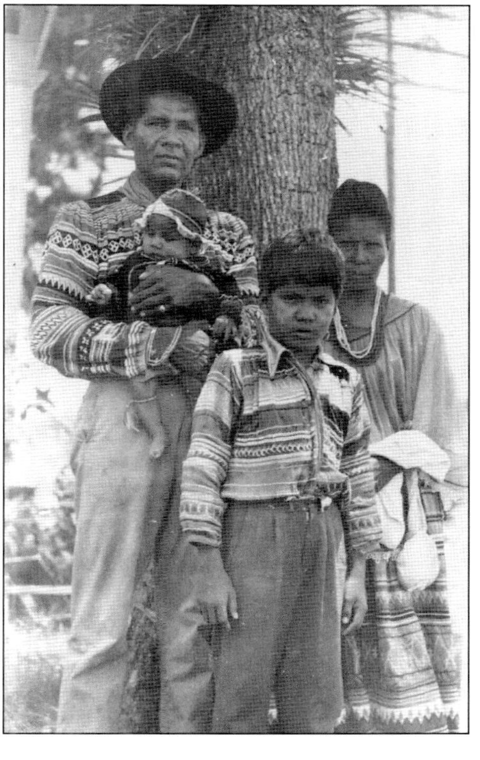

From left to right, Tom, Richard, Andy, and Maggie Buster, dressed in native clothing, are a typical Seminole family who lived here in the 1950s. Even today, Seminoles keep a cooking chickee outside of their modern homes. The chickee is made of palmetto branches spread over logs that are arranged in a circular pattern. It keeps cool underneath during the intense Florida summer heat. (FMP.)

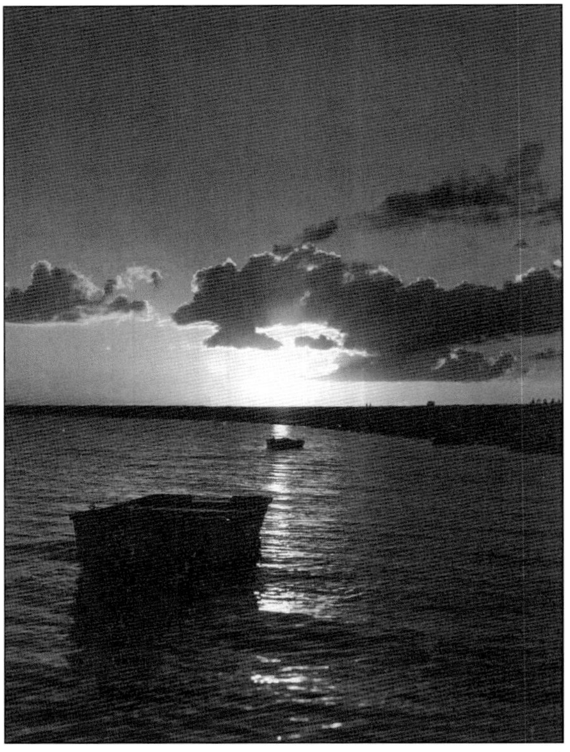

Fishermen head in bass boats for their favorite fishing holes, such as the "Monkey Box" along the Kissimmee River, to seek out their prize catches. (FMP.)

Pictured here are local Seminoles from the Brighton Reservation at the Okeechobee Rodeo. Brighton Reservation started out as a 2,500-acre tract of land known as Indian Prairie. The land was added to, and by 1938, it included 27,081 acres acquired with Resettlement Administration funds, 6,278 acres acquired with Indian Reorganization Agency funds, and 1,920 acres obtained by exchange with the State of Florida for a total of 35,643 acres. (FMP.)

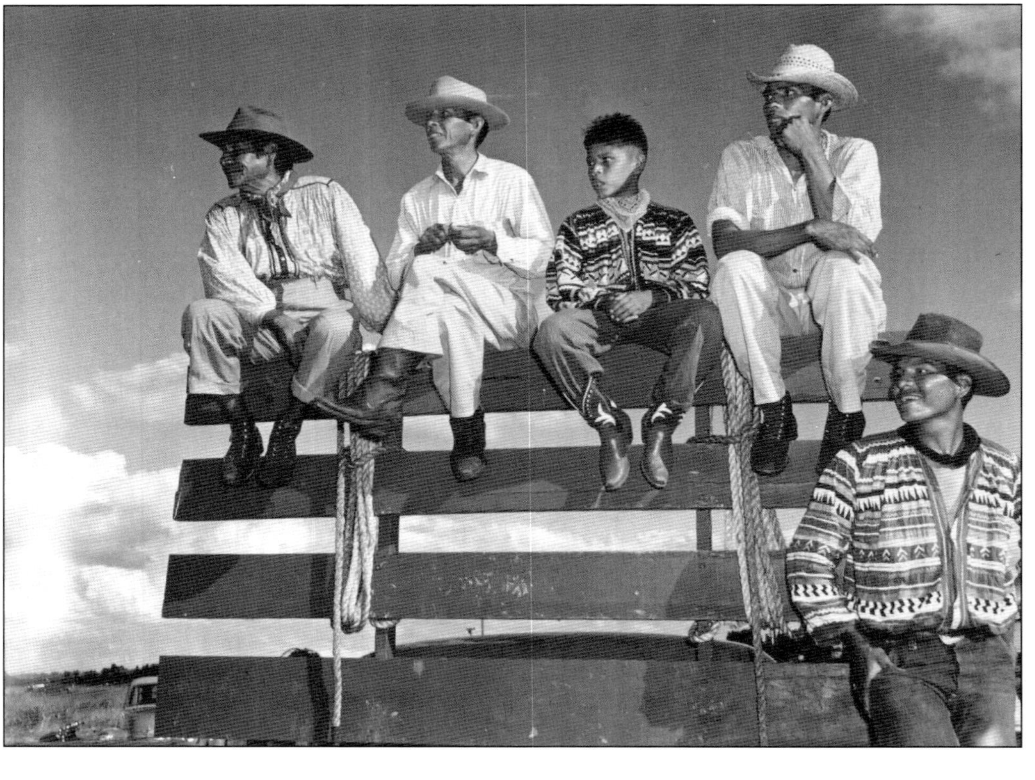

June Lowery serves Henry Lamb (left) and Vincent Boromie in Okeechobee. Okeechobee County was carved out of St. Lucie, Osceola, and Palm Beach Counties in 1917. (FMP.)

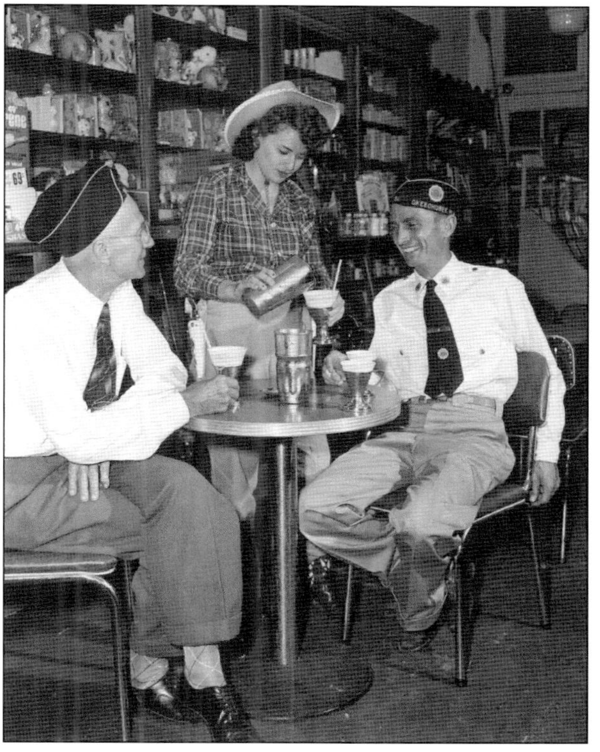

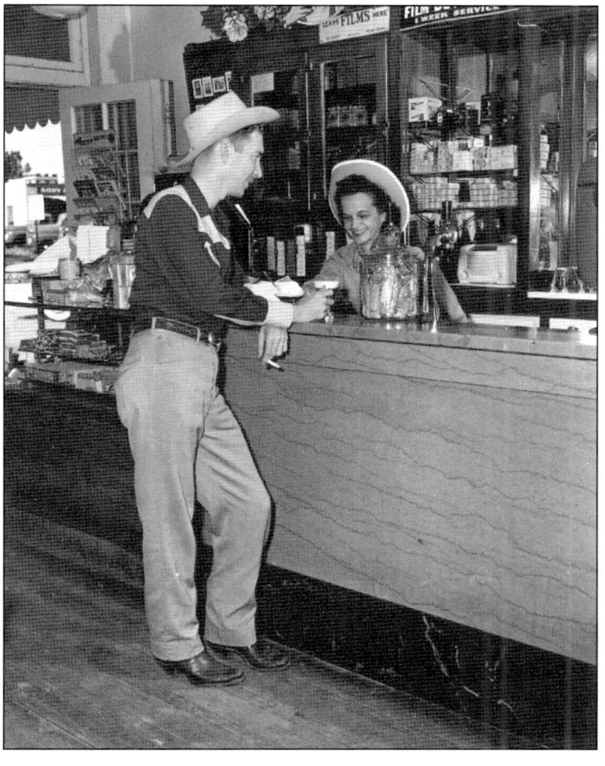

Charles Hunt and Mary Padgett socialize at the soda fountain. (FMP.)

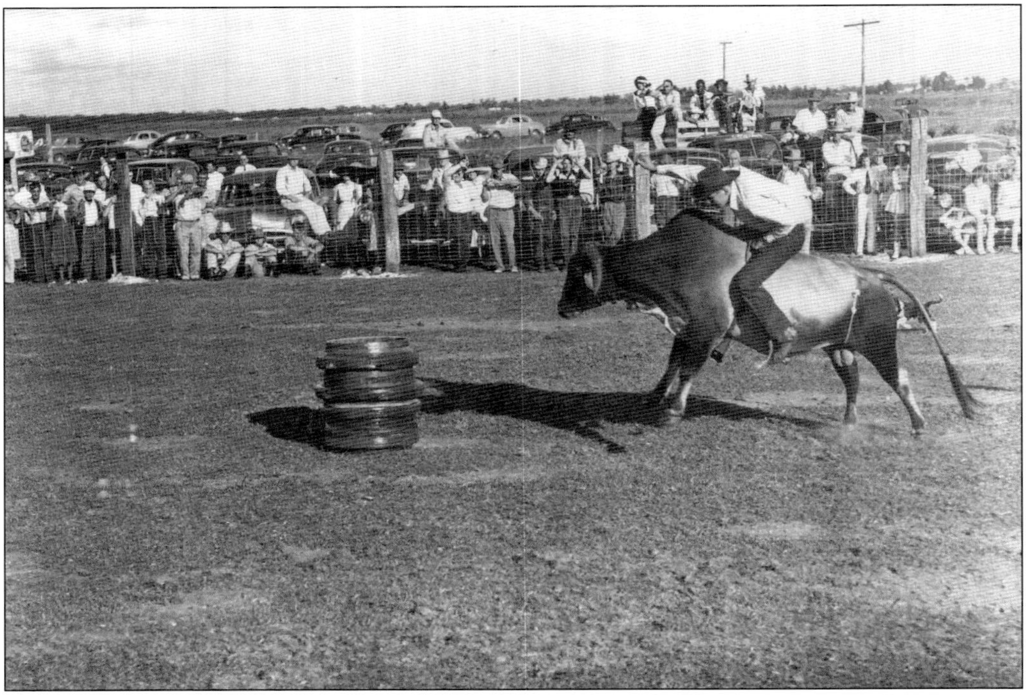

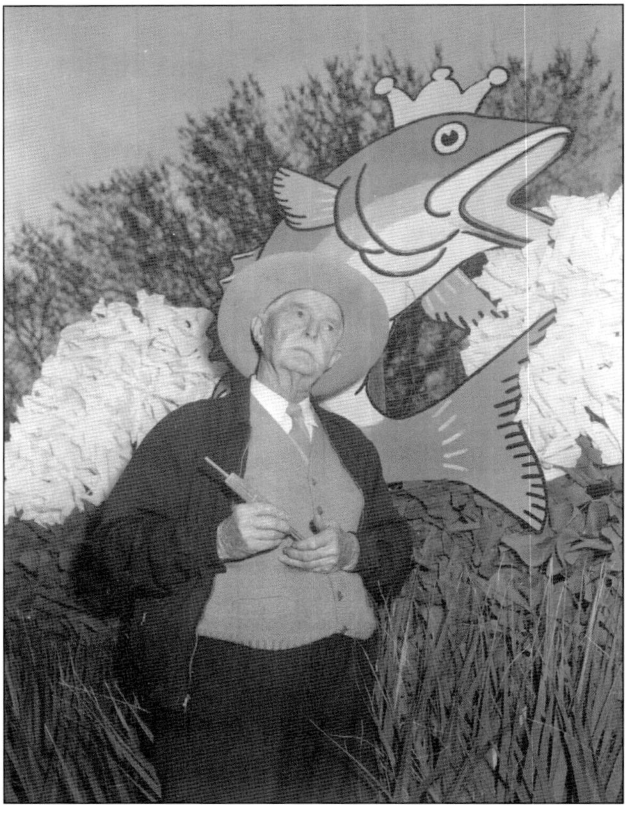

Rodeos are very popular in towns around the lake. In this photograph taken in Okeechobee, the cowboy is trying to ride and stay on the bucking bull. Bull riders compete in the rodeo circuit, and the top contenders go to the national championships in Las Vegas every year. (FMP.)

Turkey callers could blow their homemade whistles and wild turkeys would come to them. Tom Gaskins was one of the local experts. There were also Seminole Indian guides, including Billy Bowlegs III, who could "grunt up a gator." A marker on Route 27 commemorating "Cofchapkee," Billy Bowlegs III's Seminole name, reads, "1862–1965. In the Ortona Cemetery eight miles west of here lie the remains of a patriarch of the Seminole Nation. A true friend of the white man and a faithful representative of his own people." (FMP.)

Nine

Pahokee, Moore Haven, and Okeechobee

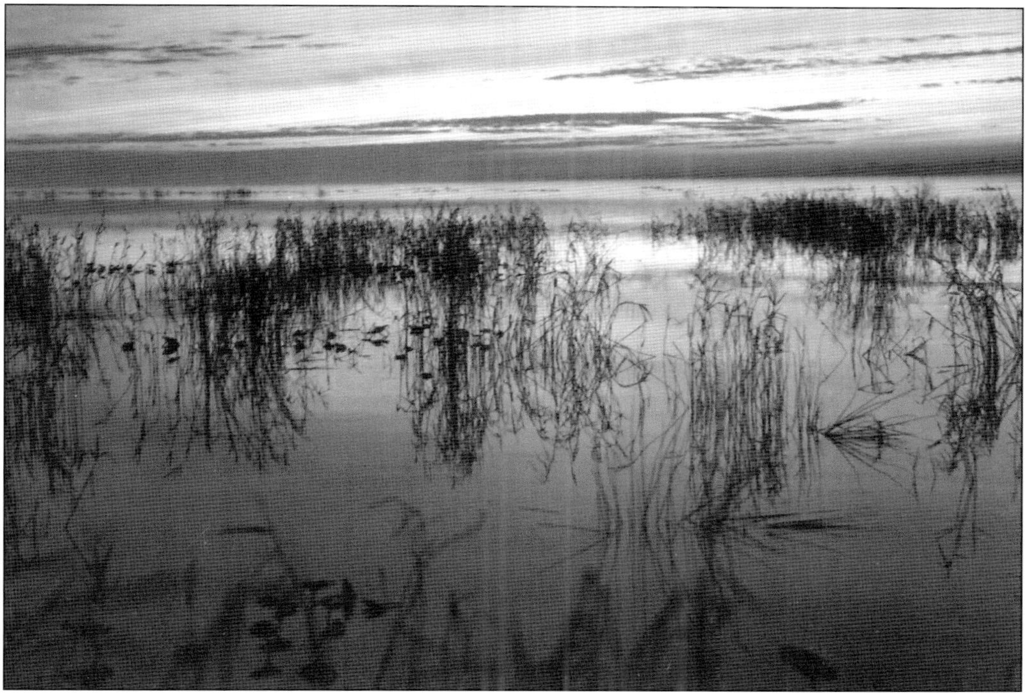

This peaceful scene shows the Pahokee docks at Lake Okeechobee. The Highwaymen were a group of African American artists who began selling their paintings door-to-door out of their cars during the 1950s. They used natural scenes of the Everglades like the setting of this photograph to portray the classic tradition of painting, a method called *alla prima*, or all at once. The group's mentor was A. E. "Bean" Backus, who had a studio in Fort Pierce. (FMP.)

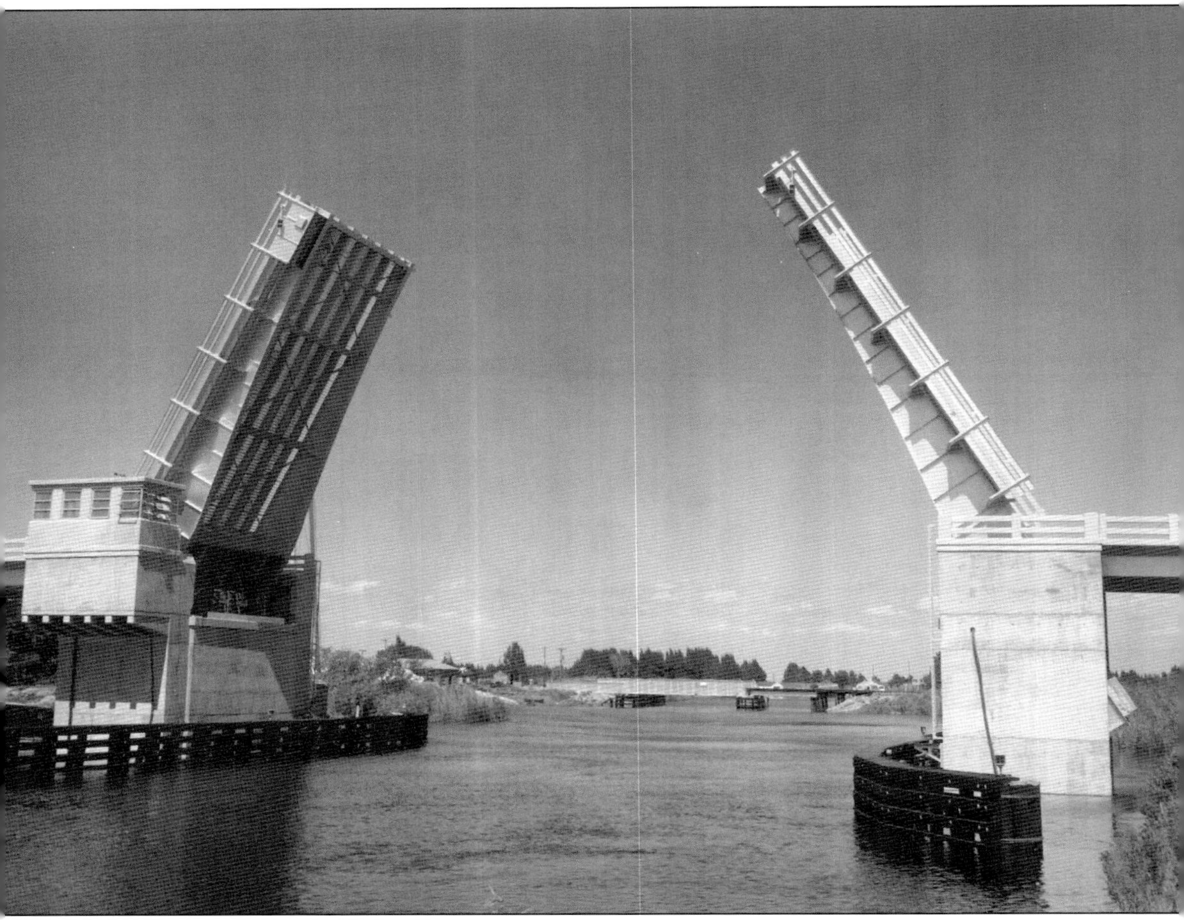

A drawbridge used to be operated in Moore Haven, but it was replaced with a permanent structure in 2000. The old bridge was dangerous when rains made it slick and was the scene of several fatal accidents. (FMP.)

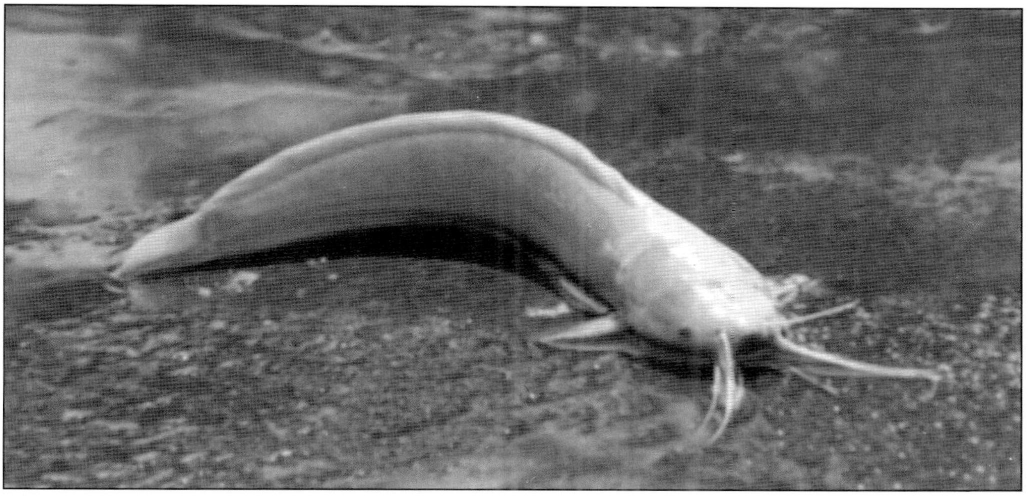

The walking catfish is an unusual creature that has adapted to Florida drought. It can cross land from pond to pond and actually "walk" by wiggling on its fins. The walking catfish was imported to Florida, reportedly from Thailand, in the early 1960s for the aquarium trade. The first introductions apparently occurred in the mid-1960s, when adult fish imported as brood stock escaped, either from a fish farm in northeastern Broward County or from a truck transporting brood fish between Dade and Broward Counties. Additional introductions in Florida, supposedly purposeful releases, were made by fish farmers in the Tampa Bay area in Hillsborough County in late 1967 or early 1968, after the state banned the importation and possession of walking catfish. (FMP.)

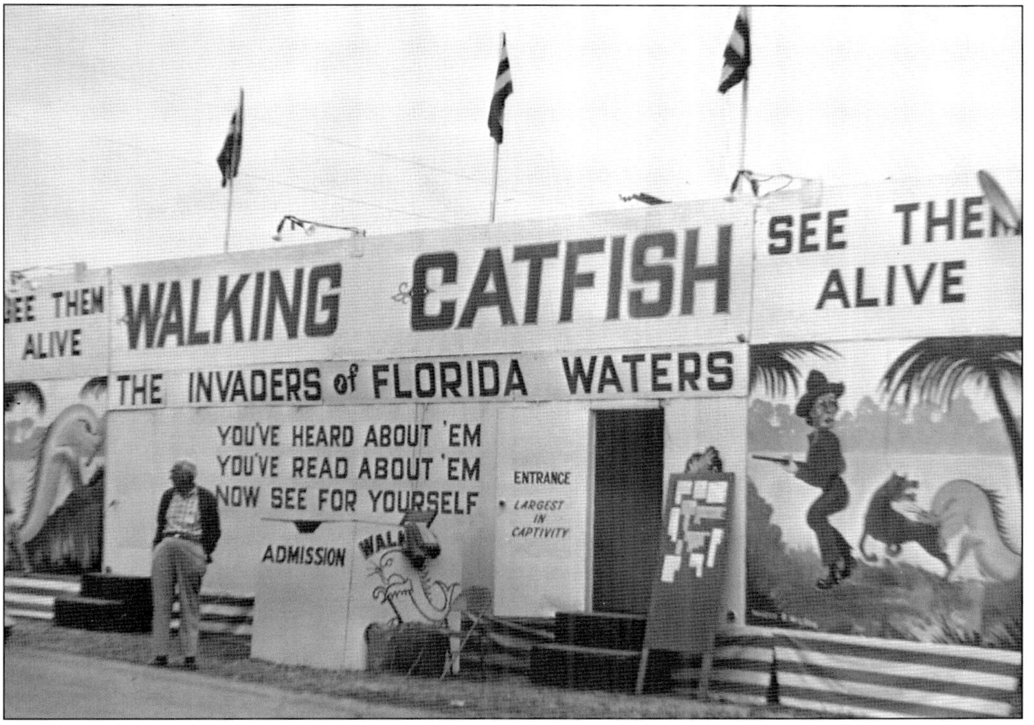

The roadside attraction of the largest walking catfish alive is shown at this sideshow. These fish are found all over Florida in the backwoods swamps and ponds that dry up in the winter. (FMP.)

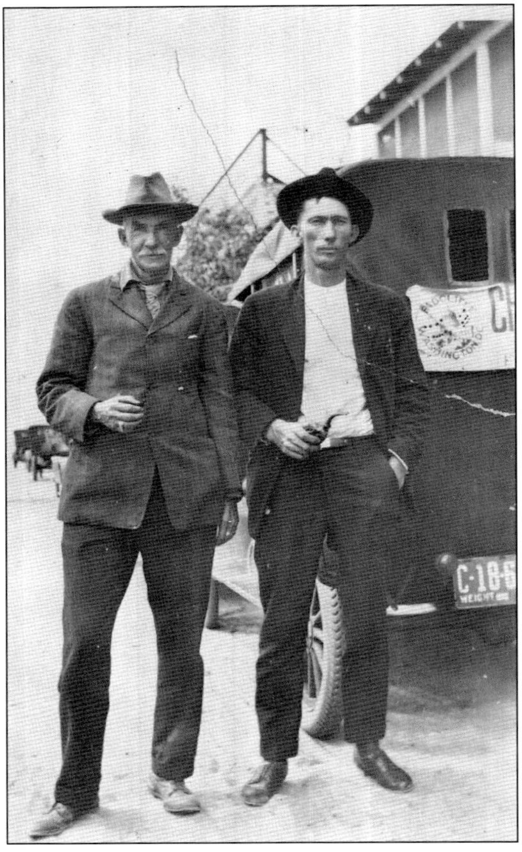

Bud Henderson (left), the first Glades County sheriff, was a city marshal as well as a DeSoto County deputy sheriff. Hendry Whidden (right) served as a constable in 1916. The first woman sheriff in the region was named Eugenia Hollingsworth Simmons, appointed by Gov. Fred Cone to fill her husband Claude's appointment after Claude died. She worked in Okeechobee but never carried a gun or arrested anyone. Moore Haven's first doctor was Irl W. Martin, who also established the Pioneer Drug Store. He left to join the armed services in World War I and never returned. (FMP.)

Here are rails being spiked while building the Moore Haven and Clewiston railroad. It was through the efforts of one of the first woman mayors in the country, Marian Newhall Horwitz O'Brien, elected in 1917, that the first railroad came to town in 1918. The Moore Haven Women's Club was formed in 1916 to start collecting books for a library, which they ran for many years. The club also exerted a great deal of influence on the community's progress by sponsoring cultural events and raising funds for the school's first cafeteria. (FMP.)

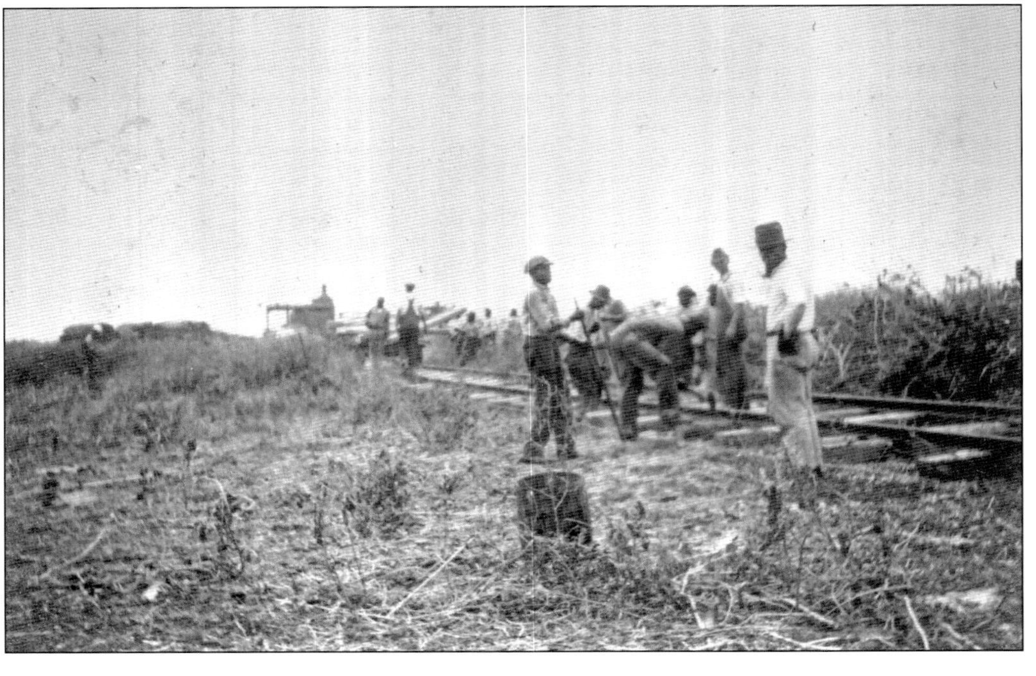

Railroads carried sand and building materials as well as passengers. This view shows the first train being loaded by mechanical shovel in Moore Haven in 1918. (FMP.)

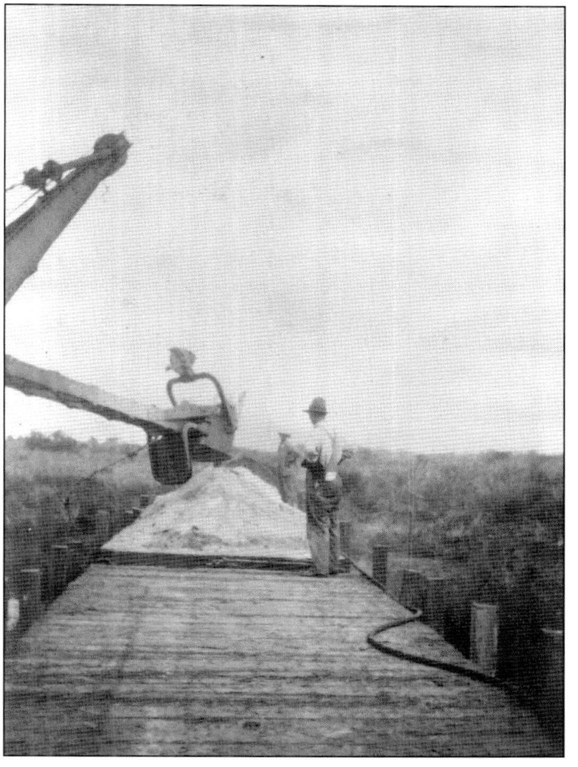

Three railroad engineers pose in a group portrait in front of the train. Early Glades trains were nicknamed the "Hinky Dink" and the "Muck Special." (FMP.)

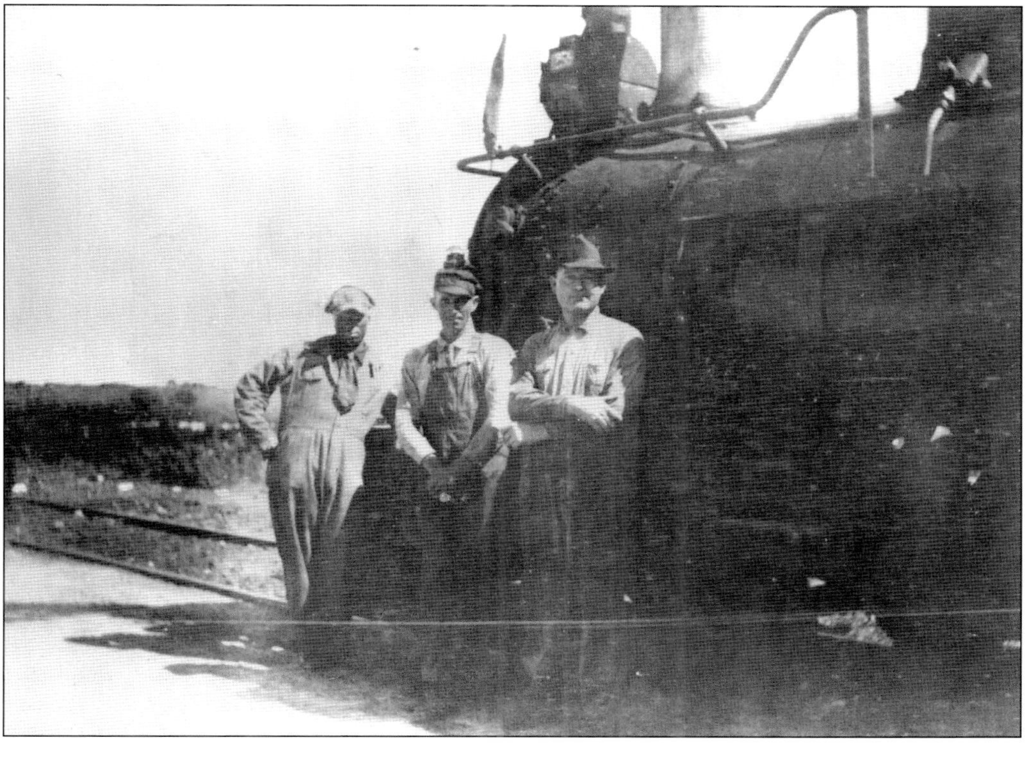

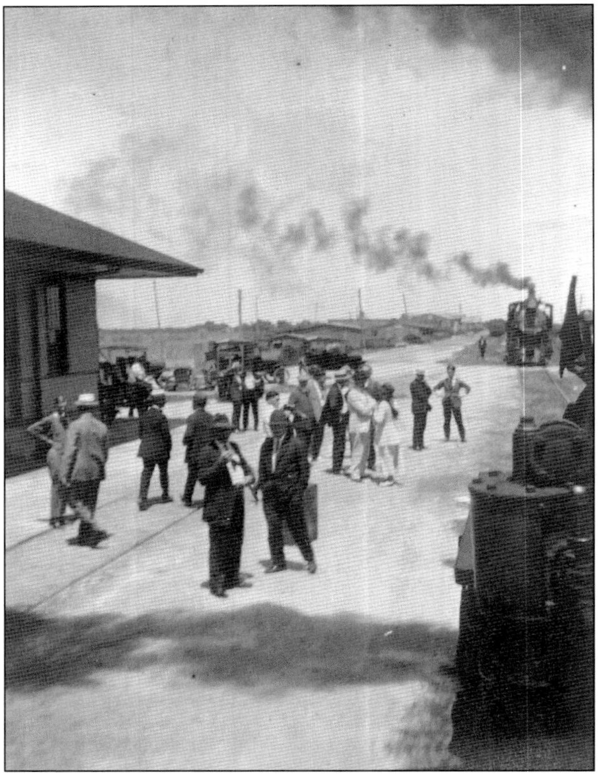

The "Muck Special" pulls into the station. The first train arrived on May 13, 1918, ninety minutes behind schedule and carrying 20 passengers and 15 freight cars. Late arrivals, schedule changes, faulty equipment, and derailments were constant sources of complaints. (FMP.)

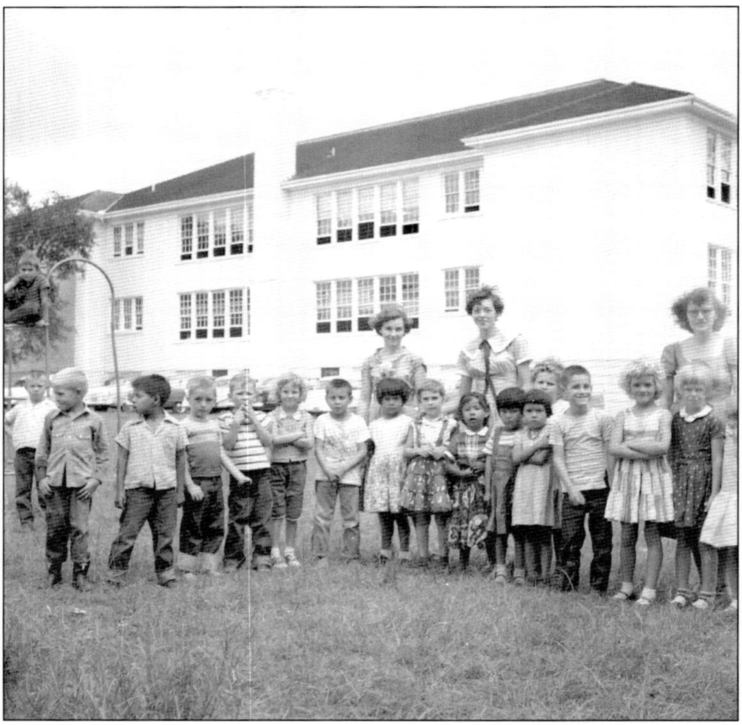

Seminole children of the Brighton Reservation congregate outside their Okeechobee school building. (FMP.)

This is the Battle of Okeechobee historic marker. On Christmas Day in 1837, over 1,000 U.S. Army and Missouri volunteer soldiers led by Col. Zachary Taylor, who would become president, attacked several hundred Seminoles and Miccosukees north of Lake Okeechobee. The battle resulted in 26 casualties and 112 wounded of U.S. Army and Missouri volunteer soldiers, and 14 American Indians lost their lives. The Okeechobee battle was part of the Second Seminole War (1835–1842), a product of Pres. Andrew Jackson's Indian Removal Act. The Battle of Okeechobee was the war's bloodiest clash. The battlefield is recognized by the National Trust for Historic Preservation as one of the top endangered U.S. historical sites. A yearly reenactment is performed on the site. (FMP.)

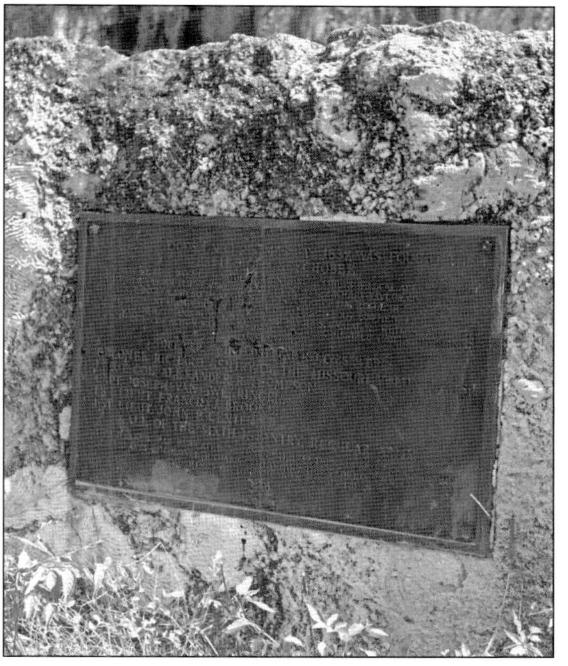

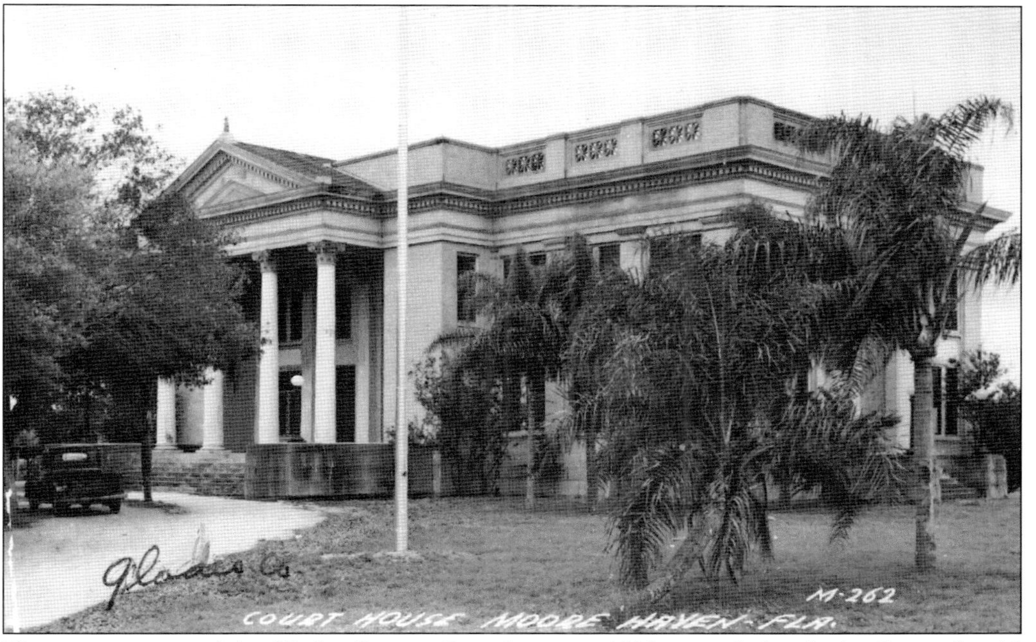

The construction of the Glades County Courthouse in 1926 coincided with the September 18 hurricane that struck South Florida with winds of over 160 miles an hour. The muck dike going from Sand Point to Moore Haven gave way, and within hours the town was covered with 10 feet of water. Buildings were ripped from their pilings, and many were demolished. Concrete blocks torn from this courthouse were not found until years later. Some inhabitants unfortunately drowned, but Vance Whidden grabbed a tree and clung to it all night, only to look up and see a bobcat sharing the same refuge. (FMP.)

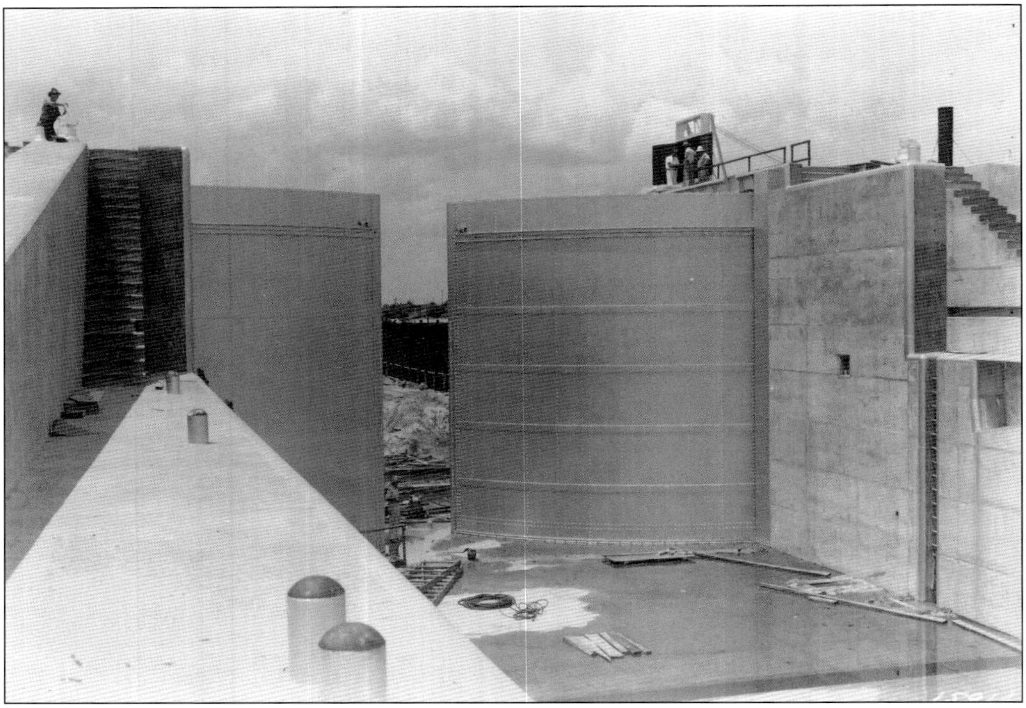

The completed upper sector gate and central panel of this lock are given an operational trial by a Lieutenant Selee. When the first locks were built here in 1918, they were a welcome improvement for the steamers that had frequently bogged down in the muck of a shallow channel. A man named Fred Flanders is remembered as the first lockmaster. A newspaper article reported that 6.5 million pounds of catfish had been shipped from Lake Okeechobee in 1924. The Pea Vine Grade Railroad reached Okeechobee and made it "the fish capital" of Florida. (FMP.)

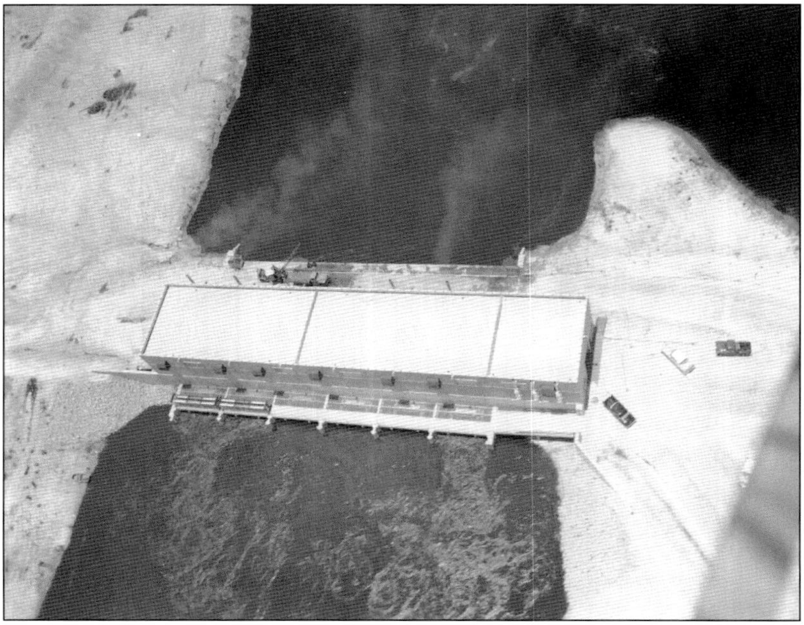

This aerial view overlooks pumping station 5A in the Central and Southern Florida Flood Control District at Lake Okeechobee in 1957. The cars in the photograph indicate the size of the facility. (FMP.)

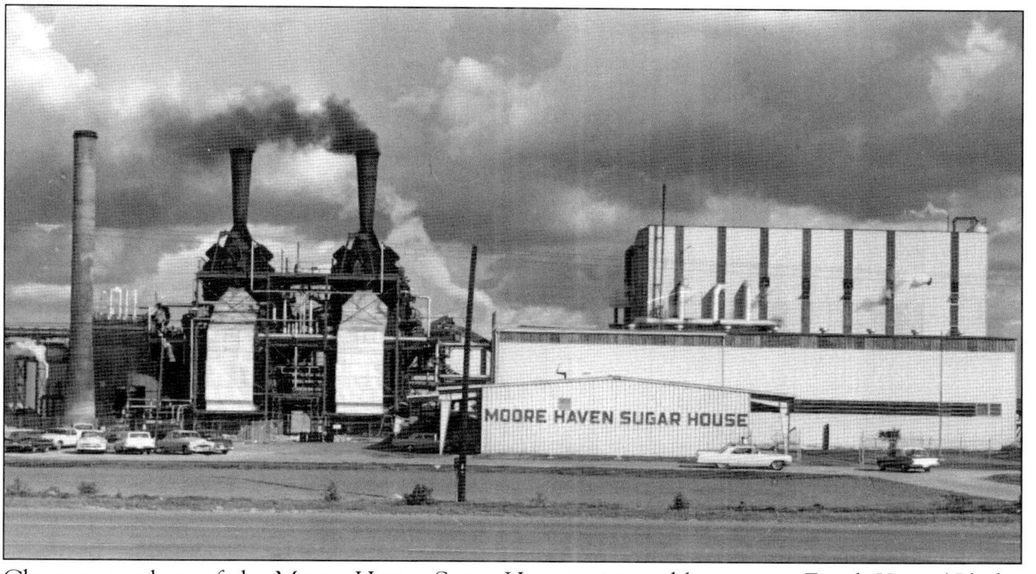

Charter members of the Moore Haven Sugar House, pictured here, were Frank Yaun (Glades County's first agricultural extension agent), Roger Weeks (Lykes Brothers), A. A. Beck, Sherman and Spurgeon Click, the Griffin family, "Uncle Joe" and sons Richard and Sammy, Monroe Thomas, W. E. Perry, Donald, Billy and Joe Peeples, Bob and Jim Beardsley, Tom Perry, Roy Lundy, Ray and Broadus Gantt, and Cecil Parkinson. Other small owners were included, many from outside of Glades County, including a few Cubans who had fled Castro. (FMP.)

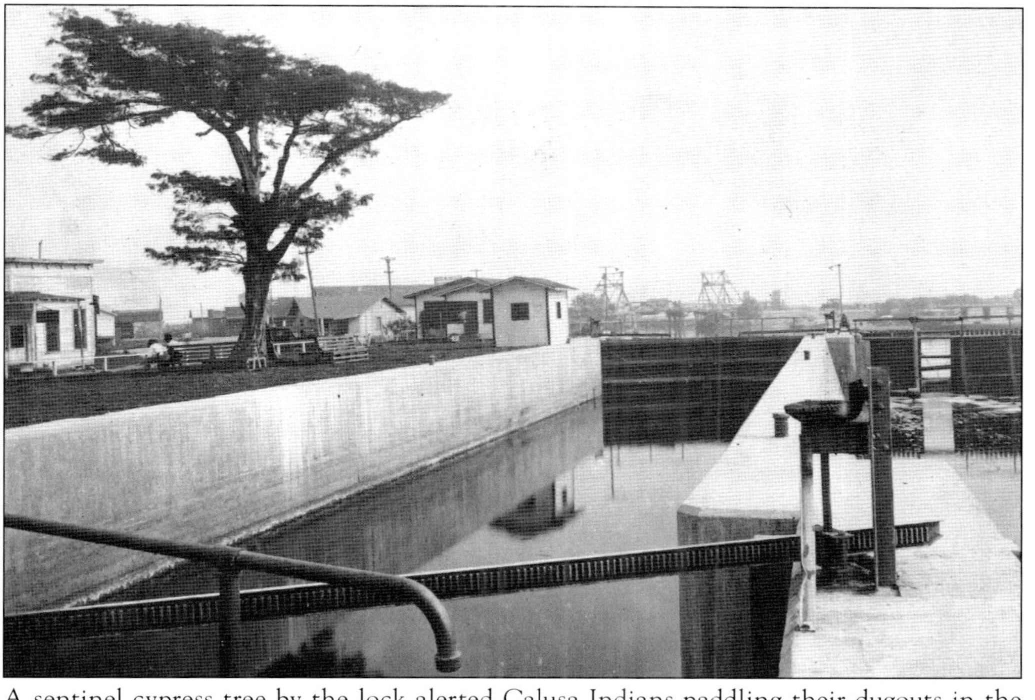

A sentinel cypress tree by the lock alerted Calusa Indians paddling their dugouts in the Caloosahatchee River that this was the entrance to the lake. Moore Haven uses this cypress tree, called the "Lone Cypress" by locals, as its symbol. (FMP.)

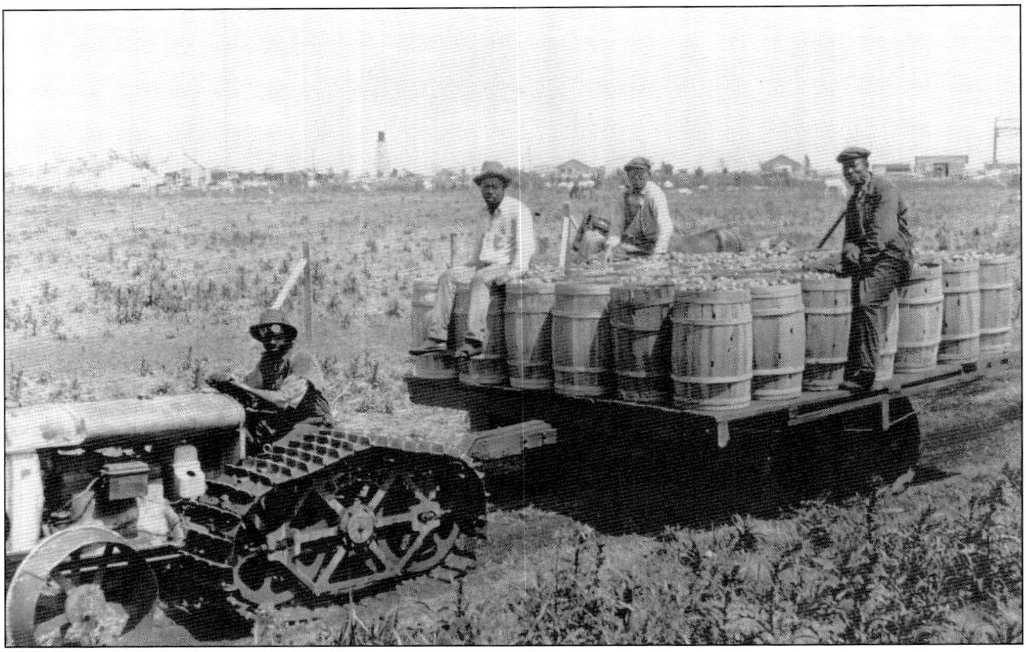

Barrels were used to store the potatoes that were hand-picked by field workers. Then the barrels were transported to the docks, where they were shipped and sold to customers on the coast. This early tractor was made in 1918. (FMP.)

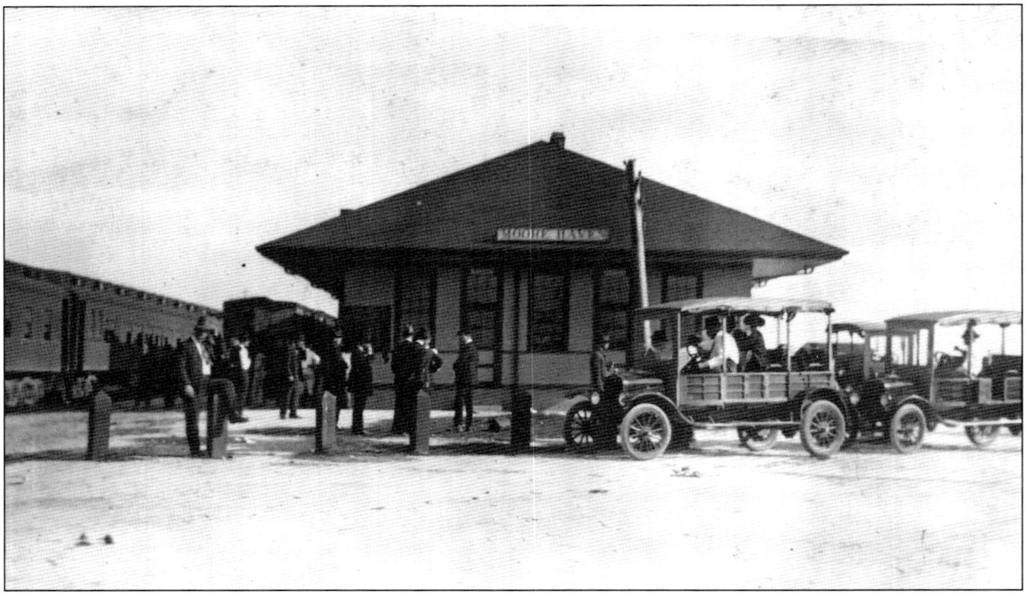

The Moore Haven train depot's first agent was R. W. Sheffield. He had to operate out of a freight car on a siding until this depot was built. A joke circulated that a middle-aged man who got off the train at Moore Haven had left Haines City as a young boy under the conductor's supervision. (FMP.)

BIBLIOGRAPHY

www.bigobirdingfestival.com

Dale, Nancy. *Would Do, Could Do and Made Do—Florida's Pioneer "Cow Hunters" Who Tamed the Last Frontier.* Bloomington, IN: iUniverse, 2006.

www.floridatrail.org

Glades County, Florida History. Moore Haven, FL: Glades Historical Society, 2008.

Gregware, Bill and Carol Gregware. *Guide to the Lake Okeecobee Area.* Sarasota, FL: Pineapple Press, 1997.

Hilliard, Joe Marlin and Barbara Oehlbeck. *The Ranch—Hilliard Brothers of Florida.* Port Salerno, FL: Hilliard Brothers of Florida with Florida Classics Library, 2005.

Morris, Allen. *Florida Place Names.* Sarasota, FL: Pineapple Press, 1995.

Mykle, Robert. *Killer Cane—The Storm of 1928.* Boulder, CO: Taylor Trade Publishing, 2006.

The Official Guide to the 17th Annual Explore Lake Okeechobee on the Big "O" Hike. Gainesville: Florida Trail Association, 2008.

Snyder, James D. *Black Gold and Silver Sands—A Pictorial History of Agriculture in Palm Beach County.* West Palm Beach, FL: The Historical Society of Palm Beach County, 2004.

Will, Lawrence E. *A Cracker History of Okeechobee.* Lakeville, MN: Great Outdoors Publishing Company, 1964.

———. *A Dredgeman of Cape Sable.* Lakeville, MN: Great Outdoors Publishing Company, 1965.

———. *Okeechobee Hurricane and the Hoover Dike.* Moore Haven, FL: Glades Historical Society, 1990.

———. *A Pioneer Boatman Tales of Okeechobee Boats and Skippers.* Lakeville, MN: Great Outdoors Publishing Company, 1966.

———. *Okeechobee Catfishing.* Lakeville, MN: Great Outdoors Publishing Company, 1965.

———. *Swamp to Sugar Bowl.* Lakeville, MN: Great Outdoors Publishing Company, 1968.

Williamson, Betty Chandler and Twila Valentine. *Strolling Down Country Roads: Okeechobee County, A Pictorial History.* Okeechobee, FL: Barnett Bank of Lake Okeechobee, 1993.

Wright, E. Lynne. *More Than Petticoats—Remarkable Florida Women.* Guilford, CT: Two Dot by Globe Pequot Press, 2001.